I0825173

ANNE BOLEYN

ANNE BOLEYN

Reputation, Revolution, Religion, and the Queen Who Changed History

MARTHA TATARNIC

Morehouse Publishing
19 East 34th Street
New York, NY 10016
www.churchpublishing.org

Morehouse Publishing is an imprint of Church Publishing Incorporated.

Cover design by David Baldeosingh Rotstein
Typeset by Westchester Publishing Services

ISBN 978-1-64065-859-2 (hardcover)
ISBN 978-1-64065-861-5 (eBook)

Library of Congress Control Number: 2025951099

Dedicated to my parents, John and Susan Smith,
who encouraged me to have big dreams and love books.

Table of Contents

Introduction: "I Want to Read That Book" ix

PART 1 The Problem with Anne

CHAPTER 1 A Brief Biography 3

CHAPTER 2 The Cutting Room Floor 9

PART 2 An Old World Falling Apart, a New World Just Beginning

CHAPTER 3 Cataclysmic Change 19

CHAPTER 4 The Role Models—Anne Had a Vision 29

CHAPTER 5 The Matter of Sex 45

CHAPTER 6 There's Something About Anne 57

CHAPTER 7 How Anne Moved the Chess Pieces of Reform 71

PART 3 She Was Dying to Start a Church

CHAPTER 8 The Enemies—Religion, Politics, and Personality 85

CHAPTER 9 Not Guilty but Not Innocent 101

CHAPTER 10 She Laughed at the King 115

CHAPTER 11 From A to E: A Bloody and Tumultuous Road Map of Reformation 131
CHAPTER 12 Her Mother's Daughter 143
CHAPTER 13 A New World, a New Church 153

PART 4 Bigger Than the Archetypes

CHAPTER 14 The Fairy Tales 169
CHAPTER 15 The Whore 179
CHAPTER 16 The Mother 189
CHAPTER 17 The Witch 199
CHAPTER 18 The Most Happy 209
CHAPTER 19 . . . Happily Ever After 219

PART 5 Only a Story

CHAPTER 20 Anne and Me; Anne and Us 227
CHAPTER 21 A Legacy of Misogyny 239
CHAPTER 22 The Riverbed 253

Acknowledgments 261
Appendix I: Key Characters 263
Appendix II: Timeline 273
Endnotes 277
Bibliography 301

INTRODUCTION

"I Want to Read That Book"

It started at the card table during Christmas break. The conversation included many of my favorite topics: gender politics, religion, strong women, and musical theater. My brother Andrew had asked me about seeing the musical *Six*, a hit on stages in the early 2020s that centers on the lives of the wives of King Henry VIII. My husband, Dan, had given me tickets for my birthday, and although I appreciated the night out, when asked to review it, I couldn't help but jump to criticizing the portrayal of Anne Boleyn.

I talked about the superficial and inaccurate depiction of the king's second wife. I rushed to describe Anne's lesser-known sides: her religious views, her role in shaping the English Reformation, and why her religious contributions are important to me as a woman and priest in the church.

Andrew interrupted me midthought. "I have literally never heard any of that before," he said, not dismissively but with genuine interest.

My brother and I grew up in the Anglican Church. His church participation as a young person was, at best, reluctant. Sometimes my mom actually paid him to go to church, and even then, he made his displeasure about being there known. Church history wouldn't be a topic toward which I would anticipate him naturally gravitating, and as my brother, Andrew has historically made for a tough audience. I expected to be on borrowed time for my impromptu soapboxing on my church hero.

"Everyone always says that the Anglican Church was started by King Henry VIII wanting a divorce," I said, encouraged by his interest. "But nobody ever talks about how the woman he lost his mind over was a reformer."

"Where is that book?" he asked me. "I want to read that book."

Lifelong Companion

My own captivation with Anne Boleyn began when I was a child. Her life had elements that typically caught my attention: glamor and magnetism, intrigue and tragedy, along with the mystery of looming unanswered questions. But she also felt like a kindred spirit. Anne was bookish, opinionated, driven, principled, ambitious. I wondered about her appeal and why she was ultimately judged as a problem to be erased. I didn't understand anything about how to be the kind of woman over whom a king would lose his mind, but I knew something about being not what people wanted or expected.

Everything about Anne told me that she, too, was someone who didn't quite fit the mold. Whereas I have learned how to make myself fit—or at least, as many women do, to manage the appearance of fitting—Anne suggested to me that there might be another way. Despite her violent ending, she made me want to be more myself. She made me want to stick to my principles and prioritize something other than conformity.

I had wanted to be a lawyer. This successful and well-paying career was custom-made for my natural studiousness and strong opinions. Unfortunately, I found myself once again out of step, detouring away from an obvious smart-girl path to law school and instead to seminary and becoming an Anglican priest. I wanted my life to go in one direction, but I couldn't deny the intractable need to become who I knew I was supposed to be.

Anne remained a powerful companion for me on my road to ordination. I gravitated to the Tudor history section of the Trinity College library where I went to seminary. In between commentaries on the Gospel of Mark and chapters from the works of famous (male) theologians like Karl Rahner, John Henry Newman, and Thomas Aquinas, my leisure reading took me to the courts of King Henry VIII. I soaked up movie and television presentations about Anne, as well as historical fiction about her and her contemporaries. I knew the accusations against her, both then and now: whore, witch, schemer, adulterer. But the more I learned about her thoroughly researched life, the more her story resonated with me, with my experience, with the life I was trying to lead, and with the work I felt called to do.

I grew up thinking that I was alone with my head full of ideas, my brain full of dreams, my imaginative landscape that felt too intense and untamed and strange for anyone else to understand. I read about Anne and wondered about her interior landscape and those of other bright, weird, challenging female figures. The great thing about growing up is finding your people, realizing that there are others who have their heads and brains and emotions overflowing with the beauty and strangeness of life too.

Told, but Not Heard

I could have walked away from that conversation with Andrew determined to write the book that my brother said he wanted to read, but that book has already been written. The information that grabbed Andrew's attention is readily available, even if not widely known. Andrew's reaction, though, is typical. I have regularly shared with people both in and outside church circles about Anne Boleyn's influence on starting and shaping the English Reformation, and with few exceptions, it is greeted with surprise.

Anne's religious convictions are behind every piece of the story that we think we know about her—including why she caught the king's eye, what happened when she refused to become his mistress, and why she died. Anne is a person of significant, controversial, and contested reputation, and even the lightest of digging into that reputation circles back to the question of faith and what vision of the church she championed. However, this has not been reflected in either the popular conception of her life or the common understanding of who history's movers and shakers have been. I don't need to write *The Untold History of Anne Boleyn* because it has already been told.

We haven't, however, been listening.

But so what? That was the question that niggled at me over the rest of the Christmas vacation. Anne is a well-known figure, so if we haven't heard the story of how she changed history, what story has dominated instead? Why would it matter that we know one story rather than another about someone who has been dead for almost five hundred years? What might our conversation say not just about Anne and her singular dramatic life, but also about us? About our patterns of talking about strong women? Why some stories get heard and others don't?

And finally, why is changing the narrative, even five hundred years later, important?

I could see in my mind's eye a cinematic montage of the countless representations of Anne that have flooded our history books and popular culture's imagination for the past five centuries. She has been the subject of best-selling books, plays, movies, television shows, and musicals. She features on TikTok. My teenage daughter informs me that Anne Boleyn is one of the two most popular historical figures to Gen Z, the other being Joan of Arc. Anne and Joan are two strong women who held positions of unusual leadership and have been labeled in ways that have shaped public consciousness and been difficult to shake.

Gen Z is hardly the first cohort to find Anne and her soap opera–esque era of Tudor England gripping. In the podcast *The Rest Is History*, Dominic Sandbrook and Tom Holland, two respected historians, closed their episode "The Six Wives of Henry VIII" by speculating about who would make it furthest as a contestant on the reality TV show *Love Island*. Anne was unequivocally voted number one.[1] She and her story have every ingredient needed to draw us in and keep us wanting more.

My brother's interest is part of a legacy of unrelenting curiosity and storytelling that has circled around this infamous English queen. The things that we have said about her and the things that we haven't are all wrapped up in that ongoing fascination. In what ways have we tried to get Anne Boleyn to conform to the usual tropes we use for problematic women? Why does she defy easy categorization? And how does our collective captivation point toward a story that needs to be understood better and the truth that doing so matters?

I know why Anne is fascinating to me, but her wider appeal is even more telling. This long-dead historical figure holds in her thrall my middle-aged accountant brother, professional historians, and my teenage daughter and her peers alike.

There has always been a cultural habit of keeping the stories of strong, uncompromising visionary women contained. But as in Newton's laws of motion, every action will have an equal and opposite reaction. Each easy categorization we have applied to Anne has been matched by an untamable interest in telling her story again, circling back, allowing a few more of the jagged contours to slip out.

We can't let her go. Anne commands our attention. She confronts us with a character that refuses to conform to expectations. She demands we do a double take on how we got to where we are today and who made it happen. She compels us to examine our talk about *her* to see what it says about *us*. Anne Boleyn is a woman who changed history.

She has the power to keep changing history, if we're willing to let her story speak.

PART 1

The Problem with Anne

In beauty she was to many inferior, but for behavior, manners, attire and tongue she excelled them all . . . But howsoever she outwardly appeared, she was indeed a very wilful woman which perhaps might seem no fault because seldom women do lack it, but yet that and other things cost her after dear.

—George Wyatt, grandson of Thomas Wyatt (Anne Boleyn suitor) and Anne's first biographer[1]

CHAPTER 1

A Brief Biography

A Simple Biographical Sketch of a Complicated Story

Sixteenth-century England was full of salacious helpings of soap-opera-like romance, political intrigue, religious upheaval, power-hungry scheming, and many of the central characters in the story getting caught up in dangerous waters, murky subplots, and deadly accusations. This history has been made even more confusing because of how well it has hooked the popular imagination. Famous movies have been directed, best-selling books written, and now viral TikTok videos litter the internet, full of half-truths and missing context that add layers of misconception and falsehood to an already complicated story.

In order to talk about Anne Boleyn, to talk about our talk about her, or to delve in any coherent way into the problem that she presents, the basic biographical details of her life need to be laid out first.

Anne was born around the turn of the sixteenth century, a time when the world was changing in cataclysmic ways. She was the child of an ambitious, noble, and cash-poor family. On both sides, her great-grandfathers were earls and dukes and her great-grandmothers the daughters of noblemen. Her father, Thomas, was the eldest son of Sir William Boleyn of Blickling, and her mother, Elizabeth, of whom we hear very little, was the daughter of the earl of Surrey.[1] The Boleyns' star had been rising steadily for generations, mostly through Anne's male forebears making strategic marriages. Anne was likely the middle child, with older sister Mary and younger brother George flanking the Boleyn birth order, although the birth years of all three siblings are disputed.[2] George and Mary would also play a part in Anne's drama, but it was George with whom Anne had the closest relationship.

The royal court in Tudor England was the place where power was wielded, relationships with other European power brokers were forged, and decisions were made affecting the lives of the whole country. There were food and fashion and social graces, but all of that was a backdrop to navigating relationships with the king and seeking his all-powerful ear. To effect change in sixteenth-century England, a person had to have access to the man with the crown.

The fact that Anne's father devoted his adult life to serving at court, and encouraged his children to do likewise, tells us that he was interested in power.[3]

Henry's birth, unlike Anne's, was carefully recorded. He was born in 1491, the second son of Henry VII. Henry's father's reign had ended the long and unsettled Wars of the Roses, a lengthy period in England's history in which the throne was consistently contested. This fact is important. The Tudor era followed a time of royal upheaval, and both Henry VII and Henry VIII, along with Henry VIII's offspring, would be on constant alert throughout their reigns for anyone seeking to make a play for the throne.

Arthur was Henry's older brother and the heir. Henry was "the spare," pegged for a life of leadership in the church. However, when Henry was just eleven, Arthur died, and the trajectory of this second son's life changed dramatically.

Marriages in Tudor England were opportunities for strategic alliances, enabling the consolidation of wealth and power between families, and in the case of royal children, marriages were arranged with careful consideration for advancing political agendas. Arthur had been married to Catherine of Aragon, a Spanish princess, and when Henry came to the throne following their father's death, he married Catherine himself. This required special permission from the pope in Rome because of Catherine's marriage to Henry's older brother, which contravened a biblical law found in Leviticus, one of the early books of the Bible.

Meanwhile, Anne's family sent her to France to receive an education in two different European royal courts. She spent her formative years there, returning to England to find a beneficial marriage and serve in the court of Catherine of Aragon, not necessarily in that order.

By the time Anne caught Henry's eye, Henry had been married to Catherine for almost twenty years and only managed to produce one living heir: a daughter named Mary. This was a problem—personally, politically, and most especially in Henry's mind, theologically. The stability of the realm rested on having a male heir, and preferably many of them. But the more time that passed and the boys didn't appear, the more that Henry began to interpret this as a sign of God's anger. Henry feared that God was unfavorably judging his marriage to his brother's widow.

Henry had several mistresses, including Anne's sister, Mary, and had a son by Elizabeth (Bessie) Blount named Henry Fitzroy. Fitzroy was the only illegitimate child Henry acknowledged, but there may have been others. Historians differ on whether they believe that any of Mary Boleyn's children were the king's as well.

Je Ne Sais Quoi

Anne came home from France with a certain *je ne sais quoi* about her. She could sing and dance. She had an intellectual mind and had been exposed to new ways of thinking. She wore trendsetting fashion. She attracted male attention easily and had admirers, at least one of them serious. It was in 1527 when Henry's attention was first documented as having landed on Anne.

The traditional story is this: Henry wanted Anne for his mistress, and Anne famously refused. Far from curtailing Henry's interest, it sparked increased obsession. We don't have access to Anne's inner thoughts on refusing the king's bed, but speculation about her motivations became its own obsession. Was she genuinely not interested in him? Did she sense an opportunity? Was she scheming for the throne the whole time? Did she simply want better for herself than an illicit affair, king or no king? Was she a manipulative schemer?

My British friend Justin suggested that I might find it interesting in my research to get my hands on the Ladybird history books that he and British schoolchildren of a certain era read in learning about their country's history. I was shocked to read this synopsis of Anne's rise to power:

> She had been well educated—partly in France—and was a good musician; but she was ambitious and unscrupulous. When she realized that she had attracted the attention of Henry, she was determined to become Queen at any cost. Perhaps if she had known that the cost was to be her head, she might have hesitated.[4]

These words would echo in my mind. This is, in a nutshell, the "problem" with Anne. The story is that she wanted Henry's attention (*She was asking for it*, we might say). And if she wanted it, then ultimately she got what she deserved. Female ambition is tidily linked to problematic moral character. A warning is implicitly sounded against such ambition, and a dose of victim blaming is added to the mix too.

This traditional narrative, and what it has taught and justified, needs to be interrogated.

Annulment and Reform Join Hands

Henry's interest in Anne turned into a religious problem. Then it wedged open the door to a religious revolution.

The dilemma was this: Henry wanted the pope to annul his marriage to Catherine, thereby reversing the papal edict that had allowed Henry to marry Catherine in the first place and declaring Henry's marriage to Catherine invalid. In the eyes of God, Henry argued, he and his first wife were never married.

There were a few problems with this. Catherine was exceptionally well-connected, and Anne was not. Catherine was a Spanish princess and the aunt of Charles V of Spain, who had been appointed Holy Roman Emperor. Charles and the pope were in a constant dance of political intrigue and power wrangling, and the pope could not afford to anger him. There was also the matter of changing the papal mind. What does it mean for the pope to challenge his own authority by reversing a previous papal decision? This was dangerous territory at a time when the pope's authority was being questioned across Europe by the tide of religious reform that was taking hold with such ferocity. The church in Western Europe had enjoyed unchallenged central authority in the figure of the pope for centuries, and now that uniformity had been fractured in recent years by Martin Luther and others.

The pope's refusal, ironically, amplified those fractures, as Henry became more intractably convinced that his marriage to Catherine was against God's law, and therefore the pope had been and was wrong. The reasons why he felt this way and what solution he ended up pursuing had a lot to do with Anne, her beliefs, the books she was reading, and the iron determination and sharp mind she possessed. Although Anne wouldn't be Henry's mistress, she did eventually agree to become his wife. This began six long years of Anne and Henry working together with their church officials—first to argue for the annulment and then to split the church in England from the authority of the pope and Rome, thus laying the groundwork for the Reformation in England.

In 1533, Anne and Henry were married. In conjunction with their wedding was the declaration that King Henry VIII was the supreme head of the English church, over and against the pope. The two developments were intimately connected to one another. With Henry in charge of the church, he could have parliament declare his annulment. He had the power then to marry Anne legally and make her queen of England.

The king's decisions were unpopular on two fronts. Religious reform had its supporters but was not well received by the masses. Catherine had been a well-loved queen, and seeing her daughter Mary set aside in such a humiliating way didn't sit well either. However, challenging Henry was a foolhardy thing to do, so ire got directed at Anne instead.

Anne came to the throne with a raft of enemies already out to get her.

And Then It All Went Wrong

Things started well. Anne was visibly pregnant by the time of her coronation. This reassured Henry that the reason for his lack of progeny with Catherine (aside from poor Mary) was God's anger with him. This belief was somewhat shaken when Anne gave birth to a girl, their daughter, Elizabeth, rather than a boy.

Other pregnancies followed, as did significant developments in the now-accelerating train that was the English Reformation. Each successive pregnancy ended in miscarriage or stillbirth. Anne used her position as queen effectively, demonstrating herself to be a devoted woman of faith, a clearheaded influencer in renewing and reforming the church, and a careful and thoughtful steward of the kingdom's business.[5]

In 1536, Anne was accused of adultery, incest, and high treason. She, along with five men who were found guilty of committing adultery with her, including her brother George, was put to death.

Henry's obsession with Anne came to a decisive end.

Our collective obsession was just beginning.

CHAPTER 2

The Cutting Room Floor

As a musical theater nerd, I had been looking forward to seeing the popular musical *Six*—a show that presents the six women "competing" for the title of best wife to King Henry VIII, only to realize that they all have voices that deserve to be heard and stories that are worthy of being centered.

It's clever and catchy. There are moments of real insight, like in the gut-wrenching picture painted of Henry's fifth wife, Katherine Howard. She sings about the liability of being a beautiful woman attracting the wrong kind of attention. She has been objectified, disempowered, disenfranchised, passed around, and ultimately becomes the victim of intimate partner violence.

My husband, Dan, knew that it was Anne Boleyn's portrayal that I really wanted to see. The lobby of the theater was set up with life-size portraits of each of the six queens. I stood in line so Dan could snap my picture with Anne. Anne's line was the longest.

As the second wife, Anne's part was early in the production. I was immediately incensed. The Anne Boleyn of *Six* is ditzy, loose, and confused. She sleeps around because she is too dumb to realize she shouldn't. She is naïvely surprised when her promiscuity gets her into trouble.

Each of the queens is given one song to articulate who they are and how their story takes shape. Anne Boleyn's song is called "Don't Lose Ur Head." This woman, who loved reading and engaging with the most radical philosophy and theology of her time, was given the indignity of a song title that can't even be bothered to spell out the word "your." I was tempted to leave the theater by the time we got to her chirpy claim, "I just wanna dance and sing." The ensemble sings back to her the question, "Politics?" to which she replies, "Not my thing."

The show's creators, Toby Marlow and Lucy Moss, define themselves as feminists and wrote the stories of all six queens as a subversive questioning of the way that history has been told and particularly how women's stories have been presented. They are clear that they did not construct this version of Anne as an accurate representation of her, her character, and her impact, but rather as a means of turning the endless gossip and speculation about Anne and her motivations on its head. What would it look like if Anne did everything of which she was accused? If she deliberately seduced the king into marrying her? If she then cheated on him? If she wasn't sorry? If she meant to do it?[1]

It's an interesting approach. Unfortunately, it lends itself too easily to continuing negative commentary about Anne specifically and about women in general. Certainly, the subversive intent was lost on me.

In this portrayal, Anne was a gold digger just out to get the crown. Anne didn't have vision and intelligence; she batted her eyelashes and pretended her head was empty in a full capitulation to the nonsense women have always been told about the need to keep their brains under wraps if they want to be attractive to men. Anne's love of a good party is a zero-sum game. If Anne is fun, then she couldn't also be serious. And if Anne couldn't keep her panties on and her sharp tongue under control, then it's no wonder that Henry killed her.

Audiences can all too easily walk away from *Six* with some of the most offensive and dangerous things we believe about women reinforced.

Cutting Anne Down to Size

Six offers one of countless examples of Anne's afterlife—how she has been constructed not just as a figure of historical study but as a character of pop-culture intrigue. As her story is continually retold, much of what is important about her is left on the cutting room floor. Her story is too big to handle, so it is edited into a manageable serving.

In *Six*, those editorial decisions might have been intended as subversive irony, but viewers can be left with the frustration of seeing on stage the same antiwoman tropes that are all too well known. Accusations of sexual deviancy get attached to women who trouble us with their strong personalities and other nonconforming qualities. Either/or categories for understanding female character and behavior are taken for granted. Either women are saintly or villainous, smart or fun, pious or evil, beautiful princess or wicked stepmother, virgin or whore.

The most popular and well-known representations of Anne have formed a general consciousness of her as promiscuous, a witch, or both. A straw poll of the average person who has a passing knowledge of popular history will reference Anne's sixth finger (interpreted as a sign of her occult dealings) or the wild rumors of the hundreds of men she entertained sexually. More nuanced portrayals have seen her as an ambitious schemer or a victim of the schemes of the men around her.

The most well-known and influential portraits of Anne from her own lifetime, or shortly thereafter, offer similarly polarized depictions. She was a whore, fighting on the side of the Antichrist. She was a pious saintly martyr, leading the charge to return the church to a truer and purer expression. She was ugly, manipulative, and sexually deviant. She was beautiful, charming, and of the highest and truest character.

The Anne Boleyn of even the most basic historical account leaves many questions in the wake of her unusual and troubling story. Why was Henry infatuated with her to such a world-changing degree? Where did all the passion and obsession that the king felt for her go? How did her fast and furious journey to become queen of England, and then treasonous criminal, happen? Because she spent the bulk of her years in three royal courts, we have a great deal of information about what her life looked like and involved, and for her last nine years, she was the subject of constant reporting. And still there is so much that we want to know. Almost everything about even the most basic facts, like when Anne was born and why she died, is contested.

The Anne Boleyn of pop culture should spark just as many questions. What assumptions are being made about Anne specifically and women in general that leave us with such radically different pictures of who she was and what she cared about?

And then, what about that lineup at Anne's picture in the theater lobby? Why is she the TikTok generation's favorite historical character? The "Don't Lose Ur Head" slang does hint at something true about the Anne of pop culture: She continues to feel relevant. She is the perpetual blank screen, despite the strange and unique details of her specific life, onto which we project our ponderings. Those ponderings center less on who Anne really was and more on our unsettled questions of female power, how women are supposed to behave, what we really expect and want of women sexually, and, most important, what we do to women who transgress expectations.

I serve the church, an institution that has had a lot to say about the proper use and place of women's voices and women's sexuality. I lead in a denomination that only relatively recently allowed women to have official authority, and we are working out the ways that women will lead and speak in this brave new world in real time. You don't have to work for the church, though, to understand that the place of women is a moving target, actively and continually contested.

Does Anne give us a role model of how to be a smart and powerful woman navigating her way with an astonishing degree of success in a man's world? Or is Anne one more manifestation of a basic archetypal warning to women who don't draw inside the lines?

If you don't behave, we'll cut off your head.

Anne Boleyn can be approached as a subject of historical study, but she can also be considered as a text. Anne was a real, historical person, and her imprint on history is substantial. And also, she is a story that we keep constructing, tearing down, and building again. We craft her story out of the things that we know about her historical context and the things that we think now. And it is in considering how she is a product of her time, how she is a product of our time, and how the contours of her life have so continuously failed to conform to the usual categories, that we have an opportunity for our curiosity and engagement to illuminate truth and transformation and wisdom.

Power and Impact: This Missing Piece

That brings me to the church, to the question of religion, and to our collective fascination with Anne. Her power and impact, as well as the controversy surrounding her and her marriage to Henry, must be understood in the context of the religious change that she championed—and that, to a remarkable degree, she successfully implemented. Of all the editorial decisions made about Anne, the omission of her leadership in religious reform is the most important. To cut out her religious passion is to miss the key explanation of Henry's desire for her, the enemies who closed in on her, the controversy that surrounded her, the conviction that ended her life, the role that was expected of her as a woman, and her failure in conforming to that role.

Anne's dramatic fall from grace has been endlessly analyzed by her contemporaries and by generations of historians. Popular accounts of Anne's story have concentrated on the lack of a son. Tales of witchcraft and Anne's bewitching of the king would be woven into the popular imagination in later years. And yet, it was in truth a potent mix of politics and especially religion that underwrote Anne's reputation at every turn.

We are left with the labels that were applied to Anne and the gossip that surrounded her, but the context for why people talked the way they did about her is missing. That talk about Anne has taken on a life of its own and follows the most recognizable and well-worn tropes used for categorizing and understanding women. As *Six* inadvertently communicates, it is more fun to cut a woman down to size by judging her as cluelessly sexy or a seductive gold digger than it is to suggest what she really wanted was to change the world, and perhaps she was smart enough to do it too.

The Text of Anne's Life

That we could still, in the third decade of the twenty-first century, put stories out into the world that conflate a woman's strong will and ambition with accusations that aren't much more elegant than stooping to calling Anne a "slut," and that we could then take from that the conclusion that women who break the boundaries deserve the violence that comes their way, is not unrelated to the stories that have been missing. The gendered nature of our collective storytelling, the history books that suggest it is just men who have shaped the world we currently inhabit, the diminishing and erasing of female power, this lays the groundwork for tolerating and excusing violence against women, as well as the many other ways that we teach women to play nice, to stay in their places, to want less, and to keep out of business that shouldn't concern them.

Anne didn't play nice, she didn't stay in her place, and she got deliberately involved in business that many wished she had left alone. This was central to both her appeal and the difficulties she has continually presented. This means that she was and continues to be judged as a problem, rather than as someone whose accomplishments deserve respect and whose end should provoke outrage for the violence and injustice committed against her.

I have been fascinated by Anne for most of my life. I have always loved studying history and poring over long-ago events to draw new through lines and connections. I write this book, though, not as a historian but as a storyteller, and most of all as a priest—a female priest, someone with skin in this game. The church I serve today would not be what it is, and perhaps would not even exist, if it weren't for Anne Boleyn. But in our seminaries and in our pews, we instead present the fiction that the faith we have was shaped almost exclusively by men.

It is also as a priest that I bring a particular skill set to the Anne Boleyn conversation. My daily work is both to probe ancient stories, looking for how they speak to us today, as well as to listen to the voices of those now crying for justice, understanding, hope, and visibility. My job is to lift up those stories so that we see new things in them, connections between them, so that we understand how those stories are connected to us. My job is *not* to give voice to the voiceless. *Just because we have failed to listen doesn't mean that there weren't things being said.* Rather, my job is to listen to the voices that have been muffled, ignored, or pushed to the sidelines, because in my faith tradition, those are the voices that speak truth.

My job with Anne Boleyn is to help us see what has been hiding in plain sight and to draw connections between recorded historical evidence and the stories we tell about her. I'm not relying on my own primary-source historical research to accomplish this. Vast amounts of that research already exist, and I am indebted to those historians and their scholarship. I am indebted to scholars like Eric Ives, Julia Fox, and John Guy for their historical excavations of Anne's life, as well as writers like Susan Bordo, who combine historical analysis with a cultural examination of how Anne's life has been portrayed and understood across recent pop culture. Historians, writers, and podcasters Suzannah Lipscomb and Natalie Grueninger are constantly in conversation on their podcasts *Not Just the Tudors* and *Talking Tudors*, respectively, with historians who are, as I write this, making new discoveries about Anne and her contemporaries and helping us to answer better the thorniest questions around why events unfolded the way they did in Anne's endlessly examined life. Grueninger's own research and writing on

Anne Boleyn has also been invaluable. This evolving body of analysis into the firsthand records of sixteenth-century Tudor England make it possible for a complex and inspiring picture of Anne to emerge and for that picture to evolve and deepen continually.

Readers may wish to complement this book with a deeper dive into that scholarship, although I am committed to representing that work faithfully and clearly for those interested in a more approachable look into Anne's life.

This story of a queen who lived five hundred years ago in England matters. It matters that we claim a more complex picture of who has shaped history. It matters that we tell stories about strong and powerful women. It matters that we interrogate the categories we often use to discuss women's lives. It matters that we allow *people's* stories, not just women's stories, to be complex and multidimensional. It matters that we celebrate those who opt for being difficult and principled and transformational rather than just being nice.

It matters to *me*. I want a fuller understanding of the people, especially women, who influenced the faith tradition I lead. I want examples of what female power and agency look like. I want to see complicated and surprising women. I want an expanded picture of history, the church, and women's lives outside of the bounds of the archetypes, fairy tales, and categories into which women so routinely get slotted.

It matters to *us*. Anne's failure to conform to the usual categories and expected archetypes illuminates truth about who we don't hear and what we fail to see. Women's voices can be easily silenced, women's rights rolled back with breathtaking speed, and there are always creative new ways afoot for keeping women's power curtailed. These missing pieces and this fuller picture of the scandalous, the inflammatory, the derided, the admired, the influential, the complex, the faithful, the controversial Queen Anne matters.

Our stories matter.

And Anne Boleyn's story is a particularly good one.

PART 2

An Old World Falling Apart, a New World Just Beginning

You cannot put a Fire out—
A Thing that can ignite
Can go, itself, without a Fan—
Upon the slowest Night—

—Emily Dickinson, "You cannot put a Fire out—"[1]

CHAPTER 3

Cataclysmic Change

Anne's Books

Anne Boleyn was a book lover.

A number of Anne's books were preserved past her scandalous death and are held today in the British Library, including her copy of Tyndale's translation of the New Testament and a French translation of the Bible. Her French Bible is decorated with the initials of HA—Henry and Anne—along with the Tudor roses.[1] Also among her prized possessions were several high-quality illuminated French manuscripts of the Epistles and Gospels, as well as *Ecclesiaste*, a French transcription and commentary of the Old Testament book of Ecclesiastes.[2]

These books are not just interesting artifacts from Anne's brief reign or even a testament to the things that she thought important. They are emblematic of her personality, as well as the time in which she was living. They reveal the most urgent and controversial conversations raging across Europe during Anne's lifespan. They contain the ideals and ideas that she herself championed. They represent the hinge time in which she lived, where old technologies—illuminated manuscripts—exist side by side with the innovation the printing press was making possible—Tyndale's English translation of the Bible and commentaries on Scripture.

These books existed in her personal collection at a time when such collections were only just becoming a thing and were sometimes a dangerous thing at that. English Bibles were still illegal in Anne's lifetime, and William Tyndale, whose New Testament translation Anne owned, was put to death for heresy just months after Anne's execution. That she owned them anyway shows her determined personality and sincere religious convictions, as well as just how uncontainable this new technology was. Books were fueling a hotbed for transformed power structures across Europe. Books were changing expectations around organized religion and vastly altering people's understanding of who God is and how God, and the spoils of heaven, were to be accessed. Anne was able to stay close to people and ideas that had formed her and to consider new possibilities because she could acquire books. Her daughter, Elizabeth, could share in the ideas most important to Anne because Elizabeth could read the same things that her deceased mother had been reading.

The Car Crash That Changed Everything

In much the same way that my generation has been shaped by the digital age, by access to computers, the World Wide Web, and by the development of social media and now AI, Anne was also living in a historical moment of massive change in technology and communication. The printing press and the books being produced were at the heart of that change.

Historian Diarmaid MacCulloch says that studying the sixteenth century is to be "present at something like the aftermath of a particularly disastrous car crash. All around are half-demolished structures, debris, people figuring out how to make sense of lives that have suddenly been transformed."[3] It's a good reminder not only of the vast—MacCulloch says "cataclysmic"—change that was happening during Anne's time, and how much violence and destruction was unleashed as a result, but also how very little was understood about where all of this might lead. These were people figuring out a new world while their previous world was smashing apart.

The history books tend to give Martin Luther top billing in both causing that car crash and providing a vision for how the demolished pieces should be reassembled. Luther was a monastic, a priest, and an academic. He was part of a zeitgeist that saw debate and the spread of new ideas bubbling up in tandem with the printing press technology.

Luther was part of an educated elite class, acting as a professor of philosophy at the newly established Wittenberg University in Germany. There, he studied the Bible in its original Hebrew and Greek languages. The more that Luther studied the Bible, however, the more he came to disagree with the institutional church. He became convinced that the beliefs he had been taught were a gross corruption of true biblical teaching.

Luther was famously known for his *Ninety-five Theses*, (possibly) nailed to the door of a Wittenberg church on October 31, 1517. However, it wasn't the act of nailing anything to the door that got the Reformation going. It was the circulation of his ideas by pamphlets, by way of the printing press, combined with a groundswell of people interested in reading what Luther had to say.

Luther's story, like Anne's, was shaped by the availability of, and access to, books.

Wildfire

The Bible is today listed as the number one best-selling book of all time, and that bestseller status got a head start five hundred years ago in Europe. Although the printing press was invented around 1440, it wasn't until approximately 1500 that people with entrepreneurial spirit began to recognize the moneymaking opportunities that printing could provide. What people wanted to buy in the new printing market were Bibles, particularly Bibles in a variety of languages other than Latin. Toward the end of the 1400s, Bibles were circulating in High and Low German, Italian, Dutch, Spanish, Czech, and French.

Wittenberg, Martin Luther's city of residence, had not received this entrepreneurial memo. The old methods of printing prevailed for many years, with the university printer producing just enough material as was necessary for the day-to-day requirements of academic life.[4] Wittenberg and its press were blissfully unaware of what was about to hit them.

This changed with the *Ninety-five Theses*. It was not unusual for academic questions to be printed, circulated, and even posted on church doors for discussion. What was unusual was the wildfire that caught with this October 1517 offering. In comparison, just eight weeks prior to his famous *Ninety-five Theses*, Martin Luther had printed *Ninety-seven Theses* against the work of, among others, Thomas Aquinas, a gigantic figure in Christian theology, whose writing in the thirteenth century had dominated Christian doctrine for centuries.[5] These arguments, as controversial as they also were, sparked minimal debate and only local engagement.[6]

The popular appetite for this second set of arguments wasn't expected or even entirely explainable. Wildfire it was though. What happened in Wittenberg became an example of sixteenth-century celebrity, of a decisive turning point in history, and a theological and commercial revolution.[7]

The Reformation began not just with a bold argument but with a lucrative product. People across Europe wanted to read what Martin Luther had to say, and entrepreneurs sought to capitalize on the masses' appetite by unlocking their printing presses' moneymaking potential. Just as they had been tuned in to the popular desire for biblical translations, so now they saw the chance for a financial windfall with this newly minted celebrity rabble-rouser. Martin Luther wrote. The printing presses of Europe printed and distributed his words. His ideas spread. Printers made money.

Indulgences: The Good, the Bad, and the Revolutionary

The nutshell read of Luther's righteous rage against the church is that he was protesting the sale of indulgences. An indulgence is based in a priest's authority, on Christ's behalf, to absolve a penitent sinner. Along with absolution, it is not uncommon for a priest to prescribe a penance that aims at mending that sinner's relationship with God.[8] Penance could, in medieval and Renaissance times, look like joining a crusade, engaging in an act of charity, giving alms, or donating to support church building.

Over the course of the two centuries leading up to Martin Luther's insubordination, an intricate set of teachings developed, with the sanction of the pope, around penance, purgatory, and the ability to purchase time off from purgatory on behalf of another person.[9] Purgatory was defined as the place the average person resided in between death and the pearly gates of heaven. Unless you were to live a blameless life, the church taught that you would spend some time getting from your deathbed to the joys of eternal life with God. Time in purgatory became associated with the imposition of penance. If the length of the stay in purgatory was indicative of the state of a person's relationship with God, then the mending of relationship and the shortening of time in purgatory were one and the same.

An indulgence was essentially a financial substitute for penance, a streamlined vehicle for making amends with God. Indulgences would be announced to support crusades, building or rebuilding churches, or occasionally for papal funds in Rome.[10] Those indulgences could then be purchased by the faithful, with the funds raised going to the project that had been announced. The purchasing of indulgences was the purchase of time off in purgatory ahead of one's death or on behalf of someone else.

Indulgences became important not just for the state of one's soul but also as an effective method of fundraising. Many of the great artistic and architectural treasures, still visible and enjoyable across Europe, were made possible by providing the faithful with a clear-cut way of addressing their sinfulness. St. Peter's Basilica in Rome, for example, was funded in its early stages of construction by selling indulgences.[11] It is one of those ironic twists of fate that this magnificent edifice at the center of Roman Catholic power and culture was being constructed by means of the very wedge that Luther would use to bring the church to its knees.

Indulgences would become a dirty word in the Christian church, but they also represent something sincere and good about pre-sixteenth-century life. Religion was a communal project, rather than a personal relationship between an individual and God. As philosopher Charles Taylor notes, "the living can pray for and otherwise bring relief to the souls of the dead. The terrifying individual destiny can be met by mutual help."[12] Likewise, the saints and the faithful departed could be asked to join in praying for the faithful who were still alive.

The church itself had raised concerns about the sale of indulgences centuries before. But as the practice became more popular and important to both church projects and the faithful, fewer and fewer voices dissented.[13]

As a scholar and as a man of his times, Luther was reading the Bible for himself, and he was incensed and inspired by what he read and didn't read. What he read was about God's dominion and grace. What he didn't read was anything about purgatory and the ability to get out of it more quickly by church fundraising. By 1518, Luther's *Ninety-five Theses* against indulgences were so popular that they were being reprinted across Europe. One of the other great thinkers of the age, Desiderius Erasmus, sent a copy of the theses to his friend and colleague Thomas More in England.[14] More shared Luther's controversial ideas with King Henry VIII. Henry was outraged.

The Ear of the King

Like previous monarchs, Henry took his religious role seriously. It was not just in England and not just in Christianity that kings and emperors were believed to play an important role in brokering an essential spiritual reality for their people. A king's relationship with God has historically been synonymous with a people's relationship with God. The king's duty to live within God's favor and to carry out his religious duties properly was not a private affair or personal choice. Religion was a collective responsibility. The monarch's job wasn't just to protect his people with military might but with religious diligence too. A people's peace, prosperity, and well-being depended on the person (usually a man) wearing the crown.

When Luther's ideas were building momentum in mainland Europe, Henry had an opportunity to shore up his significance with the power players on the Continent and gain religious traction for his people. He put his name to a tract condemning Luther and defending the pope and the Roman church.[15] As a reward, he was given the title, by the pope, "Defender of the Faith." These were the halcyon days of Henry, when he was at his most young and attractive, popular and powerful, celebrated for providing strong religious and political leadership for his people, as well as being a commanding force to be reckoned with wearing a full suit of armor in a jousting match.

Those who circulated and espoused Lutheran or reform ideas in Britain were persecuted. It was dangerous to read the Bible in English or to challenge or engage with teachings that went against Rome. Earlier reformers like John Wycliffe and then a group contemptuously labeled the "Lollards" (mumblers who talked nonsense) had not fared well. The Bible in English was banned from 1407 until the 1530s, when Henry's rule and Anne's influence finally moved that especially stubborn dial.[16] Those who put their heads above the parapet to throw their lot in, first with these earlier reformers and then with Luther and his radical ideas, could be burned as heretics or forced to live in exile outside of England, essentially running for their lives because of what they believed to be the greatest eternal truth.

But reform ideas weren't going away. People traveled and talked. Written materials circulated easily, despite dictums forbidding them and the occasional public book burning to drive the point home. The criticisms levied against the church grew louder and more prominent, as did the belief that the Bible should be available in the people's own language. Many in England's educated class became convicted of Luther's rightness and the church's wrongness. Those with financial means were acquiring translations of the Bible, even though it was technically contraband. The horses were out of the barn. No matter how much doing so was outlawed, people continued to get their hands on English Bibles and Luther's, and other reformers', writings.

There was an element to this religious rebellion that was fun and daring, particularly in the upper class of England where forbidden material circulated easily. But this was also deadly serious. If the church was wrong, then eternal life could be on the line. Despite the hefty consequences for stepping out of line, there were those who thought that getting their religious lives right was of such eternal significance that they were willing to pay the cost for standing up for these new beliefs.

The "evangelical agenda" in England found its rallying cry around a commitment to accessing English Scriptures and individuals being able to study the Bible for themselves. The publication of an official version of the English Bible was an undisputed positive achievement of the 1530s and the religious revolution sparked by Anne's relationship with the king.[17]

The reformers' other agenda items had mixed success in England. That was because of Henry. The king was not interested in a unified field theory of God and humanity. He liked to pick and choose which parts of church reform struck his fancy. Henry didn't like Luther when he wrote his diatribe against Luther in 1521, and he didn't like him later when he tried to get Luther's support for his marriage to Anne and instead got Luther's rebuke. Anyone whose views seemed too Lutheran trod on thin ice with Henry.

Henry also liked to use his absolute political power to be intimately involved in what would and wouldn't float theologically in the churches of England. Both evangelicals and Catholics were persecuted and put to death on Henry's watch. Henry's "ragbag theology of emotional preferences,"[18] couched in erratic theological rationale, would become the guiding legal and political framework for how the Reformation would take hold in England.

That meant that who had the king's ear and what ideas they were able to present to him were the foundation on which these "emotional preferences" came to be laid.

"je anne boleyn"

Martin Luther—along with men like Erasmus, John Calvin, Thomas More, and Henry VIII—would be the well-known names from this dramatic time, but women cared about access to heaven too. Women had theological opinions and insights. Women cared about what did and didn't happen to the church. Their voices haven't tended to make it into the history books, but they also shaped the new world out of the wreckage of this cataclysmic time.

Two of Anne's Books of Hours—devotional books containing selections of Christian prayers and psalms—can still be seen on display at her family's homestead, Hever Castle. One was an older hand-copied and hand-illuminated manuscript, likely passed through the family as a treasured item from the earlier fifteenth century; the second was a product of the new technology, printed in France in 1527.[19] Each contains a handwritten inscription by Anne. In the printed book she wrote:

Remember me when you do pray,
That hope doth lead from day to day.

Anne Boleyn

In the older volume, she wrote underneath a picture of the Day of Final Judgment:

le temps viendra
je anne boleyn

with a small drawing of an armillary sphere between the "je" and "anne."[20]

When she wrote these inscriptions is not known. They hint at her sense of religious conviction, that she saw herself and her role as being called by God and led by a sense of faith that was both personal and prayerful. Anne didn't come by her religious convictions in a vacuum but rather out of the exciting and fast-changing times in which she was living, and more particularly, from the smart women in whose company she grew up and who would so shape her vision for what the world could become.

Anne found herself at the receiving end of a powerful man's desire. She began to sense how that desire could carve a path of reform in the English church. She brought to Henry ideas which religious authorities in the English church, including Henry himself, had so vehemently and recently rejected.

The time will come, the second inscription read. *I, Anne Boleyn.*

CHAPTER 4

The Role Models—Anne Had a Vision

A Journey of the Times

The year was 1515, and Queen Claude of France transformed a road trip across her country into a rich spiritual encounter, as well as a seminar on the gripping intellectual questions of the day. Claude's husband Francis had been crowned King of France earlier that year, so it was also representative of the kind of court Claude wanted to lead and the principles she would champion in her reign. Teenaged Anne Boleyn had been handpicked by Claude to join her royal court, and although we have no record of Anne's impressions of the trip, the journey is emblematic of the ideas that would so deeply imprint on her.

It started with the queen's desire to visit the tomb of St. Martha and the relics of Mary Jacobi and Mary Salome at the monastic community of Tarascon in the Provence–Alpes–Côte d'Azur region. All three saints were disciples of Jesus. Jesus was a close friend of Martha and her family;

she was present at the raising of her brother Lazarus from death and is the first disciple in the Gospel of John to confess Jesus as the Messiah explicitly. The two Marys are described as being first witnesses to the resurrection, along with Mary Magdalene.

From there, Claude took her traveling court to the shrine of St. Mary Magdalene in Saint-Maximin-la-Sainte-Baume. Mary Magdalene had a central place in the life and ministry of Jesus. At both places, Claude was visibly moved and made generous financial offerings for the ministries attached to the pilgrimage sites. These holy places had attracted pilgrims for hundreds of years, dating back to at least the ninth century.

From the earliest expressions of the Christian faith, there was this sense that one could draw closer to Jesus, and therefore God, through the saints and their artifacts. Tombs and graves of the faithful became pilgrimage sites. The belief that the "stuff" of these saints—their hair, their bones, the items that they had owned—was holy and had power to draw one closer to God developed early and strongly.

Claude was a person of deep and sincere faith. These saints were important for Claude's own devotional life, and she evidently felt a desire to enter their stories with the sights and sounds and tactile reality of being in the same place where these inspiring women had served and ultimately died.

But Claude's engagement with these women's stories didn't stop there. In the spirit of the intellectual curiosity that was becoming possible in those early years of the sixteenth century, Claude had questions. She enlisted the services of Jacques Lefèvre d'Étaples and Denis Briçonnet, two early reformers, to launch an investigation into the legends and miracles attributed to Mary Magdalene. Claude had felt an emotional and spiritual connection to these sites. But her sense of wonder had other dimensions as well. Were these really places where Martha and the other Marys had come? Were the reports of miracles to be taken seriously? To what degree was any of this real, or had these legends and relics been made up by the church to manipulate the faithful?

Anne and the other demoiselles of the court, along with Claude, were treated to "impromptu seminars" on the journey back to Paris as Lefèvre and Briçonnet debunked what reformists were increasingly seeing as the church's sainthood racket—manufacturing holy artifacts to line the coffers of the church with the faithful's offerings.

It is a wonderful example of Claude's spirituality, which was pious, generous, devoted, but also probing and intellectually liberated. She seemingly felt no conflict in emotionally connecting to these holy sites but then also questioning their veracity. Claude had significant freedom in her court. She had her own power and agency—to engage controversial ideas, to provide patronage to people with radical religious leanings, to form her court into a place of learning and curiosity for the women in her care.

I recognize in this story everything that captured my imagination about religious faith when I was a young girl and teenager. I was drawn in equal parts to the stories of the Bible, particularly the singular characters at their center, as well as the mystery of what we believe and why we believe it. It was of vital importance to my faith journey to be part of a church where that kind of intellectual curiosity was not only tolerated but celebrated.

We see in this pilgrimage of 1515 something of the imprint that Claude's intellect, piety, and leadership would have on Anne. We also see the beginning of this new spirituality that was just emerging in the 1500s, which did not just involve Luther and his male compatriots (this was two years before Luther's famous theses!), and that would remake what faithfulness can look like.

Women and Reform

Occasionally I teach "Anglicanism 101" classes to newcomers at our church. One of the sessions is a history lesson, delving into the way reform unfolded in England and why it led to the creation of the Anglican church. "King Henry VIII wanted a divorce," is the rather shady origin story that I was told from the start of my Anglican life. I tell my groups that although this is the common narrative, it isn't true. The Anglican church was created not because the king wanted a divorce but because Anne became the object of the king's attention, and Anne was a reformer. She wasn't just a reformer, she was a smart, witty, articulate, and well-read reformer. She was a reformer who figured out how to use the "tale as old as time" situation in which she found herself—a woman targeted by a man who holds all the power—to enact the religious change in which she so believed.

Anne, not the king, is the primary subject in this church's origin story.

Understanding how she came to be the reformer that would catch the attention of the king and influence him to reconsider ideas that he had so vehemently rejected requires illuminating not just Anne's story, but those of the women who influenced her.

Margaret of Austria—"Noble and Excellent Womankind"

At various times in Anne's ascendancy, reign, and afterlife, she would be accused of being a "Lutheran." But it wasn't Martin Luther sparking Anne's intellectual curiosity and spiritual passion. It was a circle of powerful women, all of whom were tapping into a long legacy of spiritual vision and renewal.

These women were asking the critical spiritual questions of the age before any monks posted theses on cathedral doors. And Anne was learning from them before the marriage woes of an English king would be credited with a religious revolution.

Anne came from a titled family of significant wealth and noble bloodlines. However, Anne's father's disposable wealth was paltry in comparison to the costs associated with "keeping up with the Joneses." Advantageous marriages for the Boleyn children were a natural component of his strategizing.

A courtly education was standard fare in securing a good marriage for Anne and increasing the family's standing among English nobility.[1] Thomas was also thought to be a progressive man of his times, interested in the new ways of thinking, and believing in the value of educating his daughter.[2] Thomas's diplomatic connections afforded Anne just such an education.

Anne was first sent to the court of Margaret of Austria. Margaret was the archduchess of Austria, ruling on behalf of the Holy Roman Emperor Charles V. "It's a small world" doesn't even begin to describe the numerous connections among the ruling families of Europe. There were no six degrees of separation, but rather the multiple ties binding them to one another are dizzying. In this case, Margaret was related to Catherine of Aragon through two matrimonial alliances, and both women were aunt to Charles V. Margaret had been married to Catherine's brother John for a brief three months before his untimely death. Margaret's brother Philip had been married to Catherine of Aragon's sister Juana but had died young as well. Margaret had a hand in raising Charles, the man who would become such a powerful force in Europe and in the personal lives of Henry and Anne.

Anne's father had met Margaret the year before while on ambassadorial duty for Henry and had either requested, or had it requested of him, that Anne come to serve in her court as a *fille d'honneur*.[3]

It was heady times on the Continent, and women were engaged with the new ideas circulating. Anne was in the presence of, and shaped by, circles of female influence and philosophical debate that have been retrospectively identified as protofeminism. Margaret had a notable connection with the writing of Christine de Pizan, a provocative advocate for women from the previous century. Margaret inherited a manuscript of de Pizan's *The Book of the City of Ladies* from her mother and owned a tapestry depicting de Pizan's city.[4] The book remains a notable example of feminist thought. In it, de Pizan clapped back at the gaslighting that she experienced in being told that she was inferior to men because of her gender, despite no evidence to support that conclusion. She wrote of an imaginary conversation between her and the allegorical figures of Reason,

Justice, and Rectitude inviting her to build a city for famous women of the past and virtuous women of all times as an alternate space to the world made for men.[5]

Margaret had married twice for reasons of political convenience and was again widowed by the time Thomas Boleyn met her. Her chosen motto signaled her independence: *Fortune Infortune Fort Une* (Changes in fortune make a woman stronger).[6]

Anne made an impression on Margaret, who wrote to Thomas Boleyn herself shortly after Anne's arrival to thank him for having sent such a "clever and pleasant girl."[7] She claimed, "I am more beholden to you for having sent her to me than you are to me."[8]

In Margaret's court, Anne learned to speak French, dance, play musical instruments, and see firsthand a woman successfully operating in leadership. Margaret was a patron of the arts and owned an extensive library of fiction, romance, philosophy, Greek and Roman manuscripts, and devotional books, which the women of her court were allowed to read.[9]

Anne wrote to her father during this time to assure him that she was being diligent in her studies. She told him that "it gives me great joy to think of talking with such a wise and virtuous woman" (she might have been referring to either Catherine of Aragon or Margaret).[10] No other record of the Austrian court's influence on Anne exists, although the reports about Anne's skills and mannerisms and leadership qualities when she was back in the English courts and then at Henry's side as queen all suggest that Margaret made a profound impression on the young Anne.

Queen Claude of France—Fellow Bookworm

Queen Claude of France was a master at meeting patriarchal expectations and then carving out freedom for herself as a result. She needed to be sexually available to her husband, produce lots of babies, and avert her eyes and keep her mouth shut in the face of King Francis's legendary dalliances. She did these things in spades. She was prolific in her childbearing, producing a great brood of heirs to satisfy the anxieties of her husband, to speak to his manhood, and to assure the continuation of his royal bloodline. She tolerated his many affairs and wandering eye with little consternation or comment, at least in her public-facing role.

As a reward, she was able to guard the precious library she had inherited from her mother from her husband's clutches,[11] she operated a court that provided explicitly for the education of the girls in her charge, and she got to design trips like the one in the French mountains that was equal parts seminar and spiritual pilgrimage. She could create a haven, a free-thinking, intellectually stimulating, education-forward space for women. Men and women intermingled in the queen's household with relative freedom, in sharp contrast to the court of Queen Catherine back in England.[12] One of Claude's prized possessions was a "deluxe copy of the Dominican monk Antoine Dufour's *Vies des femmes célèbres*, a compilation of ninety-one biographies of famous women, including Joan of Arc."[13]

Anne's time with Margaret of Austria ended when Anne was enlisted to accompany the king's sister Mary to France to marry the very old and unappealing king of France, Louis XII.[14] The marriage was short-lived, with Louis dying shortly after Mary's arrival, and Francis succeeding him as king. Mary secretly wed Henry VIII's close friend Charles Brandon while still in France, creating a flurry of upset and gossip, as well as provoking Henry's significant rage. Brandon had also been involved in some scandalous flirtation with Margaret of Austria, which Anne likely witnessed. Brandon and Mary made a point of hating Anne throughout her relationship with Henry, and the theory is that this bad blood started when Anne was just a teenager, perhaps judgmentally observing these scandalous goings-on.[15]

Mary and Charles Brandon went back to England married and in disgrace. Anne joined Claude's court.[16] Claude wasn't much older than

Anne, just turning sixteen, and was already pregnant with the first heir to the French throne when Anne arrived.[17] Anne's ability to speak both English and French fluently, as well as her closeness in age to Claude, might have been the reasons for Claude to notice and select her.[18]

Francis and Claude's marriage was one of political convenience. Claude was an heiress in her own right as the daughter of the former king of France. In a different world, it would have been Claude on the throne, but having her married to the one who was to succeed her father was the next best choice.

Anne would stay for six formative years with Claude.

One of Claude's ladies-in-waiting was the protofeminist Anne de Graville, who rewrote classic texts by men "recasting women as individuals with the right to govern their own lives."[19] Queen Claude took as her role model the biblical figure of Esther, wife to King Xerxes.[20] Esther would also become a figurehead for Anne's understanding of her own role when she became queen.

Although she was not a Lutheran, Claude provided shelter and protection for reform voices. She wanted the ladies of her court, and especially the girls, to be educated and to learn to read and write. Claude's household was separate from the blatant sexuality of Francis's, and a lot less public than the household of Margaret.[21] Popular portrayals of Anne love to suggest that her time in France might have involved loose sexual living because of King Francis's reputation (and because casting Anne as a woman of questionable sexual morality has always had its appeal) but nothing could be further from the truth. Bible study and reading the Scriptures in French was the leading expectation of Claude's court, as was her engagement with ideas that challenged what were starting to be understood as the superstitious elements of the church's traditional teachings. Her court's pilgrimage to the sites of St. Martha's and St. Mary Magdalene's tombs was the epitome of the things she valued and offered the women in her circle.

Claude died at age twenty-five after birthing seven children in ten years. Cause of death is suspected to be either a miscarriage or exhaustion.[22]

Marguerite d'Angoulême—"The First Modern Woman"

Queen Claude wasn't the only strong, independently minded woman by whom Anne was molded in those formative years. Francis himself was the product of a family full of strong women. Francis's mother was Louise of Savoy, a woman known for her political and cultural opinions and influence on Francis and the country he was ruling. She was his first choice as regent whenever he was out of the country. She "exercised a vice-like grip over the royal court" and was a "ruthless politician in her own right, a woman with a razor-sharp mind and a venomous tongue if suitably aroused."[23]

Similar observations would be made about Anne when she was in power.

Francis's sister, Marguerite d'Angoulême (also known as Marguerite of Navarre), is sometimes titled the "first modern woman." Historians Julia Fox and John Guy describe her as

> Tall, slim, witty, charming and vivacious, she too was a shrewd, versatile politician, less ruthless than Louise, but an acute, clear-headed, discerning observer of all that went on in the royal courts, with a searching intelligence fully equipped to counter or repulse the slippery, deceitful devices of ambitious, predatory men.[24]

Marguerite was well educated. She was committed to promoting new humanist ideals, advocating for universal education, and fostering artistic and social development in her country. She was a political mover and shaker and a diplomat in her own right. Her most famous exploit was riding across Europe on horseback to save her brother from imprisonment and using her diplomatic skills to negotiate his release.

Marguerite is best known as an author and poet. Her most controversial work, *The Mirror of the Sinful Soul*, was initially condemned as heresy, and pressure from the monasteries was applied to Marguerite to edit her work. But her brother Francis stuck up for her, allowing the work to remain unchanged and to circulate across Europe.[25] In it, Marguerite articulated a personal relationship with Jesus as father, brother, and lover, which encapsulated the more personal spirituality that was starting to emerge.

Marguerite would write later works on the relations between the sexes but seems to have been shaping those ideas as early as these first decades of the 1500s. She talked openly—based on her own experience of having been nearly raped—about the compromised situation in which women could find themselves when men wanted to use them for sex and when a man's word was always favored over a woman's in matters of sexual assault. Women needed to be on their guard and turn to religion for guidance and fortitude.

In 1516, Marguerite was made a duke. Her brother Francis granted to her the legal status of a man.[26]

Marguerite was a regular visitor of Louise's and Claude's courts, and the royal couple also spent time with her in Argentan.[27] Anne deliberately styled herself after Marguerite and explicitly claimed her as a role model.[28]

Not only did Marguerite, Louise, Claude, and Margaret of Austria all form Anne in her most impressionable years to see how women could hold positions of power, but it is also very possible that she was shaped by Marguerite's protofeminist philosophy on a woman's need to guard her body from exploitation by men.

Decades later, Marguerite did not attend the 1532 meeting on French soil in which Anne was presented to Francis as Henry's chosen partner. This was a political decision on King Francis's part, and Anne held no ill will toward her as a result. She wrote afterward to Marguerite:

> There was no one thing which her grace so much desired . . . as the want of the said queen of Navarre's company, with whom to have conference, for more causes than were meet to be expressed, her grace is most desirous.[29]

Anne wrote in a letter to Marguerite in 1535, after she was queen, to say that her "greatest wish, next to having a son, is to see you again."[30]

Anne's personal library paid homage to Marguerite's influence. She favored evangelical tracts and Bibles translated into French by members of Marguerite's reformist circle. In one of the tracts was a written introduction pairing Henry and Francis, Anne and Marguerite, as parallel figures in England and in France.[31]

Marguerite presented Anne with the original manuscript of her famous and controversial poem, which had been published in 1531. Anne's daughter, Elizabeth, would later translate the Latin poem into English as a precocious eleven-year-old, suggesting that Anne's belongings had been passed along to her by a faithful friend or confidant from mother to daughter. Someone in Anne's circle must have known that she would have wanted her daughter to have it, perhaps communicating to Elizabeth that this writing had been treasured by her deceased mother.[32]

In Good Company

Anne didn't come from nowhere. She was formed. Likewise, these women who would imprint so significantly on her ideas of leadership and religious reform came from somewhere too. If we need to widen the lens from Anne to the women who influenced her, we also need to widen the lens from those women to the women in whose path they were continuing. Anne, Margaret, Marguerite, Louise, and Claude were all in good company.

They were in good company with the first disciples of Jesus. It is no wonder that Claude felt drawn to the pilgrimage sites of Mary Magdalene, Martha, Mary Jacobi, and Mary Salome. Women, along with men, left their homes and families behind to follow this itinerant teacher around the countryside. Women supported Jesus's ministry with their financial resources, their time and labor. They were faithful to Jesus in ways that his male disciples mostly weren't. They had insight into his teachings that the men in the group couldn't grasp.

They were in good company with those who had midwifed the birth of the church across the Roman Empire. Female leadership was a prominent feature of the nascent communities meeting mostly in the homes of hospitable and faithful women. They saw in Jesus a different sort of life and value for themselves, a new possibility of what service could look like and how relationships between human beings could be imagined.[33]

They were in good company with those who followed Jesus into an alternative, or an addition, to the prescribed roles of wife and mother. Many of the earliest martyrs—the word "martyr" means "witness"—of the Christian faith were women, some of them extremely young. The "virgin" label on martyrs of the early church was used to describe political and financial independence as much as an intact hymen:

> Virginity became a movement, the ultimate hack. As a consecrated virgin, a woman suddenly became free of many of the empire's gender laws, free to preach and to lead in their community, free to model themselves after the apostles. . . . They dressed to make a statement, sometimes adopting men's clothing and hairstyles (some sheared their heads entirely), and preached in the streets in drag.[34]

They were in good company with those who had long ago understood that renewal, a call to return to previous principles or to go forward into a brave new world, must be part of a faithful church. When Christianity became the favored religion of the Roman Empire under Constantine and was thoroughly enmeshed in both the opportunities and limitations of becoming mainstream, it was men and women of imagination and vision who fled to the deserts and created the spiritual movement of the Desert Fathers and Mothers. These were people whose radically different way of living helped to keep the rebellious spirit of Jesus alive even as Christianity was becoming more consolidated into the structures of power. This movement became the precursor to monasticism.[35]

They were in good company with those who had always yearned for a faith that would address their God-given intellectual hunger. Throughout the Middle Ages and Renaissance, as empires fell apart and as the role of women continued to be rigorously policed, it was in that monastic system where an alternative could still be embraced, where worlds of philosophy and art and music and prayer could still transform the human soul. It was in these monastic systems, too, where women sought refuge and inspiration. In the abbeys of Europe, women could wield influence, write and disseminate ideas, claim some measure of independence, and live outside of the confines of traditional assumptions about women's roles and relationships.

They were in good company. Anne was in good company.

Back to England

People would later say that Anne was elegant, witty, intelligent, and an excellent conversationalist. She was known for her singing and dancing, for playing the lute beautifully and even composing her own music.[36] I studied a piece of music in third-year music history that was attributed to her,[37] and it is likely that their shared love for and skill in music was a point of bonding between Anne and Henry. Popular lore said that "Greensleeves" was written by Henry for Anne.

The European courts had formed Anne well, including implanting in her ideas for how the world might be remade. Anne learned that women might speak freely, express sharp opinions, operate in roles traditionally reserved for men, and prioritize other qualities above being "nice." Anne learned, too, that these freedoms were negotiated; they were dependent on serving up healthy doses of traditional female offerings, namely desirability and fertility.

Anne did not go back to England with grand designs on marrying the king and upending the political and religious worlds of Britain and Europe. She went home to England to make an advantageous marriage, as was expected of her. Cardinal Wolsey, the worldly and ambitious wheeler-dealer cleric of the church and one of King Henry's closest confidantes, had arranged for Anne to marry James Butler as a convenient way of settling a dispute over lands and titles between the Boleyn family and the Butlers.[38] This would have seen Anne sent off to Ireland to make her way as a mildly titled wife. It is unclear why this marriage didn't materialize.

That doesn't mean that Anne's head wasn't also full of ideas of how women could be influential. She brought with her the religious fervor of the women who had informed her upbringing so powerfully. It is evident from the books that she was reading and the direction her life would unfold that she was passionate about seeing these ideas catch fire in her home country of England as well. While it would be a stretch to suppose that she had a master plan for how she might be able to wield influence and effect change, it is fair to say that she had seen a vision of female leadership that was inspiring and meaningful.

Opportunity of a sort came her way after the Butler marriage fell through in the form of Henry Percy, a titled and wealthy man. Percy represented a step up from the standing that her own family had. She caught his eye. It was Cardinal Wolsey, who denied their desired marriage and arranged a more beneficial marriage for Percy instead. Whether Wolsey was doing this on the king's instruction is debatable. Wolsey's biographer, George Cavendish, in his telling of Anne and Wolsey's rivalry, argued that the king already had his eye on Anne when she was the love interest of Percy and that was why Wolsey intervened.[39] However, there is no corroborating evidence of Henry's interest in Anne until a few years later. Cavendish reads like one who was taking artistic license in crafting the cardinal's story from the vantage point of knowing how it would end.

Percy would continue to reappear at key moments in Anne's life. When King Henry was obsessively pursuing Anne, Percy was brought in for questioning to speak to the nature of their relationship and whether it had been consummated. Any known sexual dalliance would have nullified Anne's prospects of being Henry's wife and queen. Percy never wavered from defending Anne's honor and insisting that their relationship never got to the bedroom. He sat on the jury at her trial, and when the verdict and sentence was announced, had to be carried out of the courtroom after dramatically fainting.

Whatever the reason for Wolsey's preventing Anne's marriage to Percy, it would have been a rude awakening for Anne to come back from Queen Claude's court with its circle of women who were joining in politics, religious reform, and the work of ruling their kingdom, to be reminded of how little power a young woman in England in the sixteenth century had. Anne had experienced a very different reality; she had touched it; she had tasted it. Now she was being treated as someone of no account, not good enough for a love match with a titled and rich man, a pawn in the schemes of people who assumed they knew better.

Wolsey was a complex figure with his own intriguing backstory and a surprising rise to power. But in the context of Anne's story, Wolsey becomes a figurehead for a whole world that has failed to take women seriously. He could not have imagined that this young courtier would change his life, his church, and the political landscape of Europe, for he had never been taught to see anything other than a picture of men being the ones who counted.

CHAPTER 5

The Matter of Sex

Prayers to St. Frideswide

In 1518, while Anne Boleyn was growing up in the French court, Catherine of Aragon was thirty-three years old and pregnant. Catherine had been pregnant at least five times prior. There had been miscarriages and stillbirths, along with the much-hoped-for boy, Henry, in 1511, who had tragically died at a month old. Mary was born in 1516. Her birth would have given Catherine hope that a boy could be next and that the string of unfortunate losses might be broken.

This wasn't just a private hope or a personal matter. If Catherine couldn't produce the needed heir, then other solutions would be found. It was not a time of middle-class respectability in thoughts about sex. Powerful men were entitled to sleep around. If heirs needed to be produced outside of marriage, then so be it.

Catherine's body and soul had been through significant hardship in these many maternal losses. At thirty-three, Catherine was knocking on the door of being an age where no more babies would be expected to come along.

Catherine was a tower of determination, however. Her faith was her source of resilience in navigating whatever heartbreaks life would throw her way. She turned to faith in this circumstance too. The Reformation was beginning in mainland Europe, but England was still thoroughly Catholic. The saints of previous generations were regarded as spiritual companions and resources in navigating life's challenges. In their exalted position from the realm of heaven, the saints could pray to God on behalf of the supplicant. Perhaps God would hear and respond, if not to the lowly mortal here on this earthly plain, then to the one who had already been found worthy of eternal life.

Catherine made a pilgrimage to the shrine of St. Frideswide, a local eighth-century saint with an interesting backstory and a track record of miracles. The unique feature of Frideswide's biography was her running from the advances of a Saxon prince. Her devotion to God was total, and she had no interest in the offer of a royal marriage.

Catherine was accompanied to Frideswide's shrine by Cardinal Wolsey. His presence in this supplication might have signaled a bond of friendship between them. Most certainly it signaled that what happened in Catherine's womb was of significant political consequence. As the man in England representing the pope, Cardinal Wolsey was the perfect person to enlist in giving Catherine's prayers the best chance of working. Together they prayed for the birth of a healthy son.[1]

Catherine gave birth to a stillborn daughter in November instead. This was her last known pregnancy.

A year later, Henry was openly having an affair with Bessie Blount, a lady-in-waiting to Catherine, and he acknowledged the son they had together, Henry, as his. (Naming this illegitimate son not only after himself but also his dead infant son didn't appear to trouble him.) After Catherine's last failed pregnancy, the king and the English people were eager to secure the succession in any way possible.

It would be at least seven years between Bessie and news that Henry's attentions had turned to Anne Boleyn, the sister of one of Henry's other mistresses, Mary. The beloved saint Frideswide's story would find a parallel in Anne's, whose own unique biography would come to public attention when she refused royal advances too.

There wouldn't have been anything initially noteworthy about Henry's interest settling on Anne, even if he had already bedded her sister. She was just another lady of the court. Although her family had land, money, and titles, these were insignificant compared to the high players of the English nobility. Anne didn't offer political alliances either. Becoming a royal mistress wasn't a bad opportunity for Anne, a relative nobody in the grand scheme of wealth and power in the royal families of Europe. Producing an heir for the king offered her a good shot at making her mark.

As the story goes, Anne refused. So began Henry's obsession. Among the many surprising and disruptive things about their relationship is that it put the project of securing male babies to continue the Tudor line on ice for an astonishing length of time. For six long years, neither Anne nor Henry were getting any younger, no sex was happening, and babies were not forthcoming. By the time Anne did get pregnant, she was, by most historians' best guess, not much younger than Catherine of Aragon when she made that "last chance" pilgrimage to St. Frideswide's shrine.

Henry and the English people needed the security of male Tudor progeny, but having Anne as his wife (and legitimate male heirs were assumed to be part of the package of marrying her) became Henry's top priority instead.

The Sex Problem

Women's sexuality is a perpetual problem in our Western world, although the assumptions of the Tudor period were different from our own. All people were thought to be ruled by barely containable lust, but women's desires were considered especially unwieldy. In Anne's time, it was women who were believed to be the ones whose libido had to be kept in check. This justified stringently managed expectations about how women could behave, what they could say, and what sexual agency they could display or suggest. These social norms were developed according to the belief that if women were left to their own devices, they would be out of control.[2]

At every turn, Anne's sexual choices were problematic. She was called promiscuous and whorish for drawing the attention of the king. She was labeled as manipulative and ambitious for refusing to have sex with him. She was accused of moral looseness because she played the game of courtly romance so well and had numerous admirers. She was a betrayer because she was said to have committed adultery, and even more dangerous, to have complained about Henry's sexual prowess (or lack thereof) in the later days of their marriage.

She was not unusual in finding herself in a no-win situation. In the *Not Just the Tudors* podcast episode "16th Century Feminists," Suzannah Lipscomb talked with Hannah Dawson, the editor of *The Penguin Book of Feminist Writing*. The two women discussed the double bind that keeps rearing its head for women across the centuries of writing that Dawson had compiled. "If a woman refuses the sexual advances of a man then she's thought of as cruel, coy, ungrateful. If she accepts them or gives them an inch, then they'll go around proclaiming to the town that she's a terrible whore. Women cannot win." Dawson also articulated how this slander is "yoked" to male violence. "The experience," she says, "is one of fleeing harassment, whether it's verbal or physical. There is continuity between cruel words and physical violence."[3] Her words caused the hair on my arms to stand up and a chill to run down my spine: The story of Henry's pursuit of Anne became the story of Henry's killing of Anne.

What is never discussed is the inner life of Anne and the conflicted feelings she must have had about a relationship with Henry, let alone sex. She was a devout and serious woman. She had a relationship with Catherine, having served in her court for at least some of the four or five years between her arrival back from France and her relationship with

Henry becoming public. To assume Anne would have found Henry attractive is to assume a lot, and she very well might have seen the prospect of going to bed with him scary or revolting.

To blame Anne for Henry's uncontrollable desire to have her is both profoundly disturbing and disturbingly predictable.

"I Want That One"

I was talking with my friend Kenneth about my fascination with Anne Boleyn. "I'm a fan of Catherine of Aragon," he offered in response, stating with conviction that "of course Anne *tried* to get Henry's attention."

Kenneth is a friend who defines himself as a feminist. However, it is a common complaint against Anne that she deliberately pursued all that came her way from the king. This complaint is then also not so subtly tied to Anne's death. If she hustled her way to the top, then she deserved to fall from those heights too.

I asked Kenneth to consider what he might be missing in his assessment. Anne returned from serving in the court of the French queen, Claude, around the end of 1521[4] and made her debut at the English court in 1522.[5] Anne, by the judgment of most historians, would have been twenty-one. She was one of four women involved in an elaborate and expensive masque in March of that year in which she played the role of "Perseverance."[6] In hindsight, the foreshadowing of this moment is rather on the nose. The occasion was a visit from Charles V of Spain, Catherine's nephew and newly minted Holy Roman Emperor. England was once again pursuing an alliance with Spain, turning on the French in doing so, and six-year-old Princess Mary was promised as a bride to her cousin Charles to seal the deal.[7]

Henry was a high-spirited participant in the performance, although whether he noticed Anne is pure speculation. It wouldn't be until the second half of 1527 that anybody in the exceedingly gossipy royal court recorded Henry's interest in Anne.

Although Anne's sister, Mary, was Henry's mistress first, it is unlikely to be the case that this was at the encouragement of Mary and Anne's father Thomas. He is often portrayed as "pimping" out his two daughters for his own political advancement—a notion that casts both Thomas and his daughters in a bad light. Rather, Thomas had been effective in securing his own advancement through his intelligence and hard work, and he didn't obviously benefit from Mary's involvement with the king.[8]

As noted, there was a problem with Henry and his reign. He hadn't secured the line of succession by producing a male heir with his wife Catherine. Although he had been actively addressing that deficiency by having at least one child outside of marriage, the question of whether God was judging him by withholding a prince haunted him. Talk of a royal divorce was on the horizon long before Anne, specifically for this reason.[9] It has been assumed that, at first, Henry's interest in Anne and the pursuit of a divorce were two separate matters in the king's mind.[10] He was interested in Anne but didn't initially see her as "wife material." Compelling new research is suggesting that we might have had that wrong and that Henry very quickly, and with great determination, went from noticing Anne to deciding that he would marry her.[11]

While Henry was obsessing about his lack of progeny, Anne had her own romantic entanglements, first with Henry Percy and then later catching the eye of the poet Thomas Wyatt, who praised her magnetic ways in his sonnets.[12] Although accusations would be whispered of Anne regarding dalliances with Wyatt, there is nothing to suggest that she returned his affections. It seems, from his poetry and from the later remembrances of his grandson George Wyatt, that Thomas was one of Anne's courtly suitors and was quite powerfully drawn to her, but that Anne's response in return was muted.[13]

What Wyatt's attraction to her does reveal is that a culture of courtly romance pervaded the Tudor palaces. It involved women being appropriately attractive and flirtatious and men falling in carefully prescribed ways for their charms. Female behavior was expected to manage a fine line between vivacity and flirtatiousness, "a certain pleasant affability" designed to please men, while never being overly suggestive or lacking modesty.[14] One of Anne's most credible biographers, historian Eric Ives, pieces together these bits of information to conclude that Henry became interested in Anne because courtier Thomas Wyatt and others were vying for Anne's attention, and this game of courtly flirtation piqued Henry's competitive spirit and sexual interest in Anne too.[15] His initial interactions with her followed the courtly love formula, a formula that was meant to be anything but serious. Real feelings developed as Henry got to know Anne—at least on Henry's part.

Popular representations of Anne have run with several hypotheses that are variations on Kenneth's casual criticism of Anne:

- Anne was encouraged by her father to put herself in Henry's sights, just as Mary had done.
- Anne herself wanted the ultimate affirmation of having the king's desire and sought to get it.
- Anne was running a master class in delayed gratification in order to secure for herself something more than just Henry's temporary affections.

These hypotheses run on some standard assumptions about how relationships between men and women operate, who has the power, and who is to blame when things go awry. While there is little to no evidence to support any of those well-worn storytelling tropes, there *is* good reason from the couple's correspondence and from the ample source material we have about Henry's personality to believe that Henry was the pursuer, and Anne had reservations about his affections.

Having said that, there is still a basic flaw in Kenneth's assessment. Regardless of whether Anne tried to capture Henry's eye in the world of courtly romance, or whether she was the world's best ten-dimensional chess player and could see a road to power from the first masque at the

English court to the day of her coronation, we should not get fooled into imagining that Anne had real choice in the matter of the king's desire for her. Kenneth fell into the all-too-easy trap of missing the forest for the trees: with trees being a woman's power to seduce and the forest being a man's power to hunt.

Consent and Kings

Thomas Wyatt wrote this poem in the Tower of London in 1536 when Anne was accused of adultery and Wyatt was rounded up in the group of suspects too:

> Who list to hunt, I put him out of doubt,
> As well as I may spend his time in vain.
> And graven with diamonds in letters plain
> There is written, her fair neck round about:
> *Noli me tangere*, for Caesar's I am,
> And wild for to hold, though I seem tame.[16]

It is insightful on several levels. Henry is compared to Caesar. Anne is marked as Henry's prey. "The thrill of the hunt" is an idea long applied to powerful men's pursuit of women they decide they want, whether they are available or not.

Consent is an increasingly important cornerstone in our understanding of healthy relationships and sexuality. It is not a concept that would have applied to the world of Anne Boleyn. It is not a concept that has historically been considered important, and in cultures where women are legally defined as belonging to their husbands, it has been largely regarded as irrelevant. Even today, insisting that consent is sexy, that it is good and healthy and desirable and leads to more passion and intimacy, has been an uphill battle.

Nonetheless, it is valuable to consider the concept of consent in looking back at some of our most beloved and well-worn stories, because it shines a different light on what is assumed to be happening. Did Cinderella consent to being the love object of the prince when she was living as a servant to her own family and the royal gaze fell on her? We know that unconscious people can't give consent, so the life-restoring kisses bestowed on Snow White and Sleeping Beauty don't pass muster. In the real world, how do we feel in the twenty-first century about a teenage Diana Spencer agreeing to marry the prince of Wales, a man she hardly knew? "This is the stuff of fairy tales," the archbishop of Canterbury famously said at their wedding. The archbishop's words have a sinister bent when we consider how widely it was assumed that Diana had reached the ultimate peak of desirability and feminine success because she became the target of the future king's interest. Few at the time were asking instead whether a barely legal Diana chose the king in return.

Anne Boleyn inhabited a world in which arranged marriages and marrying for a variety of outcomes other than romantic love was normal. That means that women, in these arrangements, were properties to be negotiated, not hearts to be won. In the wheeling and dealing of marriages, affairs, and matchmaking across the British landscape at that time, a woman's consent to being in a partnership was not a consideration either for the man making the match or for the people around judging it.

When kings were involved, the choices available to women were further diminished.

That was Anne's predicament. Like many women before her and many more still to come, Anne was the target of desire.

The question is not whether Anne herself wanted this desire, whether she brought it on herself, whether she sought it out, or whether her family sought it out on her behalf. Female consent and agency were not relevant categories of concern for the king of England in taking a partner. If the king wanted you, he would have you.

This did not leave Anne with many obvious options. The king was already married. He was married in a highly political and strategic alliance between himself and the royal family of Spain. His wife, Catherine of Aragon, was the aunt of the Holy Roman Emperor, Charles V. Anne Boleyn, a woman of no consequential fortune or political clout, would have never been considered a worthy matrimonial match for Henry, even if he had been single.[17] Ending his marriage was an option he was considering, but marrying someone like Anne was not an acceptable replacement for the royal blood of Catherine. When Cardinal Wolsey, Henry's closest advisor, went to the pope to petition for the annulment, he thought Henry was going to marry a European princess, Claude's sister, Renée, in Catherine's place.[18]

It has long been assumed that the offer Anne was fielding was to be Henry's mistress. She might have attained some of the king's protection and favor as a result, particularly if she were to bear him any children. But she would also be maligned, gossiped about, labeled, and limited about what kind of marriage she could eventually have. Anne's sister, Mary, had the protection of already having a husband when the king took up with her. If any children were produced (which they were, although whether or not they were Henry's is a question of debate) then those children had the benefit of being legitimate within the mistress's existing marriage. Anne and any children she might have would have had no such protection.

Anne was not free to choose the king. She was not free to refuse the king.

And Yet . . .

Anne refused Henry. The common story that she refused to become his mistress, and so he offered marriage instead is, as we shall see, perhaps not an accurate read of the situation. But whatever options were on the table—mistress or marriage—we do know that Anne had reservations.

We also know that she was judged as morally bankrupt anyway. The double bind was, and is, real.

To understand this choice that nobody thought was hers to make, Anne's role models shed some light.

Let's consider St. Frideswide, whose shrine was just down the road in Oxford and who had been a spiritual hope to Catherine of Aragon almost a decade earlier. Frideswide's story was of refusing the advances of a prince. Frideswide was born to royal parents and founded a monastery at a young age, taking a vow of celibacy in doing so. She was chased across the English countryside by an amorous prince. She was successful in hiding from him, and with a miraculous intervention which saw him struck blind until he gave up his pursuit, Frideswide was able to continue her monastic life.[19]

Frideswide's story was well known and popular. She is part of a long line of female saints whose virtue was defined by refusing sex. Vows of celibacy for religious purposes gave women an alternative to the pipeline to marriage that was otherwise assumed for them. Frideswide and other female mystics, martyr virgins, and desert mothers were ascribed levels of power and authority mostly not granted to women, and their chasteness was part of the spiritual parcel they were offering.

Anne was a person of deep faith and strong religious conviction, and she no doubt knew of the stories of Frideswide and other female saints like her. If Anne's story hadn't ended in such scandal, Anne's refusal of the king might have been interpreted in a more Frideswide-like light. While Anne never suggested that what she really wanted was to be a monastic, and it would be pure speculation to wonder if Anne herself were explicitly influenced by Frideswide's story, we do know of at least two other women to whom Anne looked as role models throughout her life: the biblical figure of Esther, and the sister-in-law of Queen Claude, Marguerite d'Angoulême.

Marguerite's influence can be felt in Anne's response to the king's advances. Marguerite was known for speaking openly of the vulnerability of women in the face of a powerful man's sexual desire. Her later writing explicitly counseled women to turn to their faith for strength as a shield against a man's exploitation. Her ideas were germinating during the time that Anne was growing up in France. We don't have a lot of Anne's thoughts recorded, but we do have written testimony of Anne's love for and admiration of Marguerite when Anne herself was on the throne. Anne explicitly sought parallels between Marguerite's life and her own.

Esther featured prominently in Anne's story in the final months of her life and might have been an inspiration to her throughout her time at Henry's side. Esther was also a woman chosen by a king (and a cruel king at that), and Esther used that targeting to accomplish good for her people. It isn't surprising that Esther was a touchstone for Queen Claude too, the woman in whose court Anne was raised, as well as Claude's mother before her. Anne would also find solace and inspiration in Esther, just like Claude had, in how she could use her position as queen bravely for a greater vision and deeper purpose.

At some point in Henry's pursuit of her, Anne said yes. Whether her qualms were assuaged when Henry offered marriage (as has been the traditional story) or whether Anne realized, as others in Henry's lineup of wives would also realize, that resistance was futile, we don't know. Anne might have initially rebuffed Henry because she genuinely didn't want Henry and his attentions, never imagining that he would then raise the stakes with an offer of marriage. We know from later comments Anne made that she came to believe that God's hand was at work in her relationship with Henry.

From Henry's choice of Anne came revolution. Anne and Henry's intended marriage became intimately connected to a consequential religious question, one which affected all of England and remade the political and religious map of Europe. Anne and Henry became bound together in the multiyear project of getting married, a partnership that made them coconspirators in righting Henry's—and all of England's—relationship with God.

CHAPTER 6

There's Something About Anne

She Didn't Win a Beauty Pageant

Anne Boleyn was no pageant queen. She didn't get paraded in front of the prince and chosen for her radiant, showstopping beauty. Great care was taken to erase Anne from the record of royal life as much as possible following her death, as Henry took up so quickly with his new queen, Jane Seymour. This, along with the wildly vitriolic accounts of Anne that were offered in her time and circulated after her death, means that it is difficult for us to know with any certainty what she looked like. Anne was the patron of the artist Hans Holbein the Younger,[1] but if he painted her portrait, it did not survive Anne's deliberate erasure from the Tudor court following her execution. The well-known portrait on display in the lobby at the musical *Six,* attracting its notably long line of Anne fans, is not a contemporary portrayal.

Some reports suggest that Anne was significantly disfigured—a sixth finger, a growth on her neck, a mole or birthmark on her face. These accounts were from unreliable sources, putting pen to paper with an agenda for discrediting Anne. In general, enemies and defenders alike agreed that she had attractive features, but nobody claimed she was the great beauty of the court. Details about her long dark hair, worn loose, and her dark and lively eyes are described in conjunction with noting that her skin was rather dark and her figure boyish (neither of which represented the beauty standard of the time).

George Wyatt—the grandson of Thomas Wyatt and Anne's first known biographer—wrote with affection for Anne. He said that although there was no sixth finger, Anne did have "upon the side of her nail, upon one of her fingers, some little show of a nail," and likewise "there were said to be upon some parts of her body, certain small moles incident to the clearest complexions."[2] He posited that his grandfather was attracted to Anne for her beauty and later for her "witty and graceful speech."[3]

In comparing Anne to the king's previous mistress Bessie Blount, priest John Barlow concluded that while Bessie was prettier, Anne was "more eloquent and graceful." Another anonymous writer on the English Reformation assessed that although Anne wasn't a beauty, "for her behavior, manners, attire and tongue she excelled them all."[4]

Perhaps even more surprising than her less-than-ideal looks was her age. Most scholars and storytellers peg Anne for approximately twenty-six years old when she became the King's love interest. While this would be a perfect age for a young woman in the twenty-first century to go on a reality television show like *The Bachelor*, insisting that she is ready for marriage, this is older than many of the marriages we hear about among Tudor nobility. If the main goal was children, a woman ten years Anne's junior would have been a better prospect. This means that Henry didn't marry Anne until she was over thirty. By the time she died at thirty-five, continued childbearing would not have been assumed. Catherine of Aragon's last known pregnancy took place when she was thirty-two. Even in modern times, a pregnancy after thirty-five is classified as "geriatric."

These facts challenge us to consider what was really at play. Henry was anxious to have sons. Beauty standards of that day weren't just about what was in fashion, it was also about what female package looked the most fertile. A curvy figure and youthfulness were the key ingredients to providing many kicks at the procreational can. Anne provided neither. Henry may have been driven by the need to secure his dynasty, but other factors about Anne's appeal became more important to him.

Not Ordinary Clay

The common conclusion about Anne's appeal was simply that she was sexy. There would be no other way of understanding her ability to hold Henry's interest for six years without consummating their relationship unless she had extraordinary sex appeal. Henry's desire for her—sexual or otherwise—was sufficient to make him feel that she was worth the wait. This "sexiness" has gotten bound up in ridiculous posthumous speculations about what sort of sexual techniques Anne might have learned while she was in France and the rather unoriginal thought that if the king was at Anne's beck and call, she must have been doing *something* in the bedroom to keep him interested. As we already established though, the court of Queen Claude was a modest one, and any suggestion that Anne was being schooled in sexual arts while there is pure misogynistic fancy.

That supposed sex appeal is worth unpacking more carefully. If Anne's sexiness wasn't based on appearance and the right proportion of body parts, then it would have to be a combination of other more nuanced factors—namely Anne's personality, mannerisms, wit, and her suggestion of intrigue. "She is not of ordinary clay," the king was quoted as saying to Cardinal Wolsey.[5]

There is consensus on this. Anne was noteworthy for her elegance, her sense of humor, and her ability in conversation and dancing. She had "French" mannerisms and broke fashion conventions by introducing different styles, learned on the Continent, to the court. It was her boldness, her confidence, her willingness to be different, that captivated, rather than her conformity to then-current conventions of attractiveness. Her fashion, dancing, and exposure to Europe's leading ideas weren't just aesthetically pleasing. They conveyed a message. England under Henry VIII was in the process of emerging from the century-long civil war that had isolated it from the scientific, theological, philosophical, and artistic advances that Europe had rapidly been making.[6] Anne could be seen as representing the steps England was now making to catch up with the fashion and thinking of its Continental neighbors.

The first time that Anne appeared in anybody's commentary connected to the king was in May 1527 when an ambassador reported that Henry was dancing with the daughter of Thomas Boleyn. This was not especially noteworthy. Henry danced with many women of the court.[7] Henry and Anne had traveled in the same circles for years and might have met at various occasions when Anne was living on the Continent. By 1527, she had been back in England for at least five years and was most likely serving in Catherine's court. Henry was thirty-six, hardly in his sexual prime, especially in an era when life expectancy was significantly shorter and old age set in sooner.

What happened next is astonishing. On May 17, an ecclesiastical commission was called to investigate the validity of the king's marriage to Catherine of Aragon. Anne's name was not mentioned in any contemporary reports about the king's activities or relationships. It wasn't until August 16, three short months later, that one of the ambassadors wrote to Charles V that if the marriage with Catherine ended, it would be Anne that the king would marry. In a court and culture where every move that the king made was minutely followed, gossiped about, speculated on, and analyzed, there was nothing to indicate that Anne had any relationship with Henry prior to his deciding to end his marriage with Catherine and, in short order, to replace her with Anne.[8]

Seventeen of Henry's love letters to Anne survived Anne's cancellation from Henry's court post-execution. They were saved for centuries in the Vatican archives, of all places, with fifteen of them sent to Paris during the time of Napoleon for study before being returned to the Vatican. It is theorized that one of Catherine of Aragon's supporters must have stolen them from Anne's possessions in 1528 in the hopes that they would help Catherine's cause in Henry's annulment suit against her.[9] Catherine's defenders were keen to prove that it was not religious scruples driving Henry to seek annulment, but rather just old-fashioned lust.

When the letters were written and in what order have been, as with all things about Anne Boleyn, endlessly contested. The collection offers extraordinary testimony to Henry's obsession, determination, and highly escalated state of mind, as well as the progression of his relationship with Anne.[10] Henry was someone who found the task of writing arduous, and yet each letter was written in his own hand.

Much of our understanding of the timeline of Henry and Anne's relationship has hinged on an "offer" in one of the letters in which Henry writes in French, "I will take you for my only mistress, rejecting from thought and affection all others save yourself, to serve you only."[11] The idea has long been that Anne refused Henry's offer, holding out and manipulating his desire until he agreed to marry her instead. This has been taken as proof positive of Anne and/or her family's scheming, "putting herself in the king's sights." Professor Tracy Adams has recently disputed this interpretation of the letter, arguing that the French word *maitresse* was used as a term of endearment for the woman the man intended to take as his wife. Her research suggests that the word was not understood in the way that we understand "mistress"; it was not indicative of a long-term extramarital sexual partner until after the time of Anne and Henry.

What this could mean, combined with the actual records we have of Henry's interactions with Anne, is that Henry unleashed on Anne a whirlwind of attention that escalated at an astonishing speed from courtly interactions to the decision to marry her.

Not surprisingly, the letters reveal Anne's reluctance. We don't have her responses to Henry, so we are always interpreting her actions and thoughts through Henry's lens and his feelings about what she has written to him. But he does ask for constant reassurance of her feelings toward him. We might say that he badgers and lightly threatens her into articulating the response he is looking for.[12]

Henry's words sometimes follow the script associated with courtly love and the game of romance, but they have also been interpreted as passionate, lustful, and insecure. Henry draws boyish heart doodles around Anne's initials, AB, and talks about wanting to kiss Anne's "pretty duckys" (her breasts).[13] Historians and commentators have assumed that Henry was in the thrall of a woman who had figured out how to put Henry on the back foot and call the shots. Ever since, the story has circled around exactly what it was about Anne that made Henry so fragile, vulnerable, and obsessed. "With none of his other wives would Henry rekindle the intense passion, and genuine respect he felt for this one woman," Julia Fox and John Guy wrote in 2023.[14]

There might be truth in this, but it is also true that Henry's behavior and his feelings for Anne were part of a pattern. As with his other wives, Henry's decision to marry came at lightning speed. This was a man who got what he wanted and whose wants were decisive and volatile.

The letters ultimately reveal a significant turning point. Anne sent the king a gift: a trinket of a ship with a woman on board and a pendant diamond. The ship was a symbol of protection, the diamond a signal of Anne's surrender of her heart to all that Henry was offering.[15]

I want to be clear that none of Anne's hypothetical choices deserves to be shamed or used as justification for the violence that was done to her. It is understandable if Anne refused both Henry's targeting and his offer to make her his mistress. That doesn't mean that she was a manipulative seductress. She doesn't deserve to be shamed, called a whore, or killed.

For that matter, if Anne *did* have the wherewithal to forge a master plan, to hold out for a better offer, to claim agency of her body, and to seek the best outcome that a woman in her situation could possibly gain, that doesn't warrant condemnation either. I would count that as a win for women making the best of a raw deal in times of limited options.

However, what the records of that time instead suggest stands in contradiction to either of these narratives. Henry set his sights on Anne in an obsessive and startling manner, and Anne had to make sense of the strange situation in which she found herself. This was not a man who would take "no" for an answer.

She Talked a Good Talk

Whatever the path from Henry's "that one" to Anne's "yes," once she committed to Henry's madcap plan, Anne was a force of determination.

Anne was emboldened by Henry's obsession with her to express displeasure, and even anger, with the king. Their first known fight was recorded a few years before their marriage. Anne's frustration with Henry's inability to secure the divorce, marry her, and get rid of Catherine had reached a boiling point. "I have been waiting long and might in the meanwhile have contracted some advantageous marriage, out of which I might have issue, which is the greatest consolation in this world—but alas, farewell to my time and youth," she complained.[16] She followed up her anger with the refusal to spend Christmas with Henry.

For a man surrounded his whole life by courtiers telling him "whatever you wish," Anne's whirlwind temperament must have been an intriguing novelty to Henry. He was quick to back down when she got angry with him, showering her with extravagant presents to communicate to her his regret and devotion. She was good at playing card games, and the records show that Henry spent a lot of money losing to Anne.[17]

It was Anne's religious zeal, however, that would become central to their relationship. Scholars Tracy Adams, Owen Emmerson, and Natalie Grueninger—who continue to investigate the life and downfall of Anne and are constantly challenging the prevailing narratives—speculate that it was Anne's piety, prayerfulness, intelligence, and knowledge of the Bible that was the primary draw for Henry, the reason why he so quickly and fiercely went from dancing with her to deciding she would be his wife and queen.[18]

The biggest factor in Henry's attraction to Anne was that, by 1527, Henry wasn't consumed with lust. He was consumed with the question of why he had no legitimate male heir. Leviticus 20:21 (NIV) says "If a man marries his brother's wife, it is an act of impurity; he has dishonored his brother. They will be childless." The warning appears in a long list of sexual relationships that are expressly forbidden—including sex with parents, siblings, one's own children, and animals—and in many cases, the punishment is to be much more severe than barrenness. At the time of Henry's first marriage, Catherine had sworn that her union with Arthur, Henry's older brother, had been unconsummated, which had been the basis on which the pope had allowed dispensation for Henry to marry her in the first place, despite Leviticus 20. Twenty years later, with many miscarriages in between and only one paltry daughter produced through their marriage, Henry became convinced that God was proclaiming judgment on the fundamental sin of his marriage to Catherine by denying him a male heir.[19]

Henry understood his role as monarch the way that people in general, and other kingdoms across Europe, understood the role. Being king was a religious responsibility. He had to be right with God because his role was to be a bridge for his people in their relationship with God. Henry was attracted to a woman whose religious zeal complemented his own. His love match was someone who could challenge him to think in new ways about the greatest and most eternal questions. His love match was someone who could help him right his relationship with God.

Anne read books about reformist principles. Anne was versed in Scripture and committed to the evangelical principle of reading the Bible in English. This was intoxicating to Henry. Although it is easy to read Henry backward from the incapacitated, erratic, childish, gout-plagued, abscess-afflicted man that he was at the end of his life, he was initially a king who prided himself on his intelligence. He had a habit, even to the end of his life, of being drawn toward people who were strong, intelligent, and who held opinions that challenged and informed him (even if he just as regularly tired of them and chopped off their heads).

Anne might have had little say in Henry's affections for her, but the power players of the Tudor court certainly weighed in. If Henry had put Catherine aside to pursue a match that would have been more favorable to the people of England, or if he had wanted to keep having his affairs and sire illegitimate children who could eventually be claimed as his heir, then nobody would have blinked an eye. Even Charles V, the greatest political roadblock to Henry's annulment case, wrote that if Henry were to make a more suitable marriage, rather than pursuing this folly with Anne, "he will contrive with the Pope and the Queen to annul the one contracted with her Majesty."[20] Henry's contemporaries saw Anne as someone who offered no political advantage and therefore that his desire to marry her was foolish and self-indulgent.[21]

But Henry could not be swayed from his all-consuming decision to marry Anne. He was captivated by her wit, intelligence, knowledge, and new ideas. She could see possibilities that he couldn't. In Anne, religion, power, politics, and desire came together in an intoxicating mix. As surprising as it was to everyone, Henry became unwaveringly committed to doing whatever was needed to make Anne his wife.

Coconspirators

When Anne was finally crowned queen in 1533, Henry declared his marriage to Anne to be a righting of his, and England's, relationship with God. Her coronation was carried out "as becoming the praise and glory and honor of the omnipotent God, the security of the succession and descent of the Crown."[22]

This was not about seduction, sex, sexiness, sex appeal, or the dangling carrot of deferred gratification. The power that Anne managed to hold over Henry was a literal religious pursuit, guided by Anne.

Henry was utterly convinced that his marriage to Catherine had gone against divine law and that the proof was in the procreational pudding.[23] When he applied for an annulment to the pope in 1527, he believed that Rome couldn't help but side in his favor and that marriage was right around the corner. Instead, the pope's heel-dragging dovetailed into a more significant religious question: Should the pope have more authority than the Bible, God's own Word? This was complemented by another question: Who should have the highest religious authority in the kingdom—the king or the pope?

Where did Henry get this idea? It was Hebrew scholar Robert Wakefield, brought to Henry's attention by the Boleyn family, who constructed this argument. And it was Anne who "impressed on Henry the cogency of Wakefield's arguments and persuaded him to believe them."[24] Significantly, it was Anne who bravely passed to Henry other reading material that steered him toward religious revolution.

Anne became Henry's coconspirator in bringing change to his realm, to his religion, to his kingship. They became deeply connected to one another in their religious mission, in negotiating how the church in England would function, how they would challenge the power of the papacy, and how they would eventually attain the fullness of Henry's heart's desire: marriage to Anne, unchallenged power as king, and most importantly, righteousness in the eyes of God. Together they were "committed to a single purpose, and this gave their relationship its intensity."[25] As historian David Starkey notes, "In the divorce, Anne and Henry were one. They debated it and discussed it; they exchanged ideas and agents; they devised strategies and stratagems. And they did all this together."[26]

Anne was all the things that have been noted: She was elegant and accomplished, an intoxicating mix of charism and piety, of grace and intellect. She was someone whom people noticed. But for Henry, Anne was also a person of moral bearing, which was, in Henry's mind, an inherent promise of producing sons. Anne's assumed fertility, as we have seen, wasn't especially based on her childbearing features or youthfulness. It was, rather, centered on Henry's religious conviction that Anne was of the highest moral character and that God would judge the rightness of this marriage by sending him much-needed princes.

How much Henry's passion for Anne was sexual might be questioned. Henry was plagued, throughout his reign, with questions of his virility—not just because he hadn't produced male heirs. That he was willing to go six years without bedding Anne makes me wonder whether this wasn't entirely at Anne's insistence. Henry might very well have had a low sex drive or any number of other sexual issues or insecurities.

What his passion for Anne does reveal, though, is that Henry was someone who was used to getting what he wanted. Shoring up his position of power in opposition to Rome was also enticing. Matters of sex and power were ultimately framed as a religious goal.

None of this played well for Anne. Henry's courtiers and advisors thought the king was acting irrationally and irresponsibly. They couldn't take the king to task though, so Anne was the problem. Anne was to blame. Anne was doing something to make Henry act in such a silly manner.

At the same time, the religious agenda in which the couple was embroiled meant that, although Anne had her enemies, she also had her supporters. There were players across the church and the political sphere of England who wanted to see reform come to the British church, whose own religious consciousnesses were convicted by the principles that had been taking hold in Europe and that had been so popular in the European courts in which Anne had been raised.

The more that the court of Henry attracted and supported the kinds of people whose own religious zeal was directed toward the reform that supported what Henry wanted, the more that the English court became a hotbed of new ideas, religious change, and intellectual curiosity. And Anne and Henry together presided over this exciting intellectual and religious revolution. Anne's ability to argue, to shape and put forward new ideas, to banter with Henry and to stand up to him with her own opinions, was, for many years, exactly the most appealing combination that Anne could offer to keep the king interested in her. The promise of sex was, it would seem, a peripheral concern.

No wonder Anne became convinced that she could rule England as a partner with Henry. Anne's confidence in her own power was well-founded and reinforced continually. She could now see her life unfolding in a way that mirrored what she had seen in the courts of France, in the opinionated and strong women whose ideas and skills and expertise were intricately involved with King Francis in leading that country. It must have all felt divinely ordained.

Anne began her ascent to power as the vulnerable prey of the king. But what she began to shape in response to this targeting was a role for herself of true influence and shared power. She gave Henry what he deeply wanted: perpetually stoked-up desire, intellectual engagement, and the assurance of being on the right side of God's judgment.

And in doing so, Anne got what she wanted most too. Agency. A voice. Power to enact change.

The Love of His Life (?)

This isn't a story about Henry.

Enough ink has been spilled describing the impact, legacy, and motivations of the men of history. But it is worth saying a few final things in this chapter about Henry's unbridled obsession with Anne.

Historians have noted that his passion for her had no rival. Not in any of his other matches or marriages do we see the torrent of feelings that he unleashed on Anne. He wrote her steamy and goopy love letters. He rejected the diplomatic and political advice of his previously most trusted advisors. He trusted Anne. He admired her. He defended her against attackers. He gave her surprising power in voicing her opinions, making strategic appointments in the church and in the court, and steering the religious and political direction of England. He showered her with gifts. He put his passion for her on full display.

He also killed her.

The decisive violence of Henry's feelings for Anne, as well as the hairpin turn that those feelings took, means that "love" is not a word that I would want to use to describe their relationship. While I have seen enough Tudor buffs assessing Anne as the love of Henry's life, the one over whom *he* so completely "lost his head," I would push back in saying that what he felt for her, whatever label we want to put on it, was distorted and abusive.

In talking about the six wives of this king on the podcast *The Rest Is History*, Tom Holland and Dominic Sandbrook suggested that Henry was not, as is sometimes assumed, addicted to sex. It wasn't an excessive sex drive that led him to move through six different wives, along with at least a few mistresses. Instead, they claim that he was "addicted to love."[27] This is a dangerous way to label the behavior of a man who killed two of his six wives.

Others might wonder if Henry was addicted to drama or passion. I suspect that Henry was addicted to something boring. Henry was addicted to getting what he wanted.

Anne's is not a love story. It is a story about power. It is a story about the world suddenly and radically changing. It is a story about Anne's becoming a player and power broker of that change. It is a story about religion, and how the church was so inextricably tied up in the power plays and changing worldview underway.

It is a story about how Anne's agency and impact, as well as her rise to power and her dramatic fall, was tied to a landscape of religious zeal, along with the mixed motives and strong passions that get wound into a fight for true religion, for the right knowledge of God, for laying claim to the true faith.

CHAPTER 7

How Anne Moved the Chess Pieces of Reform

Early in Henry's relationship with Anne, it became clear that it was now Anne who was the way to power in the kingdom. Anne had seen how the royal women of France had been able to exercise patronage, not just as a way of "distributing rewards, [but also] to demonstrate power."[1] She took her lead from them.

Chief among Anne's concerns was religious reform. Once she assented to Henry's pursuit, once she could imagine how her position in Henry's affections and the court of England could serve a larger purpose, Anne threw her weight behind driving forward religious revolution in England.

But the cause of reform was the most divisive and volatile of businesses. Whose ideas had the upper hand could change swiftly. And opposition on both sides of the polarizing debate was especially vicious.[2] None of the popular portrayals of Anne's life really gives any sense of the long, drawn-out danger of those years of waiting to be made Henry's wife and queen. Even *The Tudors*, the miniseries that takes two seasons to get through both Anne's rise and fall, doesn't give the audience a true sense of just how long Anne waited for what Henry promised to materialize or how perilous the waters were as she navigated her way through.

Anne didn't use that time to pick out a trousseau and select baby names. Through her ascendancy and brief reign, she was pursuing religious reform at the same point as books were being burned and reformers were being arrested and put to death as heretics. Trying to lead in liminal times, when the world is shifting under your feet every step you take, is risky indeed.

Anne, however, proved herself willing to die in every principled ditch along the way.

The Obedience of the Christian Man

Henry expected to have his marriage annulled easily and applied to Rome in 1527 to get the dispensation he needed. The rubber stamp was not forthcoming. Catherine was too important to the European political scene as the aunt of the emperor, and she was conducting her own diplomatic work, contrary to Henry's, to defend her marriage.[3] Catherine's royal blood and status with the emperor meant that she couldn't be tried and executed for treason, as was Henry's wont, not just with dissenting wives, but also with anyone who crossed his path.

I suspect, too, that the new religious landscape created by the opinionated and commercially successful Martin Luther (and others) was a factor. The pope would open a whole can of worms if he were to cancel a previous papal edict and inadvertently give more ammunition to those saying that the authority of the pope was a distortion of true Christian teaching.[4]

Other options were presented from Rome and from those working most closely on Henry's case for him. He could certainly have Anne as his mistress and legitimize any offspring they might have together. But what the pope did not want to do was to overturn the previous pope's dispensation nor anger the Holy Roman Emperor and break that key alliance in Europe.

Anne and her library offered a solution. The writing, titled *The Obedience of a Christian Man*, was published by William Tyndale in 1528. It was a ticking time bomb in Anne's hands, representing a steady influx of black-market books into England, despite the religious policing aimed at keeping reform ideas from spreading. There were many religious leaders and writers who had been forced into exile from England for holding "Lutheran" or "evangelical" beliefs, fleeing to safer parts of the Continent so that they could write and believe in relative peace.

Anne favored these sketchy materials. She got caught with Tyndale's book in her possession by one of Wolsey's henchmen. Wolsey was delighted to expose Anne's wayward ways to the king, assuming this would be her downfall.

But he miscalculated just how much Anne's influence was already changing the king. Books that would have angered Henry previously and that had been reason for Wolsey to persecute their owners were, in Anne's possession, suddenly intriguing to Henry instead.

Wolsey's plan could not have backfired more spectacularly. On Anne's orders, Henry not only ordered the precious book returned to Anne, but he also read it himself.[5] The appeal for Henry was immediate. "This is a book for me and for all kings to read," Henry pronounced.[6]

Tyndale didn't write his book to give Henry more power or to aid in the matter of royal divorces. In fact, Tyndale would be one of the English theologians who very definitely did not support Henry's marital schemes, and he would live out his days in exile, eventually arrested and put to death as a heretic. Instead, Tyndale's tract was written to challenge the authority of the pope and the notion that a human man could be considered the successor of Saint Peter on earth or should be given such commanding authority over the church.

Anne's angle, and the one that Henry seized upon, was to emphasize Tyndale's argument that the pope should not have more authority than the kings anointed to lead their people. This was meant by Tyndale to be a decentralizing of power, to disperse authority to a variety of people, anointed by God in their own realms, to lead God's people, and his overall point was in keeping with the spirit of the times. Each individual person should be obedient not to one guy in Rome called the pope but to God and the Word of God.

In the hands of Anne and Henry, Tyndale's work gave Henry a theological case for saying that he, the king, should have final dominion on all spiritual and temporal matters in his own realm. Henry should not have to be obedient to anyone, other than God. And thankfully for Henry, he was convinced that God's will was right in line with his own.

The Reformation was taking root on the Continent because people were fighting against corrupt and exploitative practices of the church and for the notion that people could have their own relationship with God, not mediated and interpreted for them by the priests of the church. Those ideas were appealing in England too, but in England those ideas had been kept underground because of Henry. Henry was opposed to Luther and to his famous "justification by faith alone" religious stance. Indulgences didn't concern him either. Henry had not imagined there to be a need for religious reform.

Anne did not apologize for reading books that she shouldn't, but instead, when caught by one of the most powerful men of the land, bravely passed along Tyndale's writing to the king. This planted exactly the right seed of revolution. Anne's reading material and influence managed to align the call to reform with an angle that Henry did care about: more power for him and an answer to his matrimonial conundrum. And this pressed the "start" button on vast religious change in England.

From there, Henry began canvassing English theologians, as well as noted evangelical leaders on the Continent.[7] His marital anxieties now had a new and expanded theological and moral framework, one that would remove the Pope's authority over the Church of England.

Anne offered steady and significant pressure to Henry to continue to pursue the end of his marriage to Catherine. When clerics Stephen Gardiner and Edward Foxe, newly appointed experts on the king's "Great Matter," were commissioned to go to Rome with a proposal for the annulment to present to the pope, Henry sent them to see Anne on their way to report to her on their arguments and progress. Henry's correspondence with Anne reveals how careful he was to communicate to her that he was working faithfully and diligently to advance their shared goal.[8]

Henry took delight in working with a team of scholars on framing his cause with the most convincing religious arguments available. He actively commissioned treatises and supervised their preparation, making his own suggestions and contributions to their final drafts.[9] Every step along the way, Anne was at Henry's side as his partner and visionary, his admiration and desire for her increased by the moral and religious conviction binding them to one another. Together they would right the monarch's, and hence the country's, relationship with God.

No Sex, No Babies

So began an interminable process of appeals to Rome, threats against Rome, Rome's counterthreats against Henry, and eventually the history-changing break from Rome. It took six years. Communications went back and forth to the pope. The question of Henry and Catherine's marriage was considered in a papal court set up on English soil. Both Henry and Anne got older: No sex was had; no babies were conceived. Gradually, and with many delays and cold feet along the way, the plan for the English church's splitting from Rome took shape.

At numerous turns, Henry appeared to back down. Henry had been thoroughly formed as a Catholic. He was superstitiously unable to extricate himself fully from the belief that the pope held power over his immortal soul. Threats of excommunication—which more than just being tossed from belonging to the church here on earth also included a ban from the joys of heaven—terrified him. It took an astonishingly long time to accomplish the split from Rome, the marriage to Anne, and the declaration of himself as head of the church.

It was Anne who drove the agenda forward when Henry's nerve wavered. It was Anne who pressured Henry to continue. It was Anne who used those "stalemate" years to get things accomplished.

It wasn't until late in 1532 that Anne and Henry finally slept together.[10] Anne had accompanied Henry to France in a spectacular meeting of the two monarchs, Henry and Francis, and in a weather-induced delay on the way home, their long years of waiting finally came to an end.[11] Rumors that they had been secretly married on the fourteenth or fifteenth of November swirled around, which would have explained why, after such a protracted and determined fight for a legal marriage, they were willing to risk it all by sleeping together.

Whether or not this secret marriage took place, Anne's sleeping with Henry proved to be the final encouragement that he needed to act decisively in splitting the church from Rome. Anne became pregnant right away, and the push to secure their marriage and therefore the legitimacy of their unborn child (assumed by both to be a boy) was on. On January 25, 1533, they were officially wed, likely by Rowland Lee, future bishop of Coventry at York Place. Henry Norris and Thomas Heneage were the king's witnesses. Anne had with her Anne Savage, later Lady Berkeley.[12]

Anne was crowned queen on June 1 in elaborate pageantry in the city of London. She was heavily pregnant at the time, which was interpreted by Henry as the ultimate validation of everything he believed to be true. He had been on the wrong side of God in his union with Catherine. Now all was made right, and princes would soon be on the way.

The Power Broker

In the meantime, there were victims. More importantly, Anne was also able to make many strategic appointments during her ascendancy.

Cardinal Wolsey was one who didn't fare well under the power of Anne Boleyn. He was a church insider, even trying to secure the position of acting pope when Pope Clement had been held captive in a prison in Rome.[13] He had excommunicated and lightly persecuted those of a reform bent, despite quite openly having a live-in mistress who functioned as his wife and birthed several Wolsey children—showing a convenient willingness to overlook church teaching, in this case on a celibate priesthood, when it suited him.

Wolsey had also long been Henry's closest confidante and advisor. But the longer that time went on and Henry was still married to Catherine, the more that Henry became converted to the idea that Wolsey was not to be trusted. Henry had Wolsey arrested on charges of treason, but Wolsey died from natural causes (likely including stress) in 1530 before he could be brought to trial. Wolsey's biographer, George Cavendish, interpreted this as Anne's revenge for the long-ago Percy marriage debacle. He quoted Anne as threatening "if it lay ever in her power, she would work the cardinal as much [similar] displeasure."[14]

Anne never mentioned holding either a torch for Percy or a vendetta against Wolsey.

In the meantime, the theologian Thomas Cranmer was brought to the king's attention in summer 1529 when Cranmer and two of his Cambridge colleagues met to discuss the king's marriage problems.[15] Dr. Stephen Gardiner and Dr. Edward Foxe had both been in Wolsey's service but, as Wolsey's demise began, jumped ship to become key leaders in securing the king's divorce.[16] Cranmer injected some fresh energy into the deliberations of the increasingly desperate Gardiner and Foxe. Through them, Cranmer soon became a man "in high favor with the Boleyn family"[17]—which was now a sure route to power. He was lodged in the entourage of Thomas Boleyn at Durham Place and charged with working on documents to argue for the annulment. Anne's father became Cranmer's patron; the Boleyn family had an eye for talent.

At the end of 1532, the archbishop of Canterbury died, leaving an important opening. The archbishop of Canterbury was the pope's senior-most representative on English soil. Once the English church had fully split from Rome, this position became second to the monarch as the most powerful office of the church. Thomas Cranmer was chosen for the role. When Cranmer tried to thank Henry for taking him from relatively unknown to top dog, Henry said "that he ought to thank Anne Boleyn for this welcome promotion."[18] Cranmer was the most exalted and important, but certainly not the only, beneficiary of Anne's religious patronage.[19]

A papal bull approved Cranmer as archbishop of Canterbury in early 1533.[20] Ironically, the pope was appointing the man whose main job would become securing England's independence from Rome and championing the end of papal authority on English soil. It is one more example of Henry's mixed bag of beliefs. He seemed to need the pope's seal of approval on appointing Cranmer before he could then dictate that Cranmer overturn the pope's authority altogether.

Cranmer would play a pivotal role in shaping the church in England and the global Anglican Communion. But first Cranmer was just a priest-scholar who came to the attention of the Boleyns and the king.

Anne saw the power vacuum. Anne identified the talent. Anne engineered a critically important person into power.

A Bigger Vision

There were others for whom Anne stuck out her neck. Each of Anne's protégés represented not just something about what she was reading and believing but also about just how vastly and quickly the religious landscape of England was changing because of her influence.

Simon Fish, a Protestant propagandist, had been exiled to Antwerp for his beliefs and for fear of Cardinal Wolsey. Fish's indiscretions included selling copies of Tyndale's New Testament from his home, vilifying the clergy as "ravenous wolves," and denying the existence of purgatory.[21] In

Antwerp, he wrote the incendiary pamphlet *Supplication for the Beggars*. Despite being banned by the church, this writing again benefited from the printing press and spread across Europe, including being smuggled into England. It was Anne's intercession that allowed Fish to return to England. Anne took Fish's pamphlet to the king after reading it herself. After spending several days with Fish's work, the king sent word to Fish's wife that he could safely return to England at the end of 1529.[22]

Fish didn't just write against the religious hierarchy and its corruption. Fish wrote for the poor. Fish's pamphlet is laden with stark economic data on the concentration of money, land, and resources in the monasteries and churches of England, and how that concentration of wealth was impoverishing the masses. He didn't just want to change the way people thought and believed, he wanted to change the material circumstances of the people. He wanted economic justice. He wanted the redistribution of wealth.

Anne brought him back from Belgium. Anne sheltered and supported him and his wife. Anne was obviously taken with his arguments. Anne's alignment with Fish's vision would cost her dearly down the road.

There Were Others

In 1559, just twenty-three years after Anne's death, John Aylmer, the future bishop of London, asserted that Anne had been:

> "the chief, first and only cause of banyshing the beast of Rome, with all his beggarly baggage," and that she had been the "crop and root" of the English Reformation, whom "God had endewed with widome that she coulde, and given her the minde that she would do it."[23]

Anne's patronage was extensive and a significant component in this later analysis. William Latymer and Nicholas Shaxton were two evangelical priests elevated to the position of bishop, and Latymer became one of Anne's chaplains.[24] These were people who had otherwise feared for their lives, circulated their ideas in secret, and worked furtively for religious change in England. Suddenly under Anne's jurisdiction they found themselves among the most powerful and prominent clergy in England.

Nicholas Bourbon was a French scholar, whose work was suppressed because of its "evangelical tendencies." Anne and Marguerite d'Angoulême worked together in seeing him released from prison and then finding him employment, first in tutoring Anne's nephew Henry Carey and later Marguerite's daughter Jeanne d'Albret.[25]

Thomas Patmore had been imprisoned for circulating copies of the English translation of the Bible, for marrying when he was a priest of the church, and for holding other reformist principles. He was condemned to die by beheading, but his life was spared by the intercession of Anne with Henry.[26]

Other protégés were William Bettes, Edward Crome, Nicholas Heath, and Matthew Parker, all known for their evangelical leanings.[27]

William Latymer later wrote *The Chronicle of Anne Boleyn* during the reign of Anne's daughter, Elizabeth, as a gift to the new queen. Anne's charitable work was described both by Latymer and later by John Foxe in his *Book of Martyrs* as being "well-organized and directed specifically to poor households instead of indiscriminately."[28] Giving money (alms) was a feature of a queen's expected responsibilities, representing God's loving care for the disenfranchised of the kingdom. What was unique about Anne's charitable action was the intentionality behind it, the way in which her monetary gifts conveyed what she cared about. The exceptional generosity of her giving was also noted.[29]

She presented herself as someone genuinely responding to specific requests of need and then forming giving plans that would make a tangible difference. Likewise, she used her charity to support education. She was particularly interested in assisting students who were "learned and of good character." Her chaplains and her almoner[30] John Skip (a man to reappear at other key moments in Anne's final months) were directed from Anne to give generous amounts of money to impoverished students.[31] In this, too, Anne consistently aligned with the humanistic version of reform that she had absorbed in her time in France.

It Came Back to Books

As Anne's access to wealth and power increased, so did her library. She might have been known for her fashion sense and extravagant jewels, but she was also passionate about book buying. Anne and her brother, George, were most interested in reformist books, especially those aligned with French reformers, some of them condemned, from several trailblazing French printers.[32] The siblings owned around forty evangelical books between them, and Anne stocked her library with deluxe devotional books and specially commissioned handwritten Scriptures.[33] She owned two works by Lefèvre d'Étaples: a French translation of the Bible (which had been condemned by the Sorbonne in France) and his *Introductory Commentary on the Four Gospels*, gifted to her by her brother. Rose Hickman, a merchant's daughter, reminisced during the time of Elizabeth that Anne used to request that her father bring back "the gospels and epistles written in parchment in French together with the psalms" on his journeys to the Continent.[34]

One of Anne's most enduring legacies and central causes was access to the Bible in English. George Boleyn was also known to have dabbled in Scripture translation. There is one soldier who recorded George's scaffold speech just before his death, saying, "Truly so that the Word should be among the people of the realm I took upon myself great labor to urge the king to permit the printing of the Scriptures to go unimpeded among the commons of the realm in their own language." Promoting the English Bible was a Boleyn family enterprise.[35] Anne kept the English Bible in her chambers for anyone who wished to read it, and doing so was encouraged,[36] much like it was in the court of Claude where Anne grew up.

Beyond her own court, protecting the illegal trade in Bibles became a signature of her rise to power and her reign.[37] Her advocacy, support, and campaigning bore fruit that she was able to witness in her lifetime. In October 1535, months before her death, the complete Bible was finally published in English by Miles Coverdale.[38] The dedication "Unto the most victorious Prynce and our most gracious soveraigne Lorde, Kynge Henry the eight . . . and your dearest iust wife and most vertuous Pryncesse, Quene Anne."[39]

While technically still illegal, and therefore published in France, the English Bible was here to stay. By 1539, the English Bible wasn't just authorized by King Henry, it was mandated for use in all of England's churches, and the title page showed Henry himself distributing the Bibles to the grateful and celebratory people.

This was one big win. The other major victory was personnel. Of the ten elections of bishops between 1532 and Anne's death in 1536, seven were reformers who were her clients. This was crucial to the future of the Reformation. Beyond Anne's death, and even beyond Henry's, the reforming bishops in office were still predominantly those patronized by Anne.[40]

This meant that come hell or high water, death or execution, reform in England was unstoppable. What Anne began in handing Tyndale's tract to Henry continued throughout her reign as queen. Reversing it would not be as simple as getting her execution orders signed. Anne was strategic. Anne used her brief hold on power with remarkable effectiveness.

Anne's impact, as a result, was not to be erased.

PART 3

She Was Dying to Start a Church

Men are afraid women will laugh at them.
Women are afraid men will kill them.

—Margaret Atwood

CHAPTER 8

The Enemies—Religion, Politics, and Personality

Not Just Another Night at Court

Two weeks before her arrest, Anne was at the center of an awkward moment at the court. It was designed to make a point about Henry and his power. It is also indicative of how quickly Henry's attitude toward Anne turned.

It was April 18, 1536, the Tuesday of Easter week. Behind the scenes, fierce negotiations had been taking place about a possible alliance between England and Spain, Henry and Charles V. What each side would need from the other—particularly in the matter of Anne's place in Henry's life and where Henry's children would each fit into the line of succession—was being considered in backroom conversations. Henry had won the power to claim religious authority over and above the pope. His nerve had weakened at times along that road, with Anne regularly bolstering his resolve.[1] Now that he had that added authority though, he was unwilling to consider relinquishing it. That was a sticking point in trying to form an alliance with a country still Roman Catholic and loyal to the pope.

In the heat of both these official and sideline negotiations, Anne was told to walk intentionally in front of Eustace Chapuys as she accompanied Henry from the royal pew down to the chapel. Chapuys was the emperor's ambassador at the court, and when the queen of England walked by him, she stopped and acknowledged Chapuys with a bow, necessitating that he respond in kind. It was a clandestine way of forcing Chapuys to acknowledge her.[2] Chapuys was one of Anne's most vocal and vicious critics, loyal to her predecessor Catherine and to the cause of the traditional church. He had never spoken to Anne himself; everything that he reported about her was secondhand. And he had never had to be directly in her presence before this moment.

The message was clear. If Chapuys wanted to negotiate some kind of alliance with the king, he would have to acknowledge Henry's chosen queen. In this most public and social of ways, Chapuys would have to signal that Anne Boleyn was legitimate and therefore that Henry's power to put her there had been valid.

It seemed like a moment of triumph for Anne. She had seen a few of her detractors vanquished over the last few years, and this was one more opportunity to hold her head high and see a longtime critic cowed.

In the shadow of this moment was another important figure, brimming with plots against Anne, and that was Thomas Cromwell. Cromwell was a lawyer who had worked in the service of Cardinal Wolsey. His first appearance in the work of furthering Henry's aims was in 1531, and he soon became Henry's parliamentary manager and chief minister.[3] Wolsey's demise had left a vacuum in Henry's service, and Cromwell made himself the answer, becoming indispensable in the nitty gritty of running the kingdom. It was Cromwell who was instrumental in finally securing the break from Rome and the annulment of Henry's marriage to Catherine.

But Chapuys's humiliation on that night in 1536 was threatening to Cromwell too. Henry's lot was tied to Anne. Cromwell, as we will see, was now one of a growing cadre of plotters intent on seeing that change.

One month and one day after this showdown, Anne was walking, not at Henry's side as his chosen queen, but alone to her execution.

The Hatred Was Complicated

Anne's enemies played an enormous role in the intrigue, gossip, scandal, and legend of her story. In Tudor England, issues of principle and policy were not expressed in open political alignment and debate. Rather, they were personalized.[4] For example, alignment with the Roman Catholic Church and conservative values was expressed as support for Catherine and Mary. Likewise, opposition to Henry's religious and political moves was expressed as vitriol toward Anne.

The reasons people directed fury toward Anne, and in some cases why her venom was turned toward them, were a heady concoction of religion, politics, and personality. Their strikes against her, and their motivations for their aggression, have become integral to the lore that has surrounded Anne ever since she walked the halls of the Tudor palaces.

Unfortunately for Anne and her legacy, the talking points each of these enemies had against her have been divorced over time from the reasons behind the chatter. Anne was vilified in most of the usual ways that women are vilified, but the fact that a significant portion of that ire stemmed from Anne's political and religious agenda has been overlooked. Anne as a person of influence and impact gets reduced to Anne as a bad woman.

As we move into the final months of Anne's life, these players offer insight into her psyche—what she was arguing about and with whom, why she made the choices she did, and how layered with bravery and determination and religious faith those choices really were. It wasn't just that she was the object of attack; Anne also had her firepower aimed and ready to launch at a target.

Anne's track record in prevailing over powerful men in Henry's circle also speaks volumes about why her downfall was met with such delight in certain circles. She wasn't a woman who had played nicely or been without her own deadly venom when she chose to bite. Anne was threatening. Anne was a powerful and dangerous foe.

Until she wasn't.

As we exhume the pile of bodies left in Anne's wake, enemies who thought they could take her down and who were instead destroyed, we can much better understand why Anne continued to fight and why she believed she would win.

Cardinal Wolsey—The One Who Underestimated Her

Cardinal Thomas Wolsey didn't take Anne seriously until it was too late.

In 1527, Henry made it clear to Wolsey that he had "deep scruples" about his marriage to Catherine. Wolsey assumed that Henry wished to make an advantageous match with the royal family of France and acted immediately.[5] He was sadly disappointed when it became clear that Anne Boleyn was the sole target of Henry's "scruples."

It would become a feature of the Anne Boleyn fables that Anne hated Wolsey and was intent from the start on bringing him down. He wasn't just the reason her engagement to Henry Percy was broken, he also represented the worst of what reformers wanted to change in the established church.

In fact, the evidence suggests that in the early days of Anne and Henry's fight for the king's annulment, they saw working with Wolsey to their benefit. He was effective, loyal, and a fixer. He was the ticket to getting things done.[6]

Wolsey no doubt believed it was unwise for Henry to take such drastic steps against Rome and Catherine of Aragon for a fleeting romance. (It turns out that Wolsey was right about Henry's changeable feelings, but by then he wouldn't be alive to say, "I told you so." Henry is unlikely to have reacted well to such a comment anyway.) It is also true that Wolsey persecuted reformers, and Anne established herself early and often as a defender of those reformers. As a cardinal, it was his job to root out heresy for the pope. As the king's agent, he curried favor with Henry in doing so because Henry had, until Anne, also been opposed to Lutherans and other evangelical ideas. With the king's support, Wolsey sought out and arrested preachers and laymen suspected of these new heresies. He publicly burned two thousand copies of Tyndale's English New Testament after raiding warehouses and arresting those found to be responsible for circulating the banned books.[7]

Anne would go toe-to-toe with Wolsey over books and bans. Anne owned copies of the same books Wolsey had burned. Anne was intent on saving reformers whom Wolsey had exiled from England. On every clash, Anne won. Henry was newly delighted by contraband books when Anne brought them to him. Henry was suddenly compassionate toward exiled reformers and, on Anne's advice, welcomed them back to England. Henry was amenable to putting reformers in the highest offices of the church, if Anne vouched for them.

Wolsey had numerous detractors. There were many ambitious men at court waiting in the wings to fill any power vacuum that disposing of Wolsey might facilitate. Wolsey had run the bus over a lot of people in his unassailable position of power at the side of Henry. When Anne realized that she was going to have to convince Henry to continue his move against Rome and to drive his own bus over Wolsey's body to do so, she had a lot of support.

In early 1529, Anne turned on Wolsey, along with the support of her brother; her uncle, the duke of Norfolk; and Charles Brandon, the duke of Suffolk.[8] Neither her uncle nor Brandon would remain on her side beyond this coup against the cardinal, and Brandon would continually undermine her throughout her time as Henry's chosen consort. Anne's motivation didn't seem to be exacting revenge for Wolsey's long-ago intervention in her relationship with Henry Percy, but rather the need to keep Henry from waffling on the English church's independence and therefore his ability legally to marry Anne.

Wolsey's comeuppance started in 1529, when he was indicted on the charge of praemunire (the ancient criminal offence of procuring proclamations from Rome to the detriment of the crown). He was removed as lord chancellor and forced to relinquish his property to Henry.[9] During the following year, Wolsey appealed to Henry's friendship to save him, as well as those of influence who he saw as having benefited from his time in power.

It almost worked. Henry had relied on Wolsey for many years and was deeply attached to him.[10] Anne was resolute though.[11] With Wolsey's enemies, she accused Wolsey of plotting with the pope, the French, and possibly even the Holy Roman Emperor against Henry.[12] Wolsey was charged with treason at the end of 1530 and died from illness on his way to London to answer the charges.

Whether the dramatic and dangerous volatility of Henry concerned Anne at the time is unknown. It wouldn't be the first or the last time that Henry would turn on his nearest and dearest with only the slightest of provocations.

Chancellor Thomas More—The One with God on His Side

Thomas More was one of the most respected minds and philosophical/theological leaders in England. Henry admired him deeply, for many of the same reasons that he was also drawn to Anne. He appreciated the breadth of More's intellectual sensibilities, his championing of new humanist ideals, and his principled religious convictions. Henry vehemently convinced More to accept the role of high chancellor in leading England after Wolsey's fall from power. More, wisely, was hesitant about accepting.

More's fight wasn't with Anne; it was with Henry, and it was ultimately a question of religious authority. Marriage to Anne had become tied to England's breaking from Rome and Henry's declaring the law of royal supremacy, putting himself in charge of the church in England. More was a staunch Catholic, loyal to the pope, and horrified at the thought of a monarch setting himself up as God's designate on earth.

More and Anne were formed by the developing humanist philosophy that had been igniting intellectual circles across Europe for decades. Despite this shared formation, they were working for opposing religious purposes. As Henry and Anne became more aligned toward religious reform, More used his position as chancellor to encourage the persecution of heretics. Nobody had been burned at the stake for fifteen years, but More brought back that particularly grisly form of execution as the strongest of signals warning against religious nonconformity.[13] He believed that the death of heretics was a small price to pay for guarding the eternal well-being of the English people as a whole.

More resigned as chancellor in 1531. He was executed less than a year before Anne also went to her grave. He was charged, along with another staunch catholic, Bishop John Fisher, for refusing to sign the Act of Supremacy, which made Henry the supreme head of the church.

More and Fisher were immediately claimed as martyrs of the Roman Catholic Church. More's influence on Anne's reputation, because of his sainted status, extended far beyond his death. More's descendants would frame Anne as the one responsible, through the intentional use of her seductive feminine wiles, to force the "king with her dalliance and pastime to grant unto her this request, to put the bishop [Fisher] and Sir Thomas More to death."[14] In truth, it was Henry who should have been the target of More's descendants' ire, not Anne. Henry was known for his rage when he didn't get his own way, and More's refusal to acknowledge Henry as the head of the church was unacceptable to him.

While superficially seeming to validate Anne's position as Henry's wife and England's queen, as well as cementing the reform that Anne championed, More's death had the effect of spurring to action more forces of opposition against Anne. And once again, it would be apparent through the rearview mirror that Henry's very changeable nature and shifting loyalties could be played for Anne's destruction too.

Eustace Chapuys—The Gossip

Chapuys served as ambassador from Charles V to England in the years surrounding Anne's rise to and fall from power. Chapuys was a prolific report writer, and so many of the firsthand accounts that we have of those tumultuous years come from Chapuys. The volume of material that he alone supplied far outweighs any other single source material from that time.

Chapuys arrived at the English court in 1529. He is described as "blessed with a cheeky smile, a sharp ear for gossip, a fertile imagination and a brilliant turn of phrase."[15] Chapuys always held out hope for the reinstating of both Catherine and Mary to power and worked steadfastly in his diplomatic role in offering protection to, and advocacy of, both. Hating Anne was central to this agenda, and he took every opportunity to cast her in the most unfavorable light possible in his prolific accounts to Charles.

Chapuys was a political and religious conservative. He hated Anne for usurping Catherine but also for instigating religious reform. In his eyes, seeing Anne as a heretic and as sexually deviant went hand in hand. She was a manipulative schemer, she was responsible for the religious demise of all of England, and therefore she was also deserving of accusatory sexual labels.

In an increasingly familiar refrain, it was far safer for Chapuys to land his criticisms at the feet of Anne rather than Henry. He blamed the woman trying to negotiate her own precarious way around the vanities of the king rather than holding to account the man signing the death warrants and pushing through parliament the bills needed to give himself more power.

This made Chapuys a notoriously biased and unreliable narrator. Anything that Chapuys wrote that casts Anne favorably is trustworthy because he was so quick to disparage her and so slow to see her as anything other than a scandal, a heretic, and a whore. But also, many of the reports that Chapuys sent of Anne's more mean-spirited, vulnerable, or disgraced moments must be filtered through the lens of knowing how much the source of these reports hated the new queen. Anne aficionados would have much less information about Anne were it not for Chapuys, but his status as "unreliable narrator" means that much of that information is tainted.

In the weeks leading up to Anne's death, Chapuys was actively trying to secure an alliance between Spain and England. To do so, he was bargaining for Mary to be reinstated as first in the line of succession over Anne's daughter Elizabeth. When Henry paraded Anne in front of Eustace Chapuys at that banquet and made him succumb to the ultimate humiliation of acknowledging his nemesis's exalted position, Chapuys must have feared that Anne had won.

But he wasn't the only one moving against Anne.

The Catholic Alliance and Edward Seymour—The Ones Who Saw an Opportunity

In the fall of 1535, the year before Anne's death, Edward Seymour and his family began to find noticeable favor with Henry. Anne and

Henry visited the Seymour estate, Wolf Hall, that fall,[16] and Henry was so taken with their hospitality and the promise that Edward, a Seymour son, showed that he appointed Edward to the staff of the privy chamber at the beginning of March.[17] The privy chamber was the private apartments of the king, and those who worked in that space had direct and personal access to his ear in ways that were envied by others wanting to wheel and deal in the politics of court and country.

The privy chamber, unfortunately for Anne, became infiltrated by those intent on removing the new queen and reinstating their more traditional agenda.[18] Nicholas Carew was the ringleader of this opposition, but Edward had resources that Nicholas didn't have, namely a sister. Jane Seymour had served in the court of Catherine and was now a lady-in-waiting to Anne. Whether Edward caught Henry's attention because the king had already fixed his eyes on Jane, or whether Jane was put forward by Edward and his family once they began to gain some leverage with the king, is unclear. But either way, an alliance formed between Edward, Nicholas, and the other conservatives to replace Anne with Jane. Jane was said to have been coached to behave accordingly.[19] (It is worth noting that Jane's agency in her own rise to power is often assumed to be minimal; that might be because she had a more malleable personality, or it might be because we have tended to see women's stories through the eyes of men.)

This conservative Catholic alliance understood itself as operating in opposition to the Boleyns. The Boleyns represented reform. The Seymours would come to be, albeit briefly, the figurehead for those seeking a return to Catholicism and to more traditional times. Ironically, by the time of Henry's death, it was obvious that Edward Seymour was a fervent evangelical.[20]

The Seymours and their cronies now had precedent on their side. Queens could be divorced. New queens could be chosen and crowned. Factions unhappy with Anne and the split from Rome were happy to stoke Henry's interest in the fresh-faced and distinctly docile Jane. Anne was fast becoming a disappointment and an inconvenience; the king was primed for moving on.

While Chapuys and Cromwell were negotiating an alliance with Spain at the expense of Anne and her daughter's interests, and while pro-Catholic sentiment in the courts and in the country were united in their hatred of Anne, the Seymours were looking to get their own person on the throne.

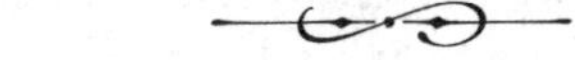

Thomas Cromwell—The One with a Venomous Bite

Cromwell's star, initially, rose with Anne's. Cromwell was able to break the stalemate in the divorce settlement and effectively move things toward the resolution that Anne and Henry both wanted. Cromwell wasn't the idea generator, but he was a "first-rate politician."[21]

Thomas Cromwell proved to be among the most venomous of Anne's enemies.

There is no evidence to suggest that Anne and Cromwell were ever close or that Cromwell felt loyalty toward Anne. As we will see, Anne would very publicly call out Cromwell and his actions in spring 1536, a month before her arrest. Anne's war with Cromwell was religious. They were both reformers, but they held differing ideas about what that reform should entail. Anne wanted social reform and economic justice. Cromwell, to Anne's mind, was working at cross-purposes to this vision.

Around the same time, Cromwell was actively exploring an alliance with Charles and Spain that would have been unfavorable to the fortunes of Anne and her daughter. To bolster his own agenda, he aligned himself with the pro-Catholic forces in the court and developed a close relationship with Chapuys. Despite Cromwell's reformed religious beliefs, he, too, saw opportunity in the possibility of Henry's affections moving away from Anne toward Jane. He aligned himself with Edward Seymour, Nicholas Carew, and the conservative faction at court.

Cromwell and Anne were ultimately fighting over something more fundamental than religion, succession plans, or European alliances. They were fighting for Henry's ear and favor. They were fighting over who would be his number one. Anne had enjoyed that position for years, but Cromwell was quick to seize an opportunity to usurp Anne as she had usurped Wolsey. Cromwell never forgot Anne's influence in removing Wolsey, Cromwell's mentor, as well as Wolsey's fatal error in underestimating Anne. If Cromwell could take her place in helping Henry rule the kingdom, and if he didn't have to go through the tiresome process of negotiating with Anne to get to Henry, then that would be the pinnacle of achievement.

Cromwell landed the windfall opportunity of not only destroying Anne but also wiping out a cadre of men close to the king's favor and ear too. This was a delicious bonus.

Cromwell eventually fell dramatically out of favor with the king too, just as almost every person in Henry's closest orbit did. Cromwell's demise, four years after Anne's own death, is often ascribed to Henry's volatility with women. Cromwell had arranged Henry's fourth marriage to Anna of Cleves. It was a political alliance, but when she arrived on English soil, Henry found she wasn't to his liking. The childish and spoiled Henry, it is popularly assumed, turned on Cromwell in his ire and disappointment at being saddled with a woman he found repulsive.

In truth, Cromwell's own fall from power was more about his closeness to the evangelical party in England and the Protestant cause in Europe.[22] He likely also died because, like Anne and Wolsey and Catherine of Aragon before him, when Henry didn't think things were going the way he wanted, he looked to the people closest to him to blame.

Cromwell was beheaded in 1540 in the grisliest fashion. It took the executioner at least three botched attempts before finally completing the task.

Nicholas Sander—Sander the Slanderer

Anne made enemies long after she was dead, and they were vicious. The Roman Catholic faction that continued to be at work in England, which felt especially aggrieved under the rule of Elizabeth I, Anne's daughter, unleashed vitriol on the late queen. Nicholas Sander was chief among Anne's posthumous enemies. He was only born a few years before she was put to death and never met her in person. Sander was a staunch pro-Catholic Englishman and devoted himself to the project of reinstating Catholicism in England. This Catholic faction found a rallying cry in their hatred for Anne.

Sander blasted Anne in his work *De Origine Ac Progressu Schismatis Anglicani* (*The Rise and Growth of the Anglican Schism*) in 1585. His biased and nonfactual commentary made its way into many of the longstanding popular narratives about Anne. Once published in Latin, it was quickly translated into French, German, Italian, Portuguese, Polish, and Spanish. It became a staple in Roman Catholic history.[23] Sander "wallowed in descriptions of Anne's body as the deformed and alluring gateway that ensnared Henry and led him through the doors of heresy."[24] Intimately woven into these accounts were fabrications of astonishing sexual depravity. He claimed that Anne had been promiscuous in the French court, nicknamed "the English mare" (a slander that was actually applied—arguably also undeservedly—to Anne's sister, Mary). Even more outrageous was Sander's claim that Anne was the offspring of an affair Henry had with Anne's mother, Elizabeth.[25]

His polemical writing fueled hatred toward Anne in Catholic circles across Europe. It was because of his influence that Anne came to be saddled with the label "witch" and for sexual depravity to become the thing that people think they know about Anne.

Anne never had an opportunity to defend herself against Sander. His complaints about Anne would take on a life of their own, minus his central issue with her: that she was the reason for the English Reformation.

Henry—The One Who Always Got What He Wanted

Long before Anne was on the scene or anything catastrophic was happening in Henry's reign, Thomas More noted to a courtier in 1520 that "having fun with [Henry] was like having fun with tamed lions—often it is harmless, but just as often there is the fear of harm. Often he roars in rage for no known reason, and suddenly the roar becomes fatal."[26] Anne made enemies. In each case, however, those enemies should have directed their ire at Henry, not Anne. But blaming the woman in a partnership is a default that has proven hard to resist.

Ultimately, it was Henry who signed Anne's death warrant. It was Henry who was the primary danger to Anne all along. He wanted her more than he wanted anything. And then he killed her.

There are specific reasons why Anne lost favor with Henry in such a violent and complete way: miscarriages, shifting political alliances, new flirtations and dalliances, a debilitating accident, enemies of Anne accusing her of heinous sexual impropriety.

Central to these specific events is Anne herself and her opinionated, visionary, outspoken, and boundary-breaking choices. She transgressed the roles assigned to her by her gender and station. When she had the opportunity to smooth troubled waters, make peace, or acquiesce for the sake of self-protection, instead Anne was "ten toes down" on standing her ground and leaning in for combat.

Which leads to some more general twenty-first-century observations about why Henry turned on her.

A lot of Anne's leverage in her climb to power was in being the one Henry was after. Her lure as the dangling carrot, the gold at the end of the rainbow, the mystical unicorn, was total. She was new and exciting and forbidden—all qualities that can be so intoxicating in an adulterous affair. When Henry finally slept with her, the thrill of the chase ended. Marriage, even for a king, involves negotiation. The hard work of building a partnership can feel disappointing in comparison to the thrill of clandestine meetings, anticipated sexual gratification, and forbidden romance. The dream of being together often pales in comparison to the reality of getting what you want.

Anne was her own tough act to follow. Once she became Henry's wife, a lot of what had made her so intoxicating was neutralized. She wasn't as exciting when she was legal and the fight in which the couple had shared was behind them. Anne was implicated in creating a precedent that would be dangerous for her and all subsequent wives. It was now an established fact that queens could be removed from the side of the king for reasons other than "'til [natural] death do us part."

There were reports that Henry had a new mistress at the end of 1534, just after Anne's first known miscarriage. At the beginning of 1535, other reports surfaced, stating that Henry was allegedly involved with Margaret Shelton, Anne's cousin. It is likely that these dalliances were limited to the tradition of courtly love, which many have thought was the start of his own rollercoaster with Anne. These "affairs" would have been unimportant except that Anne knew that her position with Henry was always contested. Because of how she herself came to power, "she was in the contradictory position of being expected to behave as a queen, but having to continue to challenge as a mistress."[27]

This added another dimension of danger for Anne. In Tudor England, it was highly unusual for marriage to be considered a romantic choice, particularly for a king. People in power married for business, not love, for consolidating land and alliances and money. People not in power also generally saw marriage as an opportunity for securing more economic or political stability in a world that could be very precarious. Henry's almost completely unprecedented choice to marry the woman he "loved," rather than have her as a mistress, meant that it was his emotions that were the foundation of the relationship, rather than strategy. Unfortunately for Anne, Henry's emotions were volatile and prone to sudden change.[28]

There are more specific observations to offer on the Henry-Anne dynamic. They aren't pretty or unusual. Anne was demanding, witty, intellectual, and opinionated. Anne was Henry's type. She wouldn't be the only woman he would marry who would draw him in with her intellectual capacities and interesting points of view. But there are downsides to this kind of person as a life partner, particularly if you are insecure and used to getting what you want, particularly if you are in a position where there are always people at the ready vying to do your will. To be married to a person like Anne, one's partner would need to possess the skills of seeing a new point of view, sharing power, admitting to being wrong, and having the strength of conviction and intellect to counter their partner's convictions with well-considered opinions.

At a certain point, the labor of being Anne's partner was too much. She became too much. Henry desired her, until he got her. He enjoyed her transgressive ways, until he felt attacked by them. He wanted her to share in his power, until she challenged him. He found her personality attractive, until it was just too much work. He loved strong women, and he loved to destroy strong women.

And through all of this was the exalted spiritual position in which Henry had held Anne. He expected that marrying her would right his relationship with God. Anne's religious convictions made her enemies; Henry's religious convictions made Anne vulnerable.

One of Henry's early love letters to Anne was accompanied by the gift of a freshly killed deer. The simmering violence in this imagery and in Henry's written word is chilling in hindsight:

> To put you even more often in mind of me, I send you by this bearer a buck, killed very late yesterday evening by my own hand, hoping that when you eat it, it will remind you of the hunter.[29]

Henry was the hunter indeed. His prey would be slain.

CHAPTER 9

Not Guilty but Not Innocent

Anne and Esther

At the beginning of April 1536, John Skip, almoner of Anne Boleyn, preached a controversial sermon claiming a parallel between Anne and the biblical woman Esther.[1] This sermon is crucial in understanding Anne, what she considered most important, how she perceived her role, and where her bravery and miscalculation left her vulnerable, exposing a flank against which her enemies attacked.

Esther was a Jewish woman living in Persia during the time of the exile. The people of Israel had been conquered by a rival army and kingdom, their temple destroyed, and their homeland overtaken.

King Xerxes was the ruler of Persia at this time[2] and had banished his first wife, Queen Vashti, from his court and from their marriage because she was disobedient. He wanted her to dance naked at a party for him and his friends, and she refused. Xerxes followed up this temper tantrum with the brilliant idea of holding a beauty pageant for all the women of his realm. He wanted to see a parade of eligible beauties so that he could pick the one he liked the best.

Esther won the pageant.

Winning meant Esther being taken from her home to serve in the king's court and bedroom. While queen, one of the king's advisors—Haman—became intent on wiping out the Jewish people within Xerxes's kingdom. Esther's relative Mordecai convinced her to speak up on her people's behalf. Esther had previously hidden her Jewish identity from her new husband, so disclosing that information was risky.

However, Esther had been sufficiently pleasing to Xerxes in the role that was expected of her, and he received her news and supplication favorably. Because of Esther's bravery, the Jewish people were spared. Haman was violently put to death for his sinister plotting.

In convincing Esther to put her life on the line to save her Jewish people, Mordecai told her this: "Perhaps you have been brought to this place for just such a time as this." Although God's name is never mentioned, this story claims that Esther's situation was not accidental but providential, a means by which God would be able to save the people of Israel.

Skip's sermon was assumed to have been crafted in consultation with his boss, Anne. Anne, like her mentor Queen Claude, identified with Esther, a fact that speaks loudly to how Anne expected her own situation to unfold. She would use her influence with the king to do the good she believed in doing. She would prevail over her detractors and those who did not have her people's best interests at heart. Anne believed she had been brought providentially to this place, the court of King Henry VIII, for just such a time as this.

A Haunting Death

It was Anne's life that inspired me and drew me to want to know more, but it was her death that haunted me. Since I was very young, I have, at infrequent intervals, dreamed of Anne's execution as if it were me going to the scaffold. The nightmares come out of nowhere and stay with me for days after; shaking them off is hard. I imagine the steel it took her to walk to her death, to speak to the thousand-plus crowd waiting to see her die, to tuck her beautiful hair into a cap, to put on the blindfold, and to kneel before the executioner's axe. It would be over so quickly; the pain would only be momentary. And then release. I find myself trying to summon the courage to be able to focus on these truths rather than succumb to the ice-cold terror of knowing my life was to end so violently and unjustly. Through the strange filter of dreamworld, my mind goes into those last moments of where Anne's life ended and, against my will, I excavate that ultimate price she paid for being exactly who she was.

The fall of Anne Boleyn has probably been discussed more than any other aspect of her life. It was shocking then, even for many of Anne's detractors. And it remains shocking now. Hers is the dark kind of fairy tale, the counterpoint to Esther, the tale that is also as old as time. It is the story of how male desire can turn lethal, how a man comes to believe that women who don't do as they're told or perform as expected, who don't affirm and receive and produce and play nice and coddle the ego appropriately, deserve to die.

There are many assumptions about what led to Anne's downfall and stories that have been popularly spun. One version goes like this. Anne refused the king's advances so he would marry her. She promised him sons in return. First, she gave birth to a daughter. Then she miscarried a deformed baby boy. She failed the assignment Henry had given her. His desire for her chilled in response. His obsession with her, coupled with her miscarriage, made him conclude that she had bewitched him, that she was poisonous and evil. This allowed an opening for Anne's enemies to move against her. They plotted; Henry believed the accusations; Anne was put to death.

There are some things here that are partly right, and there is also a lot more to the story. Anne's fate doesn't merely happen to her. Hers is a story of agency and power. She did not deserve to die. The charges against her were certainly falsified. But she was not a mere plaything thrown out by a spoiled man who no longer had use for her.

Instead, Anne's death was intimately tied to the story of her ascent. That ascent involved a man whose desires were fickle and violent. And yet, the seeming changeability of the king can mask the degree to which the reasons for his ardor for Anne and his reasons for having her killed were the same. We can overlook the fact that Anne's deliberate and intentional choices also made her the target of those whose power she threatened.

She knew who her enemies were. She knew that her choices would exacerbate their hatred toward her. But she had been given reason to believe that she could be a queen who shared in ruling the kingdom. When Henry had Anne crowned, it was with his own crown, the crown of St. Edward. No other consort has ever been crowned with the same crown as the reigning monarch.[3] The autumn prior, Anne had been made a peer of the realm in her own right. The king bestowed on her the title of Marquis of Pembroke. The conferring on Anne of the title of marquis, a male title, found its parallel in Francis's conferring on his sister Marguerite d'Angoulême the title and authority of duke. At multiple turns, Henry's trust in Anne was made explicit; she was not just his wife but the one in whom he placed the highest spiritual store.

Weeks after her coronation, Anne noted to the Venetian ambassador at court that "God had inspired his Majesty to marry her."[4] Anne saw herself like Queen Esther, brought by God to be by Henry's side. She was pious and principled and passionate and nonconforming. This was exactly why Henry was so besotted with her. That was why she had been able to claim so much power and influence.

In the face of hatred and danger, Anne leaned into her own strength, her own voice, her own vision, her own purpose. Danger be damned.

The Miscarriage

At the end of January 1536, Anne went into premature labor and delivered a stillborn—reportedly a boy. She is thought to have been at about fifteen weeks.

This event is often named as a turning point, particularly in fictional accounts of Anne's life. The king's marriage to her was prompted by his desire for a legitimate son, and when she failed to deliver anything other than a girl, her death warrant was all but signed.

It is also tied into posthumous stories of witchcraft that have become associated with Anne. It's not surprising that eventually this label, associated with outspoken women who don't conform easily to the categories we prefer for them, would eventually find its way to Anne. The stories of the baby's deformities and how this was then interpreted as a sign of Anne's witchery became layered on later but were not interpretations at the time. The baby was a miscarriage—hardly a rare turn of events in sixteenth-century Europe. Stillbirths and infant mortality were common occurrences, and Anne had already given birth to a healthy child. She was able to get pregnant easily. More babies could follow.

The eyewitness accounts of that time document that life continued for the couple after the miscarriage in ways that everyone expected. The king and queen made plans. They led their respective courts. Anne and her relatives continued to be granted prominent and lucrative royal favor, including properties and political opportunities.[5] As we saw with that interchange between Anne and Chapuys, Henry was still pushing for recognition of his marriage to her from the Spanish emperor less than two weeks before her arrest.[6] The couple argued and made extravagant purchases and saw their daughter, Elizabeth, as much as possible, even though she had her own palace and household and staff. Anne showered her child with gifts and all the finery that money could buy. Catherine of Aragon died around the time of Anne's miscarriage, and her disappearance from the pool of players vying for power had been greeted by the royal couple with celebration.[7] The truth that Anne was actually made more vulnerable by Catherine's death wasn't immediately obvious.

There were other factors shifting over the course of the first five months of 1536. And there were also choices that Anne made that were brave and dangerous.

There is definitely a connection between this miscarriage and Anne's death. Anne had at least one other failed pregnancy, thought to be a stillbirth, in 1534. That loss, along with this one in 1536, would have triggered Henry into worrying that Anne hadn't made right his relationship with God after all. Should Anne have given birth to a live baby boy, either in 1534 or 1536, she would have had protection against the king and the king's principal secretary and closest advisor, Thomas Cromwell.

A live baby boy would have saved Anne's life, but it wasn't the only reason for her death.

The Dissolution of the Monasteries

There was an event that occurred in spring 1536 that hasn't been included in the popular accounts of Anne's life, although it is well documented in the historical records. In 1536, the dissolution of the monasteries began.

Across Europe, monasteries represented heavy concentrations of land, money, and therefore power. The monasteries, being landowners whose property was never divided among inheritors (as happened to neighboring secular landowners), tended to accumulate considerable wealth and property.[8]

Tudor England isn't the only time and place when monasteries have come under attack. They have historically had too much money and power not to be seen as potential threats to the ruling authorities. Governments of a variety of countries have been known to confiscate monastic properties at times of religious or political upheaval, whether to fund the state or to conduct land reform. Even the Catholic Church has at times believed the monasteries to be a challenge to their power and has confiscated properties or disbanded communities.[9]

It was only a matter of time before England's split from Rome would result in the king's attention turning here. The monasteries represented the old authority, and their riches made them vulnerable to accusations of corruption.

In reality, these institutions were a mixed bag. They had been centers of healthcare, education, agriculture, music, arts, and literacy. Some had been guilty of mismanagement and corruption, of accumulating wealth while the general population they were supposed to serve starved. They were part of keeping education elite and guarding access to the Bible, but they had also provided an important alternative for women to be able to access education and spiritual leadership. In parts of England, the monks and nuns were fiercely loved by their people, and this love led to pockets of rebellion when Henry moved against them.

And move against them he did. The monasteries weren't just a challenge to Henry's royal supremacy; they were also an opportunity for amassing an extraordinary amount of wealth. By this time, Thomas Cromwell was Henry's chief advisor. The opportunity to line the royal coffers is usually presented as Cromwell's villainous idea, but there has been a tendency in Henry VIII's story to assume that the blame for wrongdoing should be assigned to those around Henry rather than to Henry himself. This king was not a puppet to Cromwell's puppeteering. The person who benefited from the financial windfall of the monasteries was Henry. Cromwell was doing Henry's bidding—not the other way around.

As part of the dissolution, Henry and Cromwell doled out enough gifts of lands and estates to the nobility to gain their support in the project, a smart move for keeping dissent at bay. Wealthy and powerful people amassed sufficient wealth and power that everyone whose voice counted became invested in the eventual disintegration of England's entire monastic infrastructure. Rebellion and protest arose, but Henry had all the support he needed to suppress dissent, violently if need be.

The first parliamentary bill allowing Henry to dissolve the monasteries was introduced in March 1536.

Anne had opinions about this, and she would not keep quiet.

Esther Revisited

The sermon took place on Passion Sunday, April 2, 1536, before Henry and the court at the Chapel Royal in Whitehall Palace. John Skip had recently been appointed Anne's almoner. Skip had a few Bible passages that he discussed in making his point, and the sermon is estimated to have taken upward of two hours to deliver. It was Skip's use of Esther's story that offered a pointed parallel to describe Henry and Anne's relationship, as well as to champion the causes that Anne held most dear.

Anne had enjoyed almost exclusive access to Henry throughout her rise to power and prominence. She had been the one that Henry listened to more than even the men in his innermost circle. She wanted this position of influence. She had deeply held religious convictions, and she was intimately involved in trying to steer political decision-making toward what she believed were virtuous religious ends. She thought she could and would continue to prevail over those who tried to infringe on her closeness to Henry. She was banking on it.

It was a risky conclusion to draw. It was risky because Cromwell didn't want to share his influence over the king with Anne any more than she wanted to share with him. It was risky because the things that Anne was now saying to Henry were not nearly as appealing as the things that he was hearing from Cromwell. It was risky because, although Skip looked like he was calling out Cromwell, he was really calling out the king. It was risky because Anne hadn't produced a son; she was failing the one assignment for which Henry had really hired her. Now she was criticizing

Henry publicly, and her failure in producing a son was bringing to the forefront Henry's deepest insecurity too.

Cromwell was offering Henry a windfall of money and increased power. Anne subscribed to a more pious and less lucrative vision. Anne championed voices who connected the church's break with Rome to economic justice. She believed it was wrong that so much money was concentrated in the monasteries while the British people floundered in poverty. Like Anne's role models in France, like the reformist Simon Fish whom Anne had protected from persecution and whose work she had admired, Anne saw church reform as advancing many of the basic tenets of the new humanism, including universal education and relief from poverty.

Instead, before her eyes, the religious ideals she had fought for were being leveraged into providing more wealth for the already wealthy king.

John Skip delivered his sermon just two weeks after Parliament had approved a bill for Henry to seize the wealth of approximately two hundred smaller monasteries. There was no provision in this bill for education or care for the poor, despite Anne's arguments and pleas to the contrary. There were still two weeks to go before Parliament's closing session at which the king would give his assent to the bill and make it law. Anne saw this as her opportunity to appeal one last time to the king's conscience before it was too late.[10]

It is in this context that her priest preached the sermon on Esther, using this as a blatant parable for the actual situation at court. In Esther's story, the queen used her position to bring before King Xerxes the needs of her people. Her advocacy forced the king to make a decision. Would he listen to his chosen queen or to his evil advisor? In Esther's story, she and her people prevailed, and the evil advisor was impaled for his crimes.

The parallels, with a few exaggerations by Skip, could not have been clearer. Anne was Esther. Henry was King Xerxes. And Haman, the evil advisor, was Thomas Cromwell. The choice was Henry's to make. He could either do right with his pilfering of the monasteries and use the resources for the good of the people, or he could follow Cromwell's advice and bolster his own wealth and power.

John Skip himself was hauled in for aggressive and angry questioning following the sermon but was not arrested. This message threw down the gauntlet. Either Anne or Cromwell. The king had to pick.

Anne did have precedent on her side. Chancellor Thomas More and Cardinal Thomas Wolsey had been trusted by Henry, but he had trusted Anne more. They had died, and she had stayed. She had good reason to believe that Cromwell was no match for her. After all, Henry said he loved her. Her opinions mattered to him. They were coconspirators in overthrowing Rome and in instigating this great religious reform. She had sex, desirability, the promise of more children, and God on her side.

One month later, Anne was arrested. On May 19, 1536, Anne was put to death.

The Lead-Up

Henry had other reasons for wanting to get rid of Anne. His sights had wandered to Jane Seymour, whose quieter nature could have felt like a welcome antidote to the tempestuous relationship he had with Anne. However, most signs through the early months of 1536 point to Henry's ongoing devotion to Anne, as well as his dedication to remaining true to his conviction that leaving Catherine and marrying Anne was in his, the country's, and everyone's eternal souls' best interest.

That doesn't mean that others weren't scheming for a royal divorce. The various power brokers of the English court, and especially those in the pro-Catholic faction who wanted a return to Rome and traditional ways, saw the possibility of swapping Jane in for Reformer Anne as very desirable. The relatively minor sin of championing another end to another marriage paled in comparison in their eyes to the need to bring the English church back to the true faith. If Henry could get his marriage to Catherine annulled when she no longer worked out, then surely Anne could be similarly dispatched. Anne played into their scheming by being resolutely unwilling to see her personal power over Henry diminished in any way. Anne's best bet with Jane would have been to let Henry have a courtly love flirtation with Jane and treat her as what she should have been: a passing fancy. Instead, her jealousy of Jane stoked the growing fire of Henry's interest in this woman who was in so many ways Anne's opposite. Jane went from being a dalliance to "wife material."

Thomas Cromwell was also building up a full arsenal of reasons to get rid of Anne, and it wasn't just the sermon that so explicitly declared war between them or Henry's waning affections. These reasons were happening on the European mainland. Anne had been the standard-bearer for a French-English alliance. She was known for her "French ways," which contributed to her sense of glamor and elegance. She had grown up in France, spoke French, and had been a champion of a strong and allied relationship between France and England around common values—like hating on the Holy Roman Emperor, Charles.

Anne's alignment with France had been a natural alignment for Henry too. Henry and England had split from Rome so that Anne could marry Henry. Henry's rejection of Catherine had also been a rejection of Charles and Spain, and aligning with France was both necessary for protecting Britain and a natural way of bolstering Henry's claim to ultimate authority over both his country and the church.

The French alliance, however, was consistently unstable. In 1534, Anne and Henry had both been humiliated by an embassy from France, which asked that Mary, not Elizabeth, be betrothed to the dauphin of France. It was a thumbing of the nose to all that Anne and Henry had sought to communicate about the validity of Henry's divorce, their marriage, and the new line of succession. Relations continued to cool over the course of the next year, 1535.[11] If France decided to go to war with the emperor, they would expect England to pony up with financial support, which England was reluctant to do.[12] The possibility of the pope drawing both Francis and Charles into war against Henry as punishment for his break with Rome was a looming possibility too.[13] France, unlike England, remained Catholic. Furthermore, traditional English sentiment leaned toward Spain, rather than the "old enemy," France,[14] so Anne's perception as being "French" was another mark against her in popular opinion.

Cromwell had been a saving grace for both Anne and Henry, the one who was able to catch that vision of breaking from Rome, which Anne had first presented to Henry those many years prior, and get the job done after six years of stalling. Anne Boleyn had been Cromwell's avenue into power.[15]

But Anne became more and more inconvenient to Cromwell in those early months of 1536. She had been an outspoken advocate of an alliance that was no longer politically viable or appealing, even though she had been politically astute enough in her final months to distance herself from the French. She was a vocal critic of the plundering that Cromwell was engineering as he dismantled the power of the monasteries. She was in the way of securing this vast wealth for Henry and the crown. Anne was the recognized leader of the opposition to the legislation dissolving the monasteries. When monastics wanted to appeal their destruction, Anne was the one to hear their cases. And she was considered to be directing other prominent English clerics to attack Cromwell and Henry's plans as well. Hugh Latimer, the country's premier preacher, preached before the king that the monasteries should not be dissolved but converted to better uses. Cranmer had preached a similar message earlier in the year.[16] The dissolution promised Cromwell enormous credibility in bolstering the power and the treasuries of the king, but he understood he would be hampered significantly if Anne was going to roadblock him at every turn for exemptions and protests.[17]

Just weeks after Skip's controversial sermon, Emperor Charles sent a courier to his ambassador Chapuys encouraging him to mend relations between Spain and England. Catherine of Aragon's death earlier that year created an unanticipated vulnerability for Anne. Not only did Henry not have Catherine to blame for everything wrong in his life now, but also Cromwell imagined this might present a window toward reinstating Mary without Henry's having to admit his marriage to Catherine had been legitimate.[18] If Mary could be restored to the line of succession, Henry would very likely be reconciled with the pope and allied with Spain.

This was the basket into which Cromwell was putting his political and diplomatic eggs.

Cromwell understood that Anne would never agree to compromising her daughter's position in the line of succession by agreeing to reinstate Mary. But much more critically, Cromwell was quickly made aware that Henry wouldn't agree to it either. On the night of April 18, the night Eustace Chapuys was forced by Henry to bow to Anne, Henry and Chapuys met for a conversation, a conversation that had been at Cromwell's urging.

It did not go well. Henry lost his temper with first Chapuys and then Cromwell, insisting to Chapuys that the only way he would negotiate with the emperor was if Anne were acknowledged as queen and Elizabeth's position as his heir remained intact.[19] It seemed like a victory for Anne, one more reason for her to believe Henry would continue to take her side.

Except that it forced Cromwell into a decisive corner from which the only way out was to fight. Cromwell had backed the Spanish alliance. Cromwell was suddenly on the wrong side of Henry's ego and determinations. Cromwell had ample motivation to see Anne removed from power. Cromwell was Anne's enemy, and after that sermon, everybody knew it. Anne was a visible sticking point in Cromwell's ability to deliver on a renewed alliance with the emperor. Anne, her family, and her supporters were competitors with Cromwell for the king's favor and listening ear. If the king sided with Anne on any of these matters, Cromwell's head could easily be on the chopping block instead of Anne's.

Cromwell had to plot. He had to plot quickly, and he had to be smart.

But Why Adultery?

The mysterious thing about Anne's demise is why it went in such a scandalous, violent, and final direction, and why the turn happened so quickly. The way that Anne fell wasn't just unfortunate for her. It was maximally humiliating for Henry. The entire realm was to believe that the king had been cuckolded, and badly.

There should have been easier ways to have her removed. Henry could have just had his marriage to Anne annulled and married Jane. This is what the pro-Catholic faction was angling for. However, Cromwell was reading the room much more analytically. He understood that Henry was unlikely to annul the marriage after spending a decade trying to convince everyone that Anne wasn't just an affair. Furthermore, Anne could never be relied upon to go quietly, nor was there any guarantee that Henry wouldn't be drawn back into her seemingly irresistible orbit.[20] Cromwell knew he needed to remove Anne in as final a way as possible.

Anne was already saddled with sexually deviant labels: "whore" and "concubine" the most prominent. Gossip had perpetually surrounded her magnetic ways, her skillful flirting, her head-spinning appeal. Moreover, it has always been easy to connect strong women in positions of power to accusations of sexual indiscretion. That narrative has a proven track record, across history and into our current times.

Circumstances quickly converged into offering Cromwell a perfect, decisive, and messy opportunity.

CHAPTER 10

She Laughed at the King

A Newly Fragile King

Reading about Henry VIII feels like a psychological foray into an all-too-familiar personality type, as well as a lesson in how those around this kind of spoiled and narcissistic leader operate in order to get ahead. This can lull me into thinking of Henry as dumb and oafish, easy prey to the puppeteers who knew how to get what they wanted by flattering, helping, or otherwise manipulating the king. After all, who was speaking to the king and how that connected, or didn't, with the ideas, insecurities, hopes, dreams, and desires that were front of mind for him determined who could get their ideas heard and realized—and who ended up dead. With so many people vying to be the person that Henry most needed and trusted, it is easy to imagine how Henry's volatile emotions could become pawns in other people's power plays.

Both Anne and Cromwell had risen far above their station by being exceptionally good at locking in on what was making Henry tick. When their agendas started to conflict with one another, Cromwell was the one to identify the need, not to have more convincing ideas than Anne, but to get rid of Anne. And as it turned out, getting rid of Anne with the sort of finality he was seeking had the added bonus of taking out a whole circle of others who had been in Henry's favor and taking up that precious space in his sphere of influence. Getting rid of Anne meant turning all the things about Anne that had been to her advantage—particularly the esteem in which Henry held her and the spiritual and moral rightness he had attributed to their relationship—against her.

The controversial sermon of Passiontide 1536 suggests that Anne missed the warning signs about how precarious her situation really was, or she deliberately chose to throw caution to the wind. Anne was accustomed to arguing with Henry, calling him out for behavior she didn't like, and generally being an engaged and fiery participant in their relationship and in their governance of the kingdom. Henry, for so many years, liked this about her. Anne believed that she could continue to use her position for "just such a time as this"—to accomplish good for her people.

Henry, however, had reasons for becoming increasingly insecure.

In January of that fateful year, Henry suffered a debilitating jousting accident. It had left him unconscious for several hours and with one leg crushed under the weight of his fully armored horse. On May 1, 1536, the annual May Day joust was held at Greenwich Palace. Henry was sidelined for the first time in his reign. The January accident would prove to be the end of Henry's ability to play the role of the young, golden, athletic prince of the kingdom and the start of his journey into obesity and a spiral of health concerns and mobility limitations—leg ulcers and gout, to name a few recurring problems.

Henry was not accustomed to having his power diminished. In this tournament, several of Henry's contemporaries competed as Henry himself would have liked to have done, and some of them were his age or older. Henry had put great store in himself as a powerful and athletic conquering hero. Now he had to watch from the sidelines as other men rode around the fields, representing power and manliness that was no longer in Henry's grasp. Henry Norris was Henry's oldest and closest companion, his Groom of the Stool.[1] He slept at the foot of the king's bed. He was witness to Henry and Anne's marriage. He was involved in the most intimate matters of Henry's life and body, the closest thing that Henry had to a friend.[2] But Norris was fifty-four and still jousting, and the king was only forty-five and no longer the dominant man physically that he had always been. He was suddenly a spectator, and it was deeply unsettling.[3]

Bubbling in the background of this latest humiliation was the attack on Henry's manhood that had haunted his entire adult life: He didn't have sons.

Flirting and Gossip

Cromwell was working hard at the end of April to investigate Anne.[4] He had begun plotting in earnest after the dressing down both he and Eustace Chapuys received from the king on April 18, when terms for a Spanish-English alliance were laid out and had not been to Henry's liking. Anne was being closely watched, at least by the end of April if not before, for any opportunity to build a case against her, and some courtly banter was just such an opportunity. There is a chain of gossip and flirtation that can be parsed out from the confusion of April and May that is thought to be the basis for these shocking accusations against the queen of England.

The speed with which those quiet schemes and light gossip became the era-defining scandal was breathtaking.

It appears to have started between one of Henry's courtiers, Anthony Browne, and his sister, Elizabeth Browne (Lady Worcester).[5] Lady Worcester's own sexual choices were being called into question by her brother, and she responded to these allegations with a common defense: deflection. She pointed to Anne's behavior with Mark Smeton, Henry Norris, and George Boleyn and suggested that this was the place to direct judgment and condemnation, not her.[6]

Mark Smeton, musician and groom of the privy chamber, was the first to be arrested, April 30, on the charge of committing adultery with Anne. Unfortunately, he provided exactly the right leverage needed by, upon arrest, confessing to adultery with the queen. Whether he confessed because he had been tortured, or whether he did so because he had a delusional read on his relationship with Anne, is a point of speculation. He was the only one of the men to say he was guilty.

Smeton's confession succeeded in bringing under suspicion the other men known by the gossipy court to have bantered with the queen. Despite the king's knowing about Smeton's charge and arrest, Henry and Anne attended the May Day tournament together. Suddenly at the end of the joust, Henry left. He brought Henry Norris with him, along with a few others. He interrogated Norris relentlessly on the journey back to Whitehall Palace. The court was left wondering what was transpiring; Anne was left behind with growing panic and bewilderment.

Henry Norris had been part of an ill-advised interchange with Anne, either on April 29 or April 30, just prior to the jousting tournament. Anne made the mistake of not only suggesting that Norris was interested in her, but then, within earshot of bystanders, that Norris might want to replace the king as Anne's husband, were the king to die:

> You look for dead men's shoes; for if ought came to the king but good you would look to have me.[7]

News of this exchange spread through the court, and Anne was sufficiently concerned about it that she had made Norris go to her almoner to take an oath that she was a "good woman."[8] Anne and Henry had a fight later that day, with Anne holding Elizabeth in her arms; it is assumed that she was pleading with Henry to hear her side of the story. Nonetheless, she attended the May Day joust with him the next day.[9]

Norris was arrested the day after the joust and joined Smeton, coaccused of the charges of adultery and treason. George Boleyn, Anne's brother, was arrested later that day, and then Anne herself.

It seems that those who were out to get Anne were building their case in real time, and her bafflement at being arrested served to give them ammunition as she wondered out loud with whom she might have been accused of acting inappropriately. In the list of possibilities Anne named, Mark Smeton was not on her radar, although she did worry out loud that Henry Norris had betrayed her.

William Brereton and Francis Weston were arrested two days after, implicated once the accusations had become a fully raging fire.[10] Weston had been flirty with one of Anne's ladies, Margaret Shelton, and had extended suggestive comments toward Anne too. Brereton's involvement in the mess of accusations remains mysterious, but it is interesting to note that he, too, was a competitor in the May 1 jousting tournament.[11]

This was a group of men who staffed the privy chamber, the inner circle of intimacy and influence with the king.[12] Wiping out these five men was nothing short of a coup, the removal of a whole tier of power at the court. It was also the wiping out of a circle of male competitors who were now, very clearly, physically more dominant than Henry.

Two others were arrested but eventually released. Thomas Wyatt had been known for his affection for Anne prior to her relationship with Henry, and several of his poems expressed his admiration for her with only the thinnest of veils cloaking Anne's identity as the subject of his romantic feelings. He would have been an obvious choice for ringing into the accusations. Richard Page was arrested too, a man who had risen in rank because of his support for the king's "Great Matter." Both were released. Neither was a member of the "Boleyn faction" at court.[13]

The evidence against Anne was flimsy, even by the standards of those who hated her. Chapuys, who wasn't prone to giving Anne the benefit of the doubt ever, noted that "although everybody rejoices at the execution of the *putain* [whore], there are some who murmur at the mode of procedure against her and the others, and people speak variously of the king."[14] The case hinged on flirtations, courtly crushes, and gossip.

Henry's new insecurity isn't listed among the reasons for Anne's fall, and it is admittedly speculation to connect Henry's physical limitations with the accusations brought against Anne and the men. But it couldn't have helped. There was a volatility and decisiveness to Henry's actions that speaks to tremendous fragility. Whatever Henry's psychological landscape, Cromwell's accusations against Anne, with just the slightest amount of fuel added to the fire, took on a burning life of their own.

The evidence against George was the flimsiest, with the charge of incest between the siblings based mostly on George and Anne having spent a long time together in Anne's room once.[15] George's wife, Jane Boleyn, appears to be the source of this information and was one of a group of enemies who were only too willing to turn on Anne, providing the shreds of evidence of inappropriate behavior that Cromwell would use to construct his case of adultery and treason.[16] Why Jane moved against her own family is unknown, but many theories have been woven into the speculative narratives of these dramatic last days.

Cromwell, Mastermind?

Thomas Cromwell took credit for Anne's demise.[17] While there is no doubt that Cromwell was involved, the degree to which happenstance or his own planning gave him the ultimate outcome of five accusations of adultery is debated. There is a messiness to Henry's jealousy and the court's gossip that stretches credulity in imagining that Cromwell could have possibly plotted it all.[18]

If he is to be believed, then his calculations were on point, and his stroke of genius was in understanding that the best way of getting rid of

Anne was to strike Henry hard in exactly the biggest chink in his kingly armor. At a time when Henry was on the downward spiral of health and virility, Cromwell landed the windfall of evidence against a group of men who best represented the things that Henry was losing and used them to bring down the inconveniently outspoken and domineering Anne Boleyn with accusations that used all that Henry had desired and admired about Anne against her.

Cromwell snidely and vaguely reported to a few peripheral characters that the crimes of which Anne was accused "were so abominable that I think the like was never heard."[19] The most damning and upsetting detail to emerge was at George's trial. It didn't have a criminal category. It wasn't treasonous and it wasn't adultery. But it was, to Henry, unforgivable. Anne had made fun of the king's sexual performance.

Henry was insecure about sexual matters anyway. If Anne were speaking of those matters out loud, if Anne were humiliating him—by not giving him sons and openly discussing his inadequacies—then Henry was also convinced that Anne had other lovers and was plotting his demise. "He has neither vigor nor virtue," was her reported remark. Anne and George were known to joke with each other about the king's clothing and poetry as well.[20] George laughed about the possibility that Henry wasn't Elizabeth's father, evidently based on the king's troubles in the bedroom.[21] This would have been a mightily humiliating detail to be raised before the court for Henry—especially given that he had yet to produce a legitimate male heir and could no longer perform his manhood as an athletic jouster either.

George made a startling decision at his trial, which was to read out loud the comment that he was accused of hearing from Anne about the king's impotency. George deliberately chose not to back down, even when his life was on the line, in order to make the situation as embarrassing for the king as possible.

The law at that time did not provide for a queen's adultery to be punishable by death. Anne had to be found guilty not just of adultery but treason.[22] This hinged on the argument that her adulterous behavior involved imagining the king's death and his replacement by any of Anne's supposed lovers.

Or Someone Else . . .

There is a type of movie thriller to which my brain kept circling over the time I would spend reading the different theories that have been constructed to explain Anne's demise. It's the kind of plot that leaves us with a feeling of sickened wonder for the signs that we missed, for the misdirects that caused us to be blind to what was right before our eyes.

That might be what we're discussing here. The more time I spend with the ongoing historical analysis and the careful, endless piecing together of gossip and schemes and bids for the king's favor that led to Anne and five prominent men of the court being put to death in May 1536, the more I am left with that sense of sickened wonder. Yes, there were people vying for the king's attention and for places of power. Yes, Cromwell did plot against Anne and took credit for doing so.

However, it might also have been Henry driving this all along. We have assumed that he got duped by the plots of the people around him. But maybe the one plotting was Henry. Cromwell was always the "fixer," not the "ideas man." That Cromwell was doing the king's bidding, and not the other way around, is a theory that has solid internal logic.

While many historians center their analysis on Anne's behavior, what she did or didn't do, and who was most responsible for orchestrating her death, scholar Emma Levitt makes the interesting suggestion that the men who fell with Anne were selected by Henry and were selected because they threatened his manhood.[23] They had been his closest and most trusted companions—servants of the privy chamber and combatants on the jousting pitch. With his new fragility, he no longer trusted them, and his physical humiliation translated into believing that Anne might have cuckolded him with "these glamorous, vigorous men who were still able to embody chivalric masculinity by competing in jousts."[24]

Likewise, maybe we have missed the obvious explanation for who and what came between Anne and Henry. Maybe the reason why Henry so dramatically changed his tune with a woman that he moved heaven and earth to be with doesn't require much explanation at all. As historian Natalie Grueninger piercingly notes, "[Henry] pursued her death with the same kind of vigor that he pursued marrying her." Obsessive behavior in targeting a woman with desire and then with violence is hardly new or unique to King Henry.

Anne had been Henry's partner in religious reform. He had been convinced of her moral authority and that their marriage was in accordance with God's holy law, that his relationship with her would put him right in the eyes of God and secure right relationship with the divine for his kingdom. When the princes weren't born to prove Henry right, he was humiliated. He was humiliated for the same reason he had been insecure and obsessive all along. But Henry was the king of England, so someone else had to be blamed for why Henry was left looking so inadequate.

In response, Anne's moral authority was decimated.[25] Henry's imagination ran wild with thoughts of Anne conspiring with her many lovers to unseat him from his manhood and his throne. He reported to those who would listen that Anne had more than a hundred lovers, another falsified detail that would haunt Anne's reputation long after her death.[26]

If Jane Seymour's role in Henry's life had initially been a courtly dalliance, now her contrast to Anne made her presence at Henry's side a done deal. Even as Anne was being sentenced to death, Henry was rapidly moving to make Jane his new wife. He made a show of parading to her side each night, hosting parties and celebrations and planning his wedding to Anne's replacement while his current wife was imprisoned in the tower. He also took a morbid interest in "plans for the executions, even to the making of the scaffolds" and calling for a special executioner from Calais for Anne's death.[27] It was as if Henry was intent not just on proving his manhood and virility to all who were watching, but also justifying to himself that killing his wife was moral, so long as she was the whore who ruined everything and he was killing her in the fanciest way possible.

Too Much to Say

When Jane Seymour deigned to speak up in preservation of religious houses after her marriage to Henry, he snapped at her to keep out of political matters, reminding her that her predecessor had died for her meddling.[28]

He wasn't the only one to suggest that Anne's death happened because she had too much to say. Scholars who pore over every shred of evidence from those harried and chaotic days at the end of April and beginning of May 1536 often include in their conclusions that Anne's flirtatious ways and unfiltered talk were her undoing. Her attendant in the tower, an aunt, said to her "such desire as you have had to such tales has brought you to this."[29] Eric Ives, whose careful scholarship of Anne's life couldn't disguise the admiration he felt for his subject, nonetheless noted that Anne may have suffered from "an inability to keep a safe regal distance" and that issues of "unguarded speech and gossip" had made her vulnerable.[30]

At her trial, while denying the charges with a level of self-possession and clarity that even made her enemies take notice, she did admit that she hadn't shown the king "the humility which his goodness to me, and the honors to which he raised me, merited."[31]

I hate that Anne needed to say that. I hate that for five hundred years analysts have continued to focus on the flirtatious things she said, and that has been used as proof that she misspoke or did something that would justify the charges for which she died. It parallels the questions that still go on in courtrooms about how short the skirt was of the victim of sexual assault, how many drinks she had that night, whether she had a lot of sexual partners prior to the rape.

I hate that historians can prove with a simple analysis of the facts they have at their disposal centuries later that at least 75 percent of the incidents that were constructed to bring Anne down never happened: that either Anne or the man she was accused of sleeping with were not in the place they were said to have been when they were supposed to have been cuckolding the king.[32] I hate the realization now, which certainly had to be obvious then too, that there was a "dog who didn't bark"—that is to say that nobody was accused of conspiring along with Anne to make all of this adultery happen. Queens had no privacy.[33] If Anne were really to have been sleeping with five different men over the course of her brief reign, that would have necessitated ladies-in-waiting helping her to make that happen, and they would have fallen with her.[34] No female accomplices were accused. It is the clearest tell that Anne was not guilty.

I hate that cinematic realization that all fingers might just point back to Henry. Most historians have ascribed the plotting primarily to Cromwell; they say that Henry was still behaving normally to Anne through much of those first months of 1536. He couldn't have been seriously planning to get rid of her while also making summer vacation plans and parading her in front of Chapuys. But men can plot violence to their wives and put on a charade of normalcy while doing it. From Anne's failure to produce a son to her inconvenient questioning of his flirtations with Jane and his plundering of the monasteries, Henry had a whole stockpile of reasons to find Anne tiresome, disappointing, inconvenient, enraging, disloyal, and, most of all, humiliating. Henry might have known for months that, one way or the other, he was going to be rid of Anne.

The person with whose motivations and personality we are best acquainted in the whole cadre of characters involved in Anne's downfall is Henry. That Henry was a man quick to decide he wanted a woman and just as quick to discard her is one of the most well-documented patterns of behavior we have in this whole sorry tale.

But Anne was made to apologize. She apologized for not being grateful enough, speaking up too much, and not being properly humble or deferential. Very few historians have insisted that the charges against

Anne weren't fabricated, but that hasn't stopped the victim-blaming from creeping in, nonetheless. Her big mouth, her "indiscreet" banter, and her mildly flirty ways all become fodder for judgment. She was "behaving extraordinarily incautiously" said historian Greg Walker.[35] "Pastime in the queen's chamber . . . had got somewhat out of hand," said Eric Ives.[36]

She should have known better. She should have piped down. She should have shut up. She should have wanted less. She should have been more careful.

Meanwhile, her husband, whether he plotted her demise for months or within a matter of days, chose to kill her.

Promise to Be Dazzling

There is a Taylor Swift song called "Clara Bow" in which Swift sings of the famous silent-film star to reflect on the ebbs and flows of celebrity fascination. The implication of the song is that there will always be a "next" woman to come into the spotlight and to capture the popular imagination. That time in the spotlight is fleeting; every ingenue will eventually be shoved to the side for the next new thing.

It's a constant preoccupation of Swift's, her sense of the world's adulation and how inevitable it is that she will exhaust the attention that is currently so ravenously fixed on her.

She notes this as a way of holding her own fame lightly and of calling out the capricious way the world treats famous women. But she does something else here. She also claims her own agency, the one who shapes her story and stakes out her territory as someone who matters, not because of the adulation she inspires, nor because of her ephemeral beauty, but because of her talent, hard work, and legitimate brilliance. Music critics insist that Swift's legacy won't be hinged upon the men she wrote about or the celebrity she so masterfully commanded, because she crafted songs that speak to the human heart, that tell us something not just about her experience but about our own. It is Taylor Swift's talent that we will remember about her.

They shouldn't be so sure about that. Even for one whose work has been as minutely examined and critically considered as Swift's, there is a tendency to reduce women and their offerings to questions about how effective they were in capturing the attention of the people who are seen as mattering—whether that is the mass population or whether it is men with power—and then whether their use of that attention is judged as appropriate or not.

When we held a "Taylor Swift Night" at the church in our unconventional Wednesday night worship gathering, I had to field an astonishing number of vitriolic comments about how inappropriate it was to be "celebrating" Taylor when she had slept with so many men. Her celebrity was judged as frivolous and silly. Within a matter of months, we held a "Billy Joel Night" with a similar structure to our reflections and music. Joel, who has been married multiple times to younger and younger women and made many questionable decisions typical of male rock stars, elicited not one word of protest from any corner of our congregation.

Anne Boleyn has been primarily discussed through a lens similar to the one that Swift brings to Clara Bow. What was it about Anne that captured the king's attention? Did she deserve that attention? Use it appropriately? And then how do we interpret not just the king's losing interest in her but so dramatically turning on her? Why did she inspire such passion? Was she a person who clawed her way to the top and ultimately got her comeuppance? Or was she just one more woman who was fascinating until she wasn't fascinating any longer?

What gets missed in Anne's story is that she legitimately left her mark, not as someone who captured the gaze of another, but as a talented, smart, insightful person in her own right, who in a remarkable way read the signs of the times and changed history.

Anne wasn't just someone who captured the king's attention and then failed to keep it. Anne was someone who earned her place as a decision-maker and visionary alongside the king of England and who used her power to instigate change whose effects are still visible today.

It is an interesting thought experiment to consider what, if anything, Anne would have done differently if she had known where her choices would take her.

Would Anne have had John Skip preach that sermon if she had known that the king wasn't going to side with her? She was principled and opinionated and had strong religious ideals, but it would be hard to conclude that Anne was a deliberate martyr for the religious cause she championed. She had plenty of strains of self-preservation to suggest that she might have picked her own neck rather than her principles.

Would Anne have been less flirtatious and more guarded with her language if she had understood the king's insecurities and the gossip channels of the court? There is no "there" there in Anne's behavior. It was all innocent and within the conventions of courtly banter. It was exactly this kind of witty conduct for which Anne was known and that had presumably been attractive to Henry too. But if she had understood that his feelings were shifting so completely, surely she would have been more modest in how she talked and acted.

Here is a consideration that crosses my mind though. Anne did know that Henry's eye had wandered to Jane. She must have also been aware that discussion of Henry's divorcing her was on the radar. The complaints about the king's sexual performance raised at George's trial suggest that not only was Henry tiring of her, but she was far from enamored of him either.

What if she wasn't interested in merely keeping her husband and her head? What if what she really wanted was power? An extraordinary life? The freedom to rule? Make decisions? Be desirable and influential? Would Anne have been happy to go off to a monastery to live her days out as the king's divorced wife? Would she have wanted to stay the queen but at the expense of taking on a quieter, more demure, and subservient existence?

Of course it is speculative. And of course, Anne was distressed at the dramatic turn of events that resulted in her execution. There is no doubt that Anne didn't want or seek the outcome that befell her.

But it is also possible that Anne deliberately chose to be uncompromising in her opinions and her personality, even though that choice put her in danger that she could have predicted. It is possible that, in the final analysis of all the choices available to Anne, it wasn't worth it to keep her life at the expense of being exactly who she was.

Then again, maybe this is exactly the kind of speculation that lets men like Henry off the hook. My speculations are also part of a pattern that looks to make meaning of violence, particularly violence inflicted on the bodies of women and marginalized people. What does it matter if one more woman dies unjustly and with her name destroyed if we all get what we want in the end? I want Anne's final moments to have been brave and meaningful. I want to believe that the good things that came from who she was, and even how she died, were worth it. I get to serve in a church that she made possible and that would have looked different if she had been better able to hold her tongue, bear sons, and be more agreeable.

If there is grace and goodness that has come out of Anne's life, it shouldn't diminish the cold hard truth that Anne's husband killed her. She didn't back down, she didn't fulfill the expectations of womanhood placed on her, and she stands as one more woman cut down in cold blood because men have the power to decide when they have had enough of those who threaten, talk back, don't perform, and ask for too much.

CHAPTER 11

From A to E

A Bloody and Tumultuous Road Map of Reformation

Reform Was Supposed to Have Died with Anne

Reformers in England would have had no small measure of panic when Anne was found guilty of treason and her execution warrant was signed. She was their patron and champion. She was the person of influence bringing them and their ideas forward into the power structures of the church and the kingdom.

The beginning of England's Reformation was significantly shaped by Anne's vision and convictions. Henry's religious principles were far less clear. His Catholic sympathies were visible just below the surface of the self-serving reform he had been willing to initiate. The plot against Anne was significantly facilitated by the fact that Anne had numerous religious enemies, eager to see her removed in the hopes of returning to the Roman fold. Anne's pro-Catholic enemies were rejoicing in her demise, and there was every reason for the Reformers to have believed that their cause was lost with Anne's death.

Historian Eric Ives compellingly reconstructs Thomas Cromwell's machinations in bringing down Anne as a delicate balancing act between securing allies with pro-Catholic/anti-Anne forces while ultimately committing to a continued path of reform. Despite his battle with Anne, Cromwell remained a staunch reformer. Henry, too, had his reasons for being rigidly unwilling to return to Rome. Royal supremacy had severed England's relationship with the pope and put Henry in charge of the church. The money and power now at his disposal did much to keep Henry's religious scruples firmly entrenched in the anti-Roman camp.

Cromwell had gained the confidence of a rising circle of Anne's enemies, loosely pro-Catholic, who supported the reinstatement of Mary and the promotion of Jane Seymour as part of a package deal.[1] It would be two months before these new allies realized that Cromwell did not share their views.[2] It was a bait and switch. Cromwell knew he needed these allies, but they had not realized that Cromwell, and the promotion of Jane, would not be their ticket to returning to Rome. It wouldn't be Mary's ticket to legitimacy either.

Even though Anne had so completely fallen from grace, the reform that she had stood for, spoken for, and become the figurehead of, would continue beyond her death because it had simply become too attractive for Henry to abandon.

Anne would not be given credit—by Cromwell, by Archbishop Cranmer, and certainly not by King Henry—for her spine of steel, her resolve, her vision, the chess pieces that she moved into place to secure for these men the things that they each so desired: power and money of an almost unlimited sort for Cromwell and the king, and for Archbishop Cranmer, the opportunity to be the signature leader of the religious change he so desired. These men would continue with the agenda that

Anne had begun without a backward glance at the debt that they owed her. She would be buried in an unmarked grave two feet under the ground beneath a pavement stone in front of the altar in the chapel of the Tower of London. Out of sight, out of mind.

A Kindred Spirit

While Henry was struggling in his political and religious leadership, as well as his health, another woman was quietly making her impact on who was going to rise to power, and what religious cause they would champion after Henry.

It was Kateryn Parr, the final wife of Henry VIII—the "one who survived." After Jane Seymour's death from complications in childbirth, Henry had married two more times: Anna of Cleves and Katherine Howard. Anna's was a political marriage, but she was not to Henry's liking, and he quickly had the marriage annulled. She did well by the marriage though, enjoying a life of wealth and independence for the rest of her days, including being gifted a lease to the Boleyn family homestead, Hever Castle, and taking up residence there. Katherine Howard, cousin of Anne, was also accused of adultery and put to death. She was approximately eighteen years old when she died.

Kateryn Parr was the king's final marriage. She didn't produce any children. Henry was possibly unable to consummate their union with his failing health (and with ongoing questions of impotency plaguing his reputation). Kateryn, like Anne, was a very unlikely choice for Henry's wife. She had been married and widowed twice before. Like Anne, she came from a family with some land holdings, modest wealth, and connections to nobility. Her parents had both served as courtiers, and her mother had been a loyal lady-in-waiting to Catherine of Aragon. Kateryn was named after her, and the first queen might have been her godmother. Kateryn's father died when she was just four years old, and her mother devoted herself to providing a substantial and wide-ranging education for Kateryn and her siblings, as well as modeling independent female leadership.

Unlike Anne, Kateryn was a unifying force in Henry's household. She had stepchildren from one of her previous marriages and stayed close to that stepdaughter for the rest of her life. She embraced this familial role with all three of Henry's children, developing a close friendship with both Mary and Elizabeth. Edward called her "beloved mother." Kateryn was careful about managing Henry's moods and her years as queen were the calmest and most "normal" for the family that now comprised a king in failing health, three children from three different women, and wife number six.[3]

Anne Boleyn might have named Kateryn Parr as a kindred spirit. Kateryn was scholarly and opinionated, but also astute. She led with insight and intelligence. She, like Anne, loved music and dancing, was known as a sparkling conversationalist and a woman of flair and high fashion. She enjoyed and understood the presentation of being royal: the clothes, the jewels, the elegance.

Kateryn, also like Anne, had her own agenda for power. She was a determined and passionate reformer. She had no desire to marry Henry when his finger pointed her way, and he claimed her with the proclamation: "That one!" Like the other five wives, consent wasn't part of the equation when it came to Henry's desire; she was said to be horrified by the offer. But she asserted agency in this disempowering situation by understanding her marriage to the king as a vocation. She believed that God had chosen her to be Henry's sixth wife so that she could do her part in furthering Protestant evangelical aims.[4]

Kateryn's résumé is impressive by any standard, but particularly by that of limited opportunities for sixteenth-century women. Kateryn wrote religious devotionals and one of her prayers was included in the Book of Common Prayer—still used by Anglicans across the world today.[5] She holds the distinction of being the first woman to be published under her own name in English. She commissioned biblical translations and was adept at translating Latin works into English.

Conservative factions of the court were, not surprisingly, threatened by Kateryn, especially if she were to be named regent upon Henry's death. A small cadre of conservative men plotted against Kateryn, first with the idea of accusing her of witchcraft but then settling on the charge of heresy. They managed to have Henry sign her arrest warrant but were unprepared for her charming and placating ways to win Henry's favor decidedly back.[6] The accusations didn't end in her death but may have been the reason why Henry's final will and testament appointed a group of men to act as a "Regency Council" on behalf of the nine-year-old Edward rather than Kateryn.

Kateryn enjoyed a close friendship with Princess Elizabeth and with Elizabeth's cousin, Lady Jane Grey, exchanging ideas and religious possibilities with both, and providing them with an example of female leadership and intellect. Kateryn Parr, the return to type for Henry, played a powerful hand in the direction that the country and the church would go after Henry's death. She managed to do so in a way that avoided being slapped with the labels and scandals that so beleaguered Anne both in her life and in her afterlife. Neither woman has been adequately credited for their influence on shaping the English Reformation. Kateryn did enough things right as a woman and avoided many wrong things, so her reputation hasn't needed rehabilitation in the way Anne's has. Her legacy has been easier to notice, especially since she put pen to paper, writing and publishing books.

Even with that, her scholarly contributions to the language and prayer of the Reformation, and her masterful diplomacy in negotiating a temperamental king and a venomous court, have been largely overlooked.

King Edward VI: A White-Hot Protestant and the Second Reformation

Henry's death unleashed a new version of religious reform on England. This more radical Protestantism had been waiting in the wings, biding its time, and amassing its troops. Edward, only nine years old at the time of accession, was a convicted Reformer. He and his closest circle were ready for the dawn of a new day in England.

He was profoundly influenced by these beliefs, thanks in part to Kateryn Parr and aided by Anne Boleyn's long-ago protégé, Thomas Cranmer. Cranmer proved to be a masterful politician and one of the only men in Henry's inner circle to be compliant and shrewd enough to maintain Henry's favor throughout the king's life. Even while meeting Henry's every desire with calculated subservience, Cranmer became increasingly evangelical in his beliefs as time went on.

Edward's education had been overseen first by Kateryn and then by Thomas Cranmer himself. Edward was a serious and intelligent young boy, and he was convinced their stronger Protestant belief system was in line with God's will. This included not just a fierce opposition to the Roman Catholic Church as the agent of the devil himself, but also a rejection of the traditional seven sacraments of the church and the church's long-held belief in purgatory.[7]

If Edward had lived beyond his teen years or if the woman he named as his successor—his equally Protestant cousin Jane Grey—had been successful in her bid for the throne, the church in England would have taken shape in a drastically different way, with a much more severe turn away from Catholicism.

That direction could already be seen in Edward's few years of reigning. Because he died young, history has portrayed him as sickly and weak. In fact, he was strong-willed, intelligent, and focused. He was fiery in his evangelical beliefs. Around him had rallied England's Protestant elite, including Edward's uncle Edward Seymour, along with Thomas Cranmer and John Dudley. They secured power in the final days of Henry's reign and, with the young king for whom they were providing guardianship as part of his Regency Council, they committed to a much more stringent brand of Protestantism.

This came with many heavy-handed measures. Clergy across England were forced to deliver evangelical sermons written by Cranmer himself, even though most of the church leadership would have defined themselves as traditionalists. Attendance at Mass became unlawful, and Cranmer's very Protestant Book of Common Prayer was made compulsory.[8]

The young King Edward was intent on dismantling anything in his country's churches that sniffed of superstition or idolatry. His bent was toward iconoclasm, and therefore the parish churches of England were subject to substantial overhauls—particularly of altars, crucifixes, artwork, things like rood screens that kept the congregation from being able to see the mysteries taking place around the altar, and other architectural and artistic features that suggested God could be accessed through engaging the senses, images, or sacraments.

The agenda was a clear and pious one, but it was not popular. The sentiments of the general population were of little concern as the young Edward VI and his crew pursued their mission to bring the realm in line with what the One True God would want of them. While the people of England would subscribe to the notion that their relationship with God required the faithfulness of their king, the historical record shows significant distress and confusion from the people and the majority of clergy towards these measures. These were their churches, where they worshipped and which were at the center of their devotional lives. Art and architectural features had been planned for and bought by the people. Under Cranmer's newfound power, ceremonies which had been part of people's lives across centuries were forbidden: the blessing of candles on Candlemas Day, the use of ashes on Ash Wednesday and palms on Palm Sunday.[9] Most people would have been left utterly bewildered and significantly aggrieved by these new directions.

That was the way that England was headed, however. Edward was young and powerful, smart and principled. Soon he would be wed and would produce his own heirs to the throne who could be raised to subscribe to these same fierce Protestant beliefs. His sisters, Mary and Elizabeth, were fast becoming footnotes of history.

Except then Edward died.

Lady Jane Grey—Nine Days and Two Extremes

Lady Jane Grey—otherwise known as the "Nine Days Queen"[10]—is sometimes included in the list of England's monarchs and sometimes not. She was the brainy and scholarly cousin of Edward VI. Her grandparents were Henry VIII's sister Mary and Henry VIII's close friend Charles Brandon. Jane was selected by Edward as his successor because Edward and his power brokers feared a return to Catholicism if the throne passed to his half sister Mary. Edward hoped to bypass both Mary and Elizabeth by continuing to insist that they were each illegitimate offspring of his father, the late king.

It was surprising to Cranmer and Dudley, who had helped to back Jane's bid for the crown, when Mary had something to say about who would sit on the throne of England. Displaying courage and resourcefulness that they hadn't imagined she possessed, she rallied troops, took back the throne, and locked Jane and Jane's husband, Guildford, in the Tower of London.

She also immediately put Dudley to death. Jane, Guildford, and Cranmer were killed later.

Dudley, Jane, and Guildford were not executed for religious reasons explicitly. However, who supported Mary and who supported Jane was a matter of religious conviction at heart. Jane was a fierce Protestant. Mary was the great Catholic hope, the eldest of Henry's offspring, the daughter of Catherine of Aragon, and had been raised in a court and country that was thoroughly Catholic.

Queen Mary I: Reform Undone, More Blood Shed

England was ping-ponged around by Edward's fierce reform agenda, followed (minus the nine days of Jane Grey) by the predicted return to Catholicism when Mary captured the throne. The English population had assumed the throne of England to be Mary's birthright and were generally pleased that the daughter of the beloved and ill-treated Catherine of Aragon would finally have her due.

Many of those who had been raised up, particularly in the heady days of Anne Boleyn's reign and the very beginning of reform in England, lost their heads or were burned at the stake in England's Counter-Reformation. Initially though, Mary began her reign with only cautious and moderate steps back toward the Catholicism she had steadfastly maintained throughout her life.

Mary's return to Catholicism was widely well received by her subjects, and Mary had no trouble stacking her Parliament with the traditionalists who had long been waiting in the wings. Within months, Mary had reconciled with Rome and restored the old faith. The pope was once again the ultimate religious authority in England and heresy laws were reversed to what they had been prior to the days of her father. She faced little resistance and enjoyed general popularity.[11] The people got their familiar practices back. They could return their churches to the beautiful and meaningful places of worship that they had been.

But six months into her reign, a multipronged rebellion left Mary feeling the need to be much more rigorous in her religious principles. The rebellion was prompted not by her Catholicism but by strong opinions about who she should, and should not, marry. Mary's advisors had worked to arrange a marriage for her with the Spanish Prince Philip. This was exactly the fear at the heart of having a female ruler come to fruition.

Marriage to a foreign prince could mean that England would fall under the dominion of a foreign ruler. Mary, however, interpreted the unrest as fueled by Protestants. It was at this time that Jane Grey and Guildford were executed and that Mary began to equate Protestantism with treason.[12]

By the start of 1555, those clerics who openly questioned the queen's return to Catholicism began to be arrested, brought to court, tried, and executed. Mary's lasting moniker would be "Bloody Mary" because of this sustained policy of killing that then continued until several hundred people were executed, most "obscure commoners, tradesmen, and craftsmen, incapable of posing a threat to church or state or even the leadership of their home communities."[13] It is worth noting that the blood on Mary's hands pales in comparison to the executions ordered by her significantly more violent father.[14]

She had been a well-loved monarch who had shown remarkable courage at key moments and been welcomed to the throne by a population who had loved her mother and who greeted the return to Catholicism favorably.

However, it was this turn toward deadly persecution that ultimately defined her reign. It also, ironically, strengthened the evangelical cause that she had been so enthusiastic about terminating. Every evangelical leader who went to his or her death bravely became a martyr of the Protestant cause, Thomas Cranmer most famously of all. Cranmer was burned at the stake—a method of death noteworthy for the long, torturous pain it inflicted and therefore an especially dramatic show of bravery. This is what martyrdom is best at doing: bearing witness to others that there is something worth dying for.

Mary died after five short years of ruling. One pregnancy was reported during Mary's marriage with Philip, but it is thought to have been a phantom pregnancy, caused by her deep and desperate hope for a baby and heir. When Mary breathed her last, she was childless. The result was an unexpected turn of events: Anne Boleyn's daughter Elizabeth became the queen.

Elizabeth—The Winning Formula

Nobody would have thought on May 19, 1536, that the redheaded toddler of the disgraced Anne Boleyn would ever claim the throne. That would have seemed to be decreasingly probable as Henry stampeded through four more marriages and finally produced the desperately desired healthy male heir. But even the richest of the rich were subject to the many factors of sixteenth-century life that made childhood so precarious and average life expectancy short. And despite Henry's zealous focus on securing the throne with male heirs, only Edward, Mary, and Elizabeth ever materialized as Henry's offspring. The one other child, Henry Fitzroy from Henry's dalliance with Bessie Blount, died a few months after Anne's execution. Not one of Henry's children had children of their own.

By 1558, Elizabeth was the only one left standing.

Elizabeth was a fiercely intelligent and determined ruler. Her influence politically, culturally, and religiously in England has been well documented and minutely detailed. It was during her reign that William Shakespeare received patronage and made his indelible mark on English literature. Elizabeth's court "attracted towering literary and artistic figures . . . [that] would become the envy of the world."[15] Sweeping historical accounts will say that her decisions regarding the church were both hugely influential as well as politically shrewd. Rather than pursuing the radical reform agenda of her brother, Edward, or continuing the Catholic Counter-Reformation of her sister, Mary (despite Mary's begging Elizabeth from her death bed to do just that), Elizabeth reignited religious reform, but with a more moderate approach.

Elizabeth then reigned long enough—forty-five years—for religious reform to take hold, not just in the minds and wills of the elite and intellectuals of the realm, but in the general population. By the time of her death, Elizabeth's two major achievements were an internal stability in her realm and an accepted identity—to which most of the population conformed—of what would be the Church of England.[16]

The accident of her long life and the early deaths of her siblings meant that the bloodline of Anne Boleyn, and something of her religious agenda, would rise again and leave a mark that has been more lasting than any of the opposing factions and violent men who tried to bring her down.

As a person of faith, and particularly an Anglican person of faith, I would be tempted to call that Providence rather than accident.

CHAPTER 12

Her Mother's Daughter

Actions, Not Words

Anne's name was not to be spoken publicly after her scandalous fall. But she was nonetheless influential in shaping the turbulent years between Henry VIII's and Elizabeth I's rule. Her influence was in the powerful and wily leadership of Thomas Cranmer and the many others that she had moved into positions of power; in the parallels between her and Kateryn Parr, and how this last marriage suggests that Henry was still drawn to Anne-like qualities at the end of his life; and in the reform ideas whose spark became a fully blazing fire by the time of Edward VI—Henry's son by Jane Seymour. So, too, was her influence felt in the determination of Mary, formed forever to see Anne and her ideals as enemy forces, and Mary's Counter-Reformation.

Elizabeth's feelings toward her father must have been mixed, if not contentious. The king largely ignored his daughter for much of her upbringing, and although Henry finally reinstated her in the line of succession before his death out of desperation, he had spent years determined to keep the illegitimacy of his second daughter intact and therefore out of any list of potential future rulers. But questioning Henry was not an option. The institution of the monarchy rested on the principle of the divine right to rule, and Elizabeth needed that principle to be unquestioned for the sake of maintaining the authority of her own crown. Elizabeth never said a critical word of her temperamental and violent father publicly.

This also meant that Elizabeth could say very little about Anne. Elizabeth couldn't pay verbal homage to her mother without also implicitly disparaging her father. She didn't have the decrees reversed that had annulled her mother's marriage to Henry. She didn't have her mother's body exhumed from its unmarked spot and buried in a more honorable way.

But Elizabeth's actions spoke volumes.

Elizabeth wore a locket ring with a picture of herself and her mother on either side.[1] She elevated surviving members of her mother's family—Boleyn and Howard relatives—to positions of power, keeping many of them as her innermost circle of advisors and confidants.[2] She quietly kept her mother's symbols, including the falcon, on display in her various palaces, and Anne's falcon became increasingly prominent in Elizabeth's pageantry as her reign progressed.[3] Writers who wished to curry favor with Elizabeth learned that works about Anne Boleyn's goodness and positive contributions were a sure ticket into Elizabeth's affections.

Elizabeth stayed single. This was also a telling choice in keeping her mother close. Trauma must have been a factor, having seen her father destroy the lives of so many wives, including killing both Anne and Katherine Howard. It was understandable that Elizabeth wouldn't have positive associations with how women fare in marriage. Elizabeth intentionally laid claim to the power that her mother had imagined for herself and which was so violently taken away from her. Anne briefly tasted a world where her own ideas and intellect could affect real change and be part of how decisions were made. Elizabeth was not going to risk, in marriage, giving any of her own inherited power away to a man. She was going to rule in a way that her mother could have only dreamed of.

Anne's DNA coursed through Elizabeth's body. There was a particular way of seeing and engaging the world that got cut short in Anne's life and that blossomed in Elizabeth's.

Many of the characteristics that were judged as problematic in Anne when she was shaking up the courts, the country, and all of Europe, can also be seen in Elizabeth. Both women were fiercely intelligent, witty, engaging, and magnetic as personalities and conversationalists. Both women were also demanding, opinionated, uncompromising, and quick-tempered. But as the anointed ruler, these traits became helpful and admirable. Under Elizabeth's leadership, the country enjoyed more than four decades of remarkable peace and stability. Those who were executed under her regime were convicted on charges of treason, not of religious insubordination.

Elizabeth doesn't make right the wrongs that were done to Anne. But her story is a satisfying clap back to those who wanted Anne to shut up and disappear.

The Elizabethan Age—A Quirky Version of Reform

Elizabeth came to the throne on November 17, 1558, with the death of her half sister, Mary. It had been approximately three decades of seesawing religious chaos, with people on all sides of the reform/Rome divide rising to and falling from power and often meeting violent ends.

The Church of England, and subsequently Anglicanism, eventually came to be known as "the Middle Way" and was seen as a combination of the traditions of the Catholic Church and the reforms of the Protestant church. This was not Elizabeth's vision, but Anglicans like to think this middle way took shape and came to be clearly articulated during the Elizabethan era.

What Elizabeth did bring to the throne were her own mix of beliefs about what the church should be and a few armloads of heavy baggage. That baggage included the personal trauma and precarious circumstances of her childhood and youth, along with strong religious and artistic preferences that she was now emboldened to imprint on the English church. She was young when she became queen, but she had lived through enough turbulence to know that if this was her shot, she had better take it.

The Elizabethan church coalesced around reform principles that had long been fought for and that were similar to those her brother Edward had championed. This included distrust of any of those things reformers had concluded were superstitious—like religious images and shrines, or claiming Jesus's presence in the bread and wine of the Eucharist.[4] This would surprise many Anglicans today who hear prayers from the altar asking for that bread and wine to become Jesus's body and blood, and who worship in churches that are rife with religious imagery and with grand aesthetics designed to draw the faithful into an alternate space of awe.

This is because of Elizabeth's political acumen in negotiating her people's religion once she came to the throne. Delightfully, it is also because of the religious quirks that Elizabeth left in—simply because she liked them.

On the political side of things, Elizabeth had learned some valuable lessons from watching her father and siblings negotiate their power and try to impose their will. The turmoil, unrest, and bloodshed that resulted led Elizabeth to do things more carefully than her predecessors. She was smart enough to realize that martyring those opposed to the church she wanted, as Mary and her father had done, would only make that resistance stronger.

Elizabeth knew that she was the champion and hope of evangelical England. She was expected, upon her accession to the throne, to reinstate the reforms that had been undone by Mary. However, she also had to placate, at least somewhat, the conservatives that had been so recently having their day in the sun.[5]

The outcome of this tightrope act was the Religious Settlement of 1559. This involved reaffirming the separation of England from Rome and the creation of a distinctly Protestant church in England. When Anne had handed Henry that Tyndale book almost thirty years prior, suggesting to him that splitting from Rome would be the answer to his problems, she could not possibly have known what chaos would be unleashed on the politics and religion of England, even if she herself had a clear idea of how she wanted the church to be remade.

The path that Anne and Henry then pursued together was driven by a combination of romance, self-interest, Henry's ego and arrogance, Anne's principles and convictions, and a lot of intrigue and betrayal. But through it all was an idea of legitimate and lasting theological value. "The whole basis of the Church of England's Reformation, and the reason for Anglicanism's separate existence, has always been that Rome does not know best," says historian Diarmaid MacCulloch.[6]

Those of us who have known ourselves not welcome as we are at the Roman Catholic table—for example, women in ordained leadership, divorced people, LGBTQ+ people who want faithful and blessed unions of matrimony with their partners—are ultimately grateful for this decisive act, even if it is a convoluted history that got us here.

In the Elizabethan settlement, there was sufficient softening of the legislation to prevent a crisis with the Catholics. Instead of making herself the "Supreme Head" of the church, Elizabeth instead took the title of "Supreme Governor."[7] Archbishop Thomas Cranmer's life's work came back to the church with the Book of Common Prayer. Its use was mandated by law in the Act of Uniformity. Again, concessions were made. There was a nod to Catholic understandings of the Eucharist[8] and permission to use traditional priestly vestments.[9] While this did nothing to mollify the Catholics, it appeased those with Lutheran leanings, and it also aligned with Elizabeth's sensibilities, which were more Lutheran in these specific respects.[10]

The quirks that were contained in the settlement marked the Church of England as unique in the Protestant world. Elizabeth did not dismantle the traditional threefold ministry of bishop, priest, and deacon. She also left intact the devotional life and endowments of cathedrals. It was in the cathedrals that a rich choral music tradition continued and flourished, markedly different from the simpler worship style of the thousands of parish churches dotting the countryside. The 1559 Book of Common Prayer, which essentially reproduced Cranmer's Book of Common Prayer of 1552, became the basis for the church's corporate prayer life, although Cranmer would likely have not approved of the "whole medieval shebang of deans, chapters, prebends, organs, choirs, closes" that got left with the cathedrals.[11]

Elizabeth liked those parts of the inherited faith though, so they remained. Elizabeth's temperament, born through years of tumultuous and precarious politicking, was measured when it came to religion. She had "no enthusiasm for high-temperature religion, despite the private depth and quiet intensity of her own devotional life."[12]

Elizabeth's Coattails

Who came to power in the Elizabethan church was also important in shaping what it would be.

Elizabeth made religious appointments modeled on those her mother had made a quarter of a century prior. William Latymer, former chaplain of Anne, was named Elizabeth's personal chaplain and given important titles and positions in the church. Matthew Parker, another of her mother's former chaplains, was Elizabeth's first archbishop of Canterbury.[13] Parker accepted the post reluctantly but noted later to a colleague, "If I had not been so much bound to the mother, I would not so soon have granted to serve the daughter in this place."[14] Parker finally had a visible opportunity to make good on the promise he had made to Anne in those chaotic days of spring, 1536, when she asked him to provide protection to her daughter should anything happen to her.

Cranmer had been burned at the stake during Mary's reign, as much for backing Jane Grey as for his religious convictions—which he had been quick to walk back when Mary came to power. Cranmer had no great desire for martyrdom, although when it was clear that Mary was not going to commute his sentence, he did recant his recanting, thereby going to the stake as a professing evangelical and doing much by his death for the cause of reform. Even from the grave, his influence was pervasive throughout the Elizabethan church with the reinstatement of his Book of Common Prayer. Anne's protégé and partner in championing reform would continue to have his fingerprints indelibly printed on the Church of England and then Anglicanism through his gift for language in the prayers of subsequent generations across the world.

Elizabeth and appointees like Latymer and Parker had something else in common, also born of surviving England's religious upheaval. They were people who knew how to conform outwardly to the shifting tides of theological conviction. The martyrs of Christianity might sneer at this kind of fair-weather faith. And yet, perhaps there is a way of naming, as Diarmaid MacCulloch says, "the specialized heroism of making choices about concealing opinions and compromising in dangerous times, rather than the luxury of proclaiming their convictions in unsullied purity."[15]

In other words, resistance can't be offered if everyone ends up dead.

Elizabeth was clearheaded in removing Catholic leaders from power, but she did not resume the agenda of killing that had marked both Mary's and her father's regimes.[16] Philosopher Francis Bacon summed it up in saying that Elizabeth "would not open windows into men's souls."[17] It was an earlier form of the idea that the government has no business in the bedrooms of its citizens, and as a strategy for those wielding power, it generally allows those living under their dominion a massive exhale.

Quirky or Confused?

Historian G. J. Meyer articulates a highly critical view of Elizabeth's religious leadership. Meyer claims that Elizabeth was driven primarily by her desire to assure her own survival, rather than by any clear religious conviction. Meyer would have support for this conclusion; this has been a constant complaint about Anglicanism. If it is the "big tent" of Christianity, an overarching institutional structure sheltering a wide variety of theological and liturgical expressions, then it is too big a tent. It suffers from a lack of identity. The self-deprecating Anglicans among us will agree that Anglican worship is awkward. It tries too hard. It squeezes too much in. It can feel like a cluttered jumble of different parts, and we feel beholden to keep them all in because we've been doing them for so long and each piece means something.

After Elizabeth's death, England was thrown once again into religious turmoil and confusion as different religious expressions, especially Calvinists and Puritans, fought to gain control of the church and the country, briefly pitching England into civil war, the overthrow of the monarchy, and the institution of a Puritan state and church. It was not long-lasting. The British people discovered that they didn't have any great love of the stark aesthetic and sober ways of Puritanism. They missed their pageantry and symbolism and merrymaking.

Critics of Elizabeth will lay the blame for this later conflict squarely at her feet. Where I note Elizabeth's church had "quirks," others would say it was "internally conflicted," "eccentric," or merely confused.

For many of us though, it is precisely that big-tent spirituality—both spacious and cluttered, quirky, and magnificently beautiful, with enough blurred lines to allow for big helpings of poetry and creative sensibility—that informs our lives. It is exactly that freedom of conscience and intellectual permission that we have valued and that has equipped us as people of faith. It is the both/and of this denomination that has given us the tools we need to be followers of Jesus. While it is incorrect to claim that Elizabeth intentionally created a church that would be that "middle way" and "both/and," there was enough room left in the church Elizabeth settled that this idea of Anglicanism could eventually take root.

Furthermore, those eccentricities of Elizabeth's—like the continuation of cathedrals, for example—that got imprinted on the church would be among the jewels of Anglicanism, treasured in the lives of countless people who would come to live their faith and worship their God through this religious expression. Thank God for Elizabeth's quirks and for the aspects of this faith that don't conform to a single, clear theological agenda. Thank God for a unique personality that gave rise to a distinctive religious identity. Thank God for the beauty of being odd rather than merely clear.

The Bones of St. Frideswide

There is a footnote to the story of St. Frideswide, that local saint who ran away from the advances of her royal suitor. Frideswide's afterlife would share with England in the tug-of-war between Protestant and Catholic factions that would mark the English church long after Anne handed Henry a book suggesting that maybe popes shouldn't have total authority after all.

Frideswide's remains had been enshrined at the place that became Christ Church, Oxford, and were a pilgrimage site for many faithful, including Catherine of Aragon. During the uproar of the Reformation, zeal against this kind of spirituality saw Frideswide's shrine destroyed and her remains lost. A Protestant hero, Catherine Martyr[18] was buried in a place of honor in Oxford instead, although no reformer would have dared suggest spiritual pilgrimages to her tomb. When the very Catholic Mary came to the throne, Catherine Martyr was dug up and tossed out to a nearby dunghill.

During Elizabeth's Protestant reign, the bones of Frideswide were located. An Oxford priest decided throwing around dead women's remains—saints or not—wasn't seemly, no matter what side of reform one might land on. In a stroke of brilliance and to prevent any further tampering, he mixed Frideswide's bones with Catherine Martyr's remains. Together, they were reinterred in the floor of the cathedral in an unmarked spot. Frideswide is today still celebrated as the patron saint of Oxford city and university.[19]

The unusual story of Frideswide's body's afterlife is representative of the religious turmoil that existed in the decades of Reformation and Counter-Reformation that followed Anne's death. The Catholic saint Frideswide's final resting place being a shared plot with a heroic reformer is an ideal representation of the church in which, five hundred years later, I would come to serve. When the dust finally settled, the Church of England really could best be described as a strange and beautiful mix of previously warring elements, in a combination as singular as a jawbone from Frideswide and a fibula from Catherine Martyr.

CHAPTER 13

A New World, a New Church

The Tower of London

Inscribed on a stone in the Tower of London courtyard are these haunting words:

> *Gentle visitor pause a while, where you stand death cut away the light of many days. Here jewelled names were broken from the vivid thread of life. May they rest in peace while we walk the generations around their strife and courage under these restless skies.*

Each time I have visited, I offer a moment of remembrance and respect for Anne and for the many others who were killed for holding beliefs that went against the grain, for acting in ways that were considered transgressive, for possessing bloodlines that were threatening to the one wearing the crown, or for fighting for causes that were judged as hostile.

This Tower of London memorial is a very modern way of acknowledging a history that is so different from our present. Those who were executed in this spot went obediently to their deaths.[1] They claimed their own guilt, even if they were innocent of the crimes for which they were dying. They spoke well of the king, even as he was having them killed. When their "jewelled names" had been severed from "the vivid thread of life," as the inscription notes, there was no honor paid to them, no memorial offered. They were to be erased from the public record, their lives counted as nothing other than a warning from which to be distanced, an embarrassment to be forgotten as quickly as possible.

The only hope that a condemned man or woman could claim would be in the afterlife, which would be granted to them by God, and affirming their allegiance to both church and crown before dying was the way to negotiate that passageway as smoothly as possible. It is hard for modern people to understand what would motivate someone to say these things when they already have nothing left to lose. They can't be killed twice, so the scaffold should be the place for truth telling, for any accusatory, angry thing they might want to leverage against the king and those who had brought them to this end. However, even if a person was falsely accused, they would want to have their souls in right relationship with the two institutions that represented God's power on earth: the church and the monarch.

Anne's last words and actions exemplify a way of thinking that can feel very foreign to our modern sensibilities. And yet, there were glimmers in her performance on the scaffold of the revolution of thought and consciousness that marked her lifespan and that sowed the seeds of the world we live in today.

The Seeds of Today's Fruit Were Sown Then

The truth of what pioneering media theorist Marshall McLuhan said in the 1960s has long been accepted: The medium is the message. That is, the technologies that we as a human species adopt for use, including communication technologies, don't just change how we communicate. They change how we think.[2]

Anne Boleyn was a product of living through a hinge-point of history. She was also a facilitator or midwife of the new way that was emerging. She was influenced by, and an influencer of, the transformation underway.

Philosopher Charles Taylor notes the year 1500 as the approximate point at which the Western paradigm of how the world operates began to shift. That means that the 1530s, the time of Anne's ascendancy and downfall, represent both the old and emerging way of thinking.

The old way of thinking was communal and collective. Salvation and right relationship with God were brokered in a vast interrelated system of roles, hierarchies, and power structures that were legitimized because those in power were necessary for creating access to, and favor with, God. The natural world and the institutions of society were seen as testifying to the divine purpose and action.[3]

McLuhan credited the printing press with a radical change, bringing in nationalism, industrialism, mass markets, and universal literacy and education.[4] This new sixteenth-century mindset centered the individual conscience and the need for each individual person to subscribe to the correct ways of thinking to be in right relationship with God. This new consciousness allowed individuals to challenge the status quo, including religious beliefs, gender conventions, and understandings of power and salvation.

The year 1500 is also said to be significant for church history. "Every five hundred years the church has a rummage sale," the late popular theologian Phyllis Tickle is often quoted as saying. While it is fanciful to think that history works in such neat patterns, what she means is that the changes happening in organized religion today, specifically in the mass exodus from church participation, is cataclysmic and transformative in much the same way that the split of the Roman Catholic Church in the sixteenth century was. (She traces other periods of massive transformation back through half-millennia intervals to the church's start at the turn of the common era, which again is more of an artistic representation of history than it is a true depiction of how time works.)

The reasons for the change today aren't unlike those of Anne's time, and in many ways, they are thoroughly related. Technologies have changed; work, leisure, and family have been restructured as a result. Capitalist culture favors the life of the individual and the need to maximize work and profit over relationships, communities, and people. The challenges against the institutional church and its authority which were raised in the Reformation have continued to foment and are connected to the widespread rejection of organized religion and religious belief today. It is now reasonable and common for people to conclude that the church is unnecessary to individual well-being and to question the existence of God. Today, believing in God is just one of a variety of options, and often judged as quite an unrealistic one.

I wouldn't have been able to serve as a priest of the church five hundred years ago. And there is something naïve in comparing our age to previous times without recognizing that the danger and bloodshed associated with religious change in the sixteenth century is profoundly different from any of the difficulties we might think come with modern apathy or antagonism toward organized religion that we experience in North America. Nonetheless, a certain connection to the religious leaders of Anne's day exists. It is a particular challenge, and not without measures of excitement and heartbreak, to be a leader in an institution that is noticeably in a state of collapse, where everything that we stand for professionally and personally is contested and in jeopardy.

In my work today, there is a growing realization among religious leaders that we have been concerned with the wrong problem. With church attendance, membership, and participation on a steep and dramatic decline, we have, for decades, treated this as a problem of trying to get people to church. We focus on how to be attractive, welcoming, and what sort of programming and parking lot to offer so that people want to participate.

The real problem, however, isn't about getting people to come to church. The real problem is communicating the living God to a world that has come to view reality primarily through a rational, physical, and secular lens. The principles of collecting and believing the data that can be attained with our five senses are paramount, and the idea of a God who acts and intervenes in our world, along with questions of what happens after death and what the soul is, are treated as individual, private, and interior concerns.[5] The central spiritual question, both for those who participate in organized religion and those who do not, is very basic: *Does God exist?* Other questions of specific religious dogma, attendance in public worship, and how much any of these questions or answers really impact one's eternal soul, follow.

This was not the focal question of sixteenth-century people. The church was central to people's lives; public space and public activities were infused with religiosity. Religious belief was not one option among many options; it was the only option. Not believing in God was a virtual impossibility.[6] Doing and believing the right things in this life was essential in securing the right kind of place in the afterlife. That driving concern should factor into all interpretations about how Anne and the other key players in her story were acting.

That is not to say that people weren't also motivated by the timeless desires for power, status, wealth, material possessions, love, sex, and acceptance. These needs and desires are fundamental and should be acknowledged too.

What I would caution against, though, would be setting up an analysis of choices and behaviors as a zero-sum game, an "either this or that." We might be tempted to ask whether Anne wanted power or whether she was a sincere evangelical reformer. It was almost certainly both. In Anne's time, religious zeal and the quest for power were tied to one another. This doesn't make religious zeal any less authentic. Power structures were intimately woven into the collective imagination around how right relationship with God, and ultimately eternal life, would be navigated for a whole people. Likewise, desire can't be teased out as a separate thing from status, acceptance, material goods, love, and sex, from spiritual and eternal considerations.

And for the record, these things still get knotted up with one another. I have no experience of religious faith existing in some kind of pure form, separate from the many other things that concern us and drive us. We believe in and serve God as human beings, not as one-dimensional, paper-doll versions of idealized selves, flattened out from the complications of living the messy, interconnected, bodily, biology-driven, emotion-forward lives that we do.

Among the many things that make Anne Boleyn's time so fascinating is that the seeds of modernity were also being planted in those three-plus decades that she lived on earth. Anne's story is a collision between these premodern ways of thinking that are so different from our own and the emerging worldview that we so thoroughly inhabit today.

A Small Detail, a Larger Vision

Anne was almost incoherent with terror when she was arrested. Her confusion was so great that she wondered out loud, rambling and panicky, about which of her actions and with whom had been twisted into these monstrous allegations. Her words, unfortunately, helped to give fuel to her accusers' fire as Constable Kingston—Anne's jailor—passed along her outbursts to those making their case against her and rounded up those she had named to place them under arrest too.

As Anne began to calm and come to terms with what was happening to her, Kingston continued to interpret Anne with utter seriousness, rather than realizing that Anne was using humor to distract her from the severity of her situation. He interpreted her robust laugh in response to his assuring her that she would receive justice as a sign of madness.[7] The night before her death, she suggested that her enemies would have the pleasure of remembering her as "*La Royne Anne sans Tete.*"[8] When she talked about having a "little neck" and so could probably enjoy a painless death, Kingston responded rather unctuously that the executioner's axe would be "subtle."[9]

As far as coping strategies go, humor might have been one of the more effective in trying to reconcile herself to the incomprehensible nature of her circumstances. She was jailed in the same palace where she had stayed the night before her coronation. She had been pursued relentlessly by the man who was so desperate to have her that he instituted religious and political revolution, only to kill her three years later. Just days before, she had been surrounded by servants and palaces and jewels and a place in the machinations of the kingdom's rule, and mere months prior she had been proudly carrying in her belly what she thought to be the heir to that kingdom. Now she was to see it as an act of mercy that a swordsman from Calais had been brought across the Channel for her execution.

By the time Anne went to trial, defended herself, and walked to her death on the scaffold, her composure was remarkable not just to her friends but also her enemies. She exhibited notable poise and eloquence in the most dire and confusing of circumstances. Recognizing the ultimate futility of trying to defend herself against the charges at her trial, Anne eloquently stated, "But God knows, and is my witness, that I have not sinned against him [the king] in any other way. Think not I say this in the hope to prolong my life, for He who saveth from death hath taught me how to die, and He will strengthen my faith."[10]

It is an idea that has become very appealing among the Anne apologists of history that she was presented with a deal prior to her execution that could have saved her life. If she had been willing to have the king declare their marriage annulled, then she could have lived, but that would have meant her daughter Elizabeth would have been declared illegitimate. Anne's refusal of this deal is imagined as her final act of bravery in choosing to die rather than compromise her daughter's future. It was part of the Anne Boleyn lore that I found especially gripping as a child learning her story for the first time.

This deal was unlikely to have been offered to Anne, and if it was it evidently wasn't sincere. Thomas Cranmer, archbishop of Canterbury, did visit Anne prior to her execution, and the content of that visit has been the source of much speculation. Whether he offered her any sort of possibility of escaping with her life though, the marriage was declared invalid, and Elizabeth was made illegitimate. The Parliament that ruled on this at no point indicated that Anne's permission had been needed to make its decree.

Elizabeth, at the age of three years old, had been the heir apparent of the kingdom, graced with her own palaces and households and every fine thing that money could buy, the subject of political alliances and marriage deals with European princes. Overnight, she became an embarrassing reminder of Henry's wild passions and temper, his impulsivity and foolishness, his unshakeable belief that Anne was going to make Henry and the whole kingdom right with God, only then to believe her the most corrupt of sinners. On the day of Anne's death, suddenly illegitimate Elizabeth had no prospect for anything other than a marriage to someone with a modest amount of land and money and a quiet life outside of the hallways of power.

Anne asked to be shriven and to receive Communion before her death. It is a small detail, but it suggests a religious vision that was distinctly different from that of Lutheranism or of some other reform agendas that were vying for power through her lifetime. As the sands of the hourglass were fast running out on Anne's life, what was of essential importance to her was to receive the sacraments of confession and Communion.

This represents something of the kind of reform that was so influential to Anne and that is visible in her own religious attitudes and practices throughout her adult life. On the *Not Just the Tudors* podcast, Suzannah Lipscomb discussed Marguerite d'Angoulême—the woman whose person, ideas, and leadership Anne held in such high regard—with Dr. Emily Butterworth. Butterworth defines Marguerite as a "reforming Catholic." Marguerite and others in her circle wanted to see reform of the church from within the church; they never "made that step into schism." Marguerite held to the Catholic understanding of the Eucharist and supported monasticism, while also holding beliefs that became associated with Protestantism, namely the primacy of the Scriptures and the inability of the human being, through their own efforts, to "attain" salvation.[11]

Whereas Marguerite published some of her religious beliefs, Anne didn't. We have to piece together Anne's religious faith from her behaviors and her influences. We can see that right up until her death, reform for Anne included room for and adherence to the sacraments and practices of the church that had formed her and her people. When she was on the throne, theologian Tristram Revell had tried to dedicate to the queen an English translation of a writing which denied the presence of Christ in the Mass. Anne refused the request.[12]

There are those who would argue that Anne had to walk a strategic tightrope in navigating Henry's strident opposition to anything that seemed too Lutheran. I would draw a different conclusion: Anne's version of humanistic reform was widely consistent with the ideas, vision, and principles that were so much a part of her formational years in the presence of Marguerite, as well as Queen Claude. The church that she knew and championed was a middle way between the Catholicism that had come before and the more radical versions of reform that would follow.[13]

In Anne's final days, there is a glimpse of the church that was just being born and that would take centuries to blossom more fully. It was a church that would continue in established traditions while also committing to a path of transformation, change, and renewal. It was a church that had room for sacramentality and a church that would continue through the centuries ahead to connect the faithful to God not just through a commitment to God's Word but through a bodily engagement in seeking and living out relationship with God.

Six-Toed Jesus

Elizabeth and Mike, friends and colleagues in ministry, both attended Virginia Theological Seminary. They were married in the VTS chapel and ordained in the Episcopal Church in the United States, which is the American version of the Anglican church.

In the VTS chapel was an unusual stained glass window depicting Jesus with six toes. The students of VTS, including Elizabeth and Mike, interpreted this stained glass as a sly nod to the influence of Anne Boleyn on creating what would become the worldwide Anglican Communion. Popular lore about Anne has included the apocryphal description of her six-fingered hand. It is delightful to think that five hundred years later in the chapel of a seminary across the Atlantic Ocean from where Anne lived that this inaccurate but well-known detail of Anne's life would be used to signal her impact on creating Anglicanism.

The chapel burned down in 2010, but the stained-glass window of the six-toed Jesus survived.[14]

I will be the first to admit that a lot of water has gone under the bridge in the time between Anne Boleyn and the Anglican Church of today. Many different voices, desires, beliefs, and political agendas took their turn in molding the church of the sixteenth century into the church of the twenty-first. To suggest that there is a straight line back from the church I inhabit today to Anne, Marguerite, Elizabeth, and others is fanciful.

Anne wasn't fighting for the version of the church that Elizabeth would eventually have such a strong hand in creating. Anne did not argue one way or the other (that we know of) for an understanding of what was happening to the bread and the wine in Christian worship and how that was related to Jesus. She wasn't, according to any record we have, concerned about religious imagery and its use in churches. Furthermore, the church that Elizabeth shaped is a lot different from the church that I now serve. The idea of an Anglican "middle way" between Protestantism and

Catholicism was a later conceit. Many of the aspects of this church that I hold most dear were only glimmers in Anne's leadership and weren't particularly integral to Elizabeth's church.

And yet, I can't help seeing connections between those things that mean so much to me about the church I inhabit and the singular personality of Anne Boleyn. The idea that the church is the creation of male ideas, male leadership, male voices, has been largely fanciful too. It has involved enormous blind spots, deliberate or otherwise, in failing to see the influence and hear the voice of women shaping our Christian faith. It is important and valid and good to include other imaginings too, to be intentional in naming a connection between the vision one strong and brave woman of five hundred years ago offered and what we have today.

Anne came to have such a significant voice in the political and religious direction of her country through strange and personally fraught circumstances. Bound up into the start of the Anglican Church was a hotbed of human passion, ambition, self-interest, danger, persecution, and intrigue. The Church of England, and then the Anglican Church, got shaped not just by ideas, but by personalities, and by very flawed and compromised human beings trying to navigate their way through exceptionally turbulent waters.

There is a resonance between the Bible study Anne promoted and encouraged in her ladies-in-waiting, the books and animated discussions she enjoyed in her chambers, and the intellectual curiosity that allows so many to find a home in the Anglican church today.

There is a resonance between Anne's protégé Thomas Cranmer and the poetry and love of language that is baked into Anglican DNA.

There is a resonance between the intellectual curiosity enjoyed in Queen Claude's court and encouraged in the flow of cutting-edge reading materials and theological debate in Anne's court, and the relief many experience in our churches when realizing that science and reason don't have to be checked at the door.

There is a resonance between the ritual and sacramentality that speak today to the part of our souls that ultimately needs more than words, and the way that Anne had learned on the Continent and continued to champion in Henry's court: that the traditions of the church didn't need to be abandoned but renewed. We could, as people of faith, be both a work in progress and inheritors of the gift of faith passed across generations.

There is a resonance between the practical reform that Anne defended and the Anglican Church that allowed me as a teenager to be challenged into considering social justice issues that precious few people in my small town were interested in. At her best, Anne saw reform not as a reorientation of people's individual beliefs but as an economic reordering of society, with better opportunity and access to education for all.

At the Anglican Church's best, there is an alignment with addressing climate change, calling out and ending human and sex trafficking, admitting to wrong and seeking reconciliation with Indigenous peoples, championing both Band-Aid crisis-management solutions and being an advocate for structural change in ending poverty. The church defends equal marriage, speaks up for trans people's rights and healthcare, engages thoughtfully with the hottest of hot-button issues like abortion and medically assisted death, and seeks not to proclaim but to listen. At its best, the church articulates our experience of a God who walks with us and our conviction that following Jesus has something to do with making the world materially better for all people. That the church's record on inspiring real change on any of these fronts is spotty doesn't diminish the church's desire to be this kind of voice in the world.

There is a resonance between the church that ultimately gave Anne solace and strength in facing grief and loss and death, and the church that remembers that our structures and prayers need to be oriented toward helping people to know the God who loves them.

There is a resonance between the fiery, dramatic, complicated personalities of Anne and Elizabeth, of Anne's role models Claude, Marguerite, Margaret, and Louise, of the various men who got swept along into their influence and causes, and the strange, weird, awkward, sometimes nonsensical Anglican Church that we have today.

The history of the Anglican Church since its birth in sixteenth-century Tudor England has been complex and global. Many influences can be cited on who shaped the church that we have today and why.

Six toes on a stained-glass Jesus in Virginia might be a rather too subtle way of including Anne in those credits. But it's a start.

What She Said at Her Death . . . and Didn't Say

There was confusion about the day on which Anne was to be executed, which meant that Anne spent two full nights holding prayer vigil. She first thought that she was to be executed on the morning of Thursday, May 18, the feast of the Ascension of the Lord. Instead, another full twenty-four hours passed before she was finally escorted to her death. She received Communion one last time and made her final confession to her priest. She swore twice on the Sacrament that she was innocent of the crimes of which she was accused.[15]

I imagine Anne holding prayer vigil in those long night hours before her morning execution. In those troubled prayers, I picture her receiving a momentary vision of something that lay ahead, of her little girl taking up her own version of that fight to reimagine the church for a new dawn. I hope for her that she had some flash of insight, of knowing that there would be more to this story than the finality of the executioner's axe.

Anne's last words followed the formula convicted people were to say before their execution. Mostly. She did make sure to say what was required about her husband, the king:

> I pray God save the King and send him long to reign over you, for a gentler nor a more merciful prince was there never: and to me he was ever a good, a gentle and a sovereign lord.[16]

These words sound ludicrous to our ears, given that the "gentle" and "merciful prince" was having her put to death. But Anne could not afford to jeopardize her soul by using her final moments to ream him out. She also didn't want to say anything that could affect her daughter's now limited prospects or lead Henry to take revenge on her remaining family members.

The shocking thing about her final speech, however, is where it deviated from the expected formula. The crowd was stunned into silence.[17] Anne did not admit her guilt. She did not refer to her crimes at all. She did not even cop to being a sinner.

This omission reveals Anne's self-possession and authenticity. She should have said she was guilty and bought herself a little more assurance of being on the right side of eternity when the axe came down. But she wouldn't bring herself to admit guilt that she didn't have. It is also one more glimmer of the new age that Anne was such a key player in ushering in—an age in which the individual's relationship with God through their own conscience, not mediated through the mechanisms of crown and church and the correct formulas, was becoming paramount.

The execution of an anointed queen of England was unprecedented. As Anne knelt down before the axe, she glanced over her shoulder several times. Observers wondered whether she was anticipating what was to come or if she thought that Henry might deliver a commuted sentence at the last minute.[18] The crowd might have also expected some eleventh-hour drama. But the king was already absorbed in preparations for his next marriage and future queen. No mercy or second thought was shown.

The last words on Anne's lips were "Jesu, receive my soul; O Lord God have pity on my soul."[19] And then she had no more words.

PART 4

Bigger Than the Archetypes

I used to be Snow White, but I drifted.

—Mae West[1]

CHAPTER 14

The Fairy Tales

Fairy-Tale Ingredients

Before I knew about Anne Boleyn, I knew about Cinderella. I sought out as many different versions of the fairy tale as I could find. The Brothers Grimm described the wicked stepsisters mutilating their feet in the hopes of extracting a marriage offer from the prince.[1] I shuddered at the thought of their sliced off heels and toes, blood pooling in the glass slipper as the girls were whisked off in the prince's carriage—until the stains of their secrets became unavoidably visible and they were returned to the wicked stepmother in disgrace.

Each account featured a heroine of good heart who achieved surprising recognition and validation after years of obscurity, neglect, and abuse. The endings of the tale varied. Sometimes poetic justice brought down the evil stepmother and stepsisters. And sometimes Cinderella's goodness was so all-consuming that even her abusive family members were swept up into her happy ending.

Fairy tales articulate humankind's most deep-seated desires. There are things forbidden. There is justice served ("the execution of wicked kings and evil stepmothers"[2]). There is the presence of magic, giving a mystical sheen to the human realities being described. There is grace, the sudden turn, the consolation, the happy ending.[3]

Our fairy tales also provide ways of talking about female power. They describe appropriate, if magical, avenues for women to ascend beyond their station and gain their heart's desire. They make it clear that if that power is inappropriately gained or misused then society will vanquish them with the sword, push them down a bottomless pit, or perhaps cut off their heads. Fear around female agency is channeled into stories about bad women who get their comeuppance. Romantic love becomes a gloss over the terrifying experience countless women have faced of being married off to old, bad, abusive, ugly men.

But also, fairy tales are stories, and they can be revolutionary. They might give voice to the world the way that we think it should work, but like it or not, our stories also end up telling us how uncontainable and complex life really is. Fairy tales can transgress expectations and challenge prescribed categories.

In the realm of popular folk stories told, collected, and curated, both women and men were the creators of fairy tales, so fairy tales were a way for women to talk.[4] Woven into popular compilations were stories that gave voice to women's anxieties over being married off to ogreish men. In these "magical" stories, women did not have to accept this as business as usual, but could turn their partners from frogs into princes or could escape the clutches of evil boorish men altogether. Women could dress up as men. Women could challenge boundaries. Women could be agents in their own salvation. The magic and enchantment of these fairy tales could be a screen for detailing subversive behavior and claiming a different "happily ever after" in which women were able to be happy and fulfilled in ways that weren't typically on offer.

Supervillain

Anne's story isn't a fairy tale, but there are contours of her biography that loan themselves well to a fairy-tale treatment. There are several familiar arcs and archetypes that could be pulled from Anne's life, and each one, emphasized on its own, could say something based in truth. Anne was selected by the king to move from relative obscurity to a position of surprising prominence. If the story hadn't led to execution and four other marriages for the king, her story could have been a real-life version of Cinderella, complete with the happily ever after of a long-fought-for wedding.

As it was, Anne has more easily and regularly been slotted into the archetype of supervillain. She was the evil stepmother who eventually got her just desserts. She was the cruel sorceress, using her powers to manipulate and bring ruin to the kingdom.

Those who hated Anne had plenty of material for casting her in these roles. She argued relentlessly with Henry. The king was said to complain to Anne's uncle, the duke of Norfolk, about Anne's domineering ways, "begging . . . 'with tears in his eyes' to mediate between them."[5] She was not a wife to turn a blind eye to his penchant for side dalliances and insisted jealously that he be faithful to her. She threatened to fire servants.[6] In the lead-up to her marriage with Henry, she had her livery servants embroider their coats with an arrogant version of a motto she had learned from Margaret of Austria: *Ainsi sera, groigne qui groigne*— "Let them grumble, that is how it is going to be!"[7]

She wasn't always nice to her father. Anne seems to have had a very close relationship with Thomas Boleyn, despite the long-standing popular assumption that he was a power-hungry schemer. But dear Dad, too, came against the "rough edge of [Anne's] tongue" on occasion.[8]

Anne was reviled and criticized for her obvious delight in the riches offered to her by Henry and the court. Anne was experienced as haughty and arrogant and demanding and difficult. Under her reign there were excessive displays of wealth and material riches. She was showered with jewels and gowns.

Several years before Henry was able to marry Anne, the couple commissioned the building of an extravagant new palace. This was formerly York Place, the lavish enough residence of Cardinal Wolsey. When Wolsey fell from grace, the residence became Henry's, who then rebuilt and expanded it, calling it Whitehall. Until the building of Versailles, its fifteen hundred rooms made it the largest palace in Europe.[9] It was an opulent display of the king's wealth and devotion. It could also be seen as a trophy—a physical reminder of Anne's triumph over Wolsey and a warning to others who might cross Henry or his new queen.

One of the features of the new palace was a cockfighting ring. This was for Anne. Anne had a taste for watching animals fighting to the death.[10]

Anne may have used her position to champion universal education and to address poverty, but she was also not above using innocent creatures and people for her own gratuitous entertainment. In the fairy-tale genre of storytelling, this anecdote is great ammunition for casting Anne as the villain. Snow White and Cinderella speak to the birds. Anne delights in watching our feathered friends fight to the death while she bets on which one is more likely to peck the other's eyes out. In Disney, Brothers Grimm, or Charles Perrault, the heroine would never be the one enjoying the cockfight.

"I Don't Want to Be Dismissed That Easily"

Dorothy Day once said that she didn't want to be considered a saint because she didn't want to "be dismissed that easily." Despite being so vilified and so associated with accusations of sexual wrongdoing, Anne has also been pictured by those who claimed common cause with her as being so spotlessly good that one wonders whether they are talking about the same person who wanted a cockfighting ring built in her new palace.

Anne had her defenders. Those who shared her religious viewpoint, who sought religious reform, who viewed her as the champion of their cause, or who had experienced persecution and loss due to their Protestant beliefs, saw Anne as nothing less than a martyr or a saint. Her refusal to sleep with Henry wasn't evidence of manipulation and ambition but of her principled religious beliefs. Anne the studied flirt, the witty and humorous conversationalist, the one who loved music and dancing and fashion, was downplayed. What was emphasized instead was the modesty of her ladies, their charitable acts, and their study of Scripture.

John Foxe's *Book of Martyrs* detailed how Anne invested thoughtfully and intentionally in acts of private charity and in the distribution of alms to those most in need—whether to buy livestock or food. She was known to have sent her almoner to the towns around her residences "to get lists of the poor householders and distribute money accordingly."[11] Similarly, he described the "decorum of Anne's household and the pious behavior of her ladies," with "the ladies occupied in sewing clothing for the poor."[12]

These accounts ultimately suffered from the same kind of editing that historians now use to discredit those who were most intent on vilifying Anne and debunk their accusations against her. Foxe's accounts of her religious piety and sincere and visionary faith can be verified independently. However, historian Thomas Freeman notes that:

> There is not a glimpse to be seen in Foxe's account of Anne the polished, accomplished courtier; of Anne the skillful and opportunistic politician; of Anne the patron of humanist art and writing; to say nothing of the outspoken, imperious and fiery queen who intimidated even the leading peers at court.[13]

Foxe's version of Anne didn't really "take" in the Anne Boleyn canon because those who knew her didn't recognize her in his one-dimensional description. And although this portrayal might be flattering in a way, it also says something about power and how to contain it. Anne must be edited down to size in order to be admirable. It is assumed that her power and agency need to be blurred out if she is to have anything good to offer or if anything that she did is to be taken as important and significant.

If I wanted to do so, I could call each of the nastiest things that have been said about Anne—her temper, her sharp tongue, and her enjoyment of cockfighting—into question right here and now. I could argue that the stories of yelling and causing tears, of arrogance and haughtiness, were all misconstrued, misinterpreted, and even manufactured. The most negative reports about Anne were from people who had axes to grind about religion and politics, and they were jealous of Anne's influence with the king. I could easily craft a picture of Anne that is more appealing, and I could offer a plausible justification for doing so.

But also, I want the not-nice parts included in the picture we paint too. I want the jagged edges. I want the bits that don't sit well. I want the complexity and the color and the imperfections. I want the whole picture of Anne, and I want it to stand in defiance of the ways that we have tried to contain her story specifically and the stories of women generally. I don't want nice or neat or blandly palatable. Anne doesn't need a reputation makeover just so she can be relegated to the dustheap of irrelevancy. Anne needs to be allowed to draw outside of the lines of the archetypes we have used for understanding and controlling women.

As Dorothy Day noted, saints are admirable, but easily dismissible.

Anne's Afterlife

As Anne's afterlife unfolded, layers of the mystical, the magical, the enchanted got painted onto her. She was a ghost haunting the Tower of London, carrying her head under her arm. She was a sorceress whose portrait is included in the hallways of Hogwarts Castle in the Harry

Potter movies. Sixth fingers, third nipples, birthmarks, and growths under her chin have variously been described and exaggerated. She didn't conform to traditional standards of beauty, and so her desirability must have been manufactured by nefarious means. She was the manifestation of evil itself.

Every decade or so, an offering of pop culture comes out that passes for a time as the authoritative version of Anne. *Anne of the Thousand Days* from 1969 is still referenced as one of the best Anne representations. Geneviève Bujold sympathetically portrays her as a passionate, articulate, brave, and strong-willed woman, whose heart is eventually won over by the king, only to have him reject her for not giving birth to a son.

In the early aughts, *The Tudors* became iconic in the Boleyn imagination, dealing with Henry and his court in the manner for which it seemed custom-made: as a serial drama. With the luxury of several seasons and twenty episodes, the creators had the opportunity to spin out the political and romantic machinations of Anne and Henry's relationship. Natalie Dormer would transition from playing Anne to establishing a career of portraying strong-willed royal women, and her knowing, slightly leering smile and confident tilt of her head did justice to this woman, who was historically described not as beautiful but as magnetic (although Dormer is traditionally beautiful).

These portrayals leave a lot on the cutting room floor, but they generally offer a more nuanced and interesting picture of Anne Boleyn. In contrast are the best-selling book and movie *The Other Boleyn Girl* by Philippa Gregory or the earlier *The Autobiography of Henry VIII* by Margaret George. The Anne Boleyn of these stories leans into the accusations of scheming, sexual deviancy, and suggestions of the perverse and occult associated with her.

There is a dynamic connected to this and noted by some observant scholars, which is a backlash in Anne's reputation exactly as her character and actions started to be more clearly seen. As historians of the 1990s and early aughts were rediscovering how influential Anne had been on English politics—"not just a catalyst in the Reformation, but a key player"[14]—popular depictions of Anne began playing up the more negative sides of Anne's personality, happy to give credence to the notion that Anne was involved in deviant and dark dealings.

"Virtuous Anne" has been one way of framing Anne's story, but ultimately not a popular one. "Villainous Anne" has been easier to construct. So has Anne the sexual and spiritual deviant. It makes for good entertainment. It sells books and movies. It fits other things we understand about how women and the world work. It has been done so often and in so many contexts that we all know how to read the stories for what they are: warnings to women who don't behave or play nicely.

Inconsistent Anne?

Anne has been portrayed as a victim, a villain, a beautiful heroine, an evil manipulator, a saint, a slut, a seductress, a protofeminist, a femme fatale, and a figure of warning to other upstart women. Boleyn storytelling circles around the same thing that fairy tales describe: power. How is it supposed to be used? By whom? When is it good and when is it bad? How do we distinguish one from the other? What happens when the wrong people use power? And what happens when power isn't used by the people we want or expect for the purposes we have deemed acceptable?

There is a temptation to treat Anne Boleyn as one more character in the fairy tale, varnished with that sheen of distance, packaged into familiar archetypes that tell us something about how we are to understand the world. Anne has provided ample fodder for each of the prepackaged prototypes we most like to apply to women.

Indoctrination about appropriate female behavior continues to happen in a powerful, if more subtle, way for women of the twenty-first century. Anne lived five hundred years ago, but the story of her life and how we have discussed it remains relevant.

And also, the best kinds of stories, "fairy" or otherwise, refuse to be neatly contained and have a way of holding a mirror up to ourselves, not just to tell us something about how the world should work, but also how it could work, and how magical it can be when we give permission to see the strange beauty of people being different from what we have been told to expect.

Eric Ives, the historian whose work on Anne Boleyn has widely been seen as her definitive biography, concludes his seminal book *The Life and Death of Anne Boleyn* with this note:

> To us she appears inconsistent—religious yet aggressive, calculating yet emotional, with the light touch of the courtier yet the strong grip of a politician. . . . [She was] a woman in her own right—taken on her own terms in a man's world; a woman who mobilized her education, her style and her presence to outweigh the disadvantages of her sex; of only moderate good looks, but taking a court and king by storm.[15]

It is a good summary of Anne and what made her extraordinary. What I find interesting is the conclusion that these characteristics then come across as "inconsistent." I would argue that Anne is only inconsistent if we fail to recognize that she is a human being. She isn't a trope or an archetype or a label. She most certainly isn't a fairy-tale heroine or villain. She is extraordinary, and the contours of her life were dramatic to the extreme. But there is nothing about her personality and choices that seems inconsistent with what I know about my own life and what I observe in the lives of other complex, nuanced, flawed, and grace-filled human beings. People are religious *and* aggressive, calculating *and* emotional, political *and* personable. People fall in love for a variety of reasons other than merely being drawn to the best-looking person in the room. People have dreams and ambitions, and they live out possibilities that defy the categories we might want to slot them into and escape the confines of our expectations for them.

People are like this. Women are like this.

Anne was like this.

CHAPTER 15

The Whore

A Promiscuous Afterlife

The Tudors television show offers a scene in which Anne covertly petitions the king of France on an important trip Anne and Henry took to secure French-English relations just prior to their marriage. She takes Francis aside and quietly asks him not to reveal to Henry any of the indiscretions that she committed while growing up in France. It is implied that King Francis was among those indiscretions.

While the trip to France was an important part of Anne and Henry's relationship arc, the conversation between Anne and Francis depicted in this episode is fiction. Francis's court had a reputation for its spicy sexual behaviour, but Queen Claude's did not. Francis was certainly a notorious womanizer, but Anne Boleyn was not among his conquests.

That this is fabricated is the least problematic thing about this scene. *The Tudors*, a mainstream television offering, created a storyline that implies that a teenage girl, entrusted to the care of the French court to receive an education, could be passed around by the men of the court and the king of France himself, and that this would be a sign of *her* sexual promiscuity. The blame we so routinely ascribe to victims of sexual violence and exploitation is a story that we might be more careful about telling in the twenty-first century, but it remains an all-too-popular trope.

In the two seasons it takes *The Tudors* to tell Anne's story, the creators still could not be bothered to give even the slightest of nods to the cutting-edge ideas of religion and philosophy to which Anne was exposed by the female leaders in the French court. Instead, this mecca of feminine power, influence, and leadership is brutally distorted into a tale of female sexual sin.

The work of Joanna Denny provides an interesting contrast to *The Tudors*. Her book, *Anne Boleyn: A New Life of England's Tragic Queen*, portrays Anne so favorably that it resembles the hagiography of John Foxe writing about Anne in the time of her daughter Elizabeth's reign. While presenting true things about Anne's religiosity and religious influence, it downplays or explains away the more hardheaded aspects of Anne's personality. Denny is quick to ascribe purity to Anne's intentions and actions that bears little resemblance to the more complex personality revealed in the historical record.

What is most troubling about Denny's work, however, is the way that it frames Anne's purity in contrast to the other women around her. Catherine is described as a manipulative liar. Princess Mary is immature and temperamental. Mary Boleyn, Anne's sister, is labeled as promiscuous, with her sexual ethics and behaviors of the lowest sort.

Anne's reputation is carefully rehabilitated in Denny's book, but still the need to slut-shame and victim-blame proves too hard to resist. This author falls into the patriarchal trap of pitting women against one another so that one can be considered good and worthy, but only in contrast to those who are judged morally loose.

Both Denny's saintly Anne, as well as the more common sexual name-calling applied to Anne, say something about female sexuality and how it is understood. Women are not judged well for refusing men's advances, and Anne was labeled a whore because she was seen as being a manipulative tease. However, those who give in to those advances and become a mistress (like Anne's sister, Mary, whose feelings about being the king's love interest, mistress, and then rejected mistress, are lost to history) fare no better.

The Whore of Babylon

The label "whore" wasn't just about what Anne was or was not doing in the bedroom with the king. It was also about Anne's religious views and how powerfully she was shaping those views politically. Rolling female assertiveness into sexual name-calling has a proven track record of keeping women in their place. And there is a long and varied history of using the metaphor of a prostitute to describe what is seen as religious faithlessness.

The Hebrew Scriptures regularly describe the people of Israel as a prostitute when they are disobeying God's law.[1] The metaphor of the "Whore of Babylon" in the Book of Revelation follows many of the same patterns of the Hebrew Bible in personifying cities or ruling powers as women who commit adultery or engage in prostitution.[2] There are a number of clues in this biblical book to suggest that "Babylon" was code for the Roman Empire and for calling out the power that was persecuting Christians. That doesn't make the imagery any less upsetting: This woman is denounced, left naked, burned, and her flesh is eaten by the people.[3] It is one of the more gruesome and dangerous descriptions of violence against women from the pages of the Bible.

Ever since the words were first written onto parchment and circulated, there have been religious leaders intent on applying this metaphor and its imagery to whatever worldly power they see as undermining the church and the "true faith." During the Reformation, reformers labeled the Catholic Church as the Whore of Babylon. An image from the 1545 edition of Luther's Bible depicts the whore as wearing the papal tiara.[4] Henry's daughter Mary was equated with the Whore of Babylon by angry reformer John Knox when she came to the throne and returned England to the Catholic faith. Still today, there are anti-Catholic Protestant voices who will claim that what the author of the Book of Revelation prophetically had in mind in the "Whore of Babylon" was calling out the faithlessness of the Roman Catholic Church.

I have my own strange story of the "Whore of Babylon" imagery being mobilized when I was not expecting it. Shortly after I began my first pastoral charge at an Anglican-Lutheran church in Orillia, a couple of hours north of Toronto, I was four months pregnant, new to the city, and just settling into the leadership role. My amazing colleague at the church, Pam, suggested that we should attend an ecumenical prayer breakfast to which we had been invited.

We were the only two women who came to the breakfast. The male pastors exclusively represented churches of the more charismatic/fundamentalist bent. After the grace was said and we had each gone through the self-serve continental breakfast line, the conversation took a surprising turn. Several of the men began describing visions that they had been having of a terrifying female creature, part serpent, part Medusa of *The Little Mermaid*, and definitely reminiscent of Revelation's Babylonian whore, holding the city of Orillia in her clutches of evil. They reached a consensus when one of the men decided that it would be up to them, and their churches, to cut off this whore's head, thereby freeing the city from her evil death grip and delivering their people safely into the arms of Jesus.

I had a lot on my mind at the time: new job, new baby on the way, new home, new community. I didn't say it out loud, but I did wonder if Pam and I were the implied target of their graphic imaginings. We were not the right gender; we were known for supporting equal marriage and other agendas considered by these pastors to be wrongheaded and faithless. Pam and I left the breakfast eager to laugh off the whole bizarre situation and decided we could do without those kinds of colleagues and connections in our city and never went to another prayer breakfast. My guess is that was an outcome not unwelcome to this group.

Anne: The Wrong Kind of Woman

The conflation of religious and sexual faithlessness as synonymous was well established in the Christian consciousness by Anne's time and is still troublingly popular. Anne was the wrong kind of woman, and the reason why she was the wrong kind of woman was because of sex.

Sexual labels and sexual accusations have continually stuck to her—both before and after her death. During her ascent and time as queen, the court, political ambassadors, dignitaries, and even the general population chattered about Anne as a sexual deviant: "a goggle-eyed whore," a "naughty paikie" (prostitute), a "*grande putain*" (French for "prostitute"), and "the concubine." Eustace Chapuys continued to call Anne "the concubine" and a "*grande putain*" even after she had been Henry's wife and queen consort for years.[5] By the time she was accused of adultery and incest, disparaging Anne's sexual behavior was already a well-entrenched habit. When Anne was long dead, her name was smeared across Europe as a "Jezebel," a "Salome," and "the Great Whore."

Detractors like Nicholas Sander would be among those most responsible for this smearing. His main complaint was with Anne's daughter Elizabeth and her return of England to Protestantism. He wanted to discredit Elizabeth by tearing down her parents and the relationship that split the church from Rome. His book introduced Anne as having "sinned with many before marriage, and after her marriage with the king she sinned with her own brother. She was always a Lutheran."[6] In the next paragraph he claimed that Anne was the product of incest, Henry's own daughter by an affair he had with Anne's mother. This is a logistically impossible claim: Henry would have been little more than a child when he supposedly sired Anne. But Sander would go to any lengths to show that holding the wrong kind of beliefs and being a sexual deviant are two sins cut from the same cloth.

Sex sells. Sander's work spread across Europe with pro-Catholic supporters who likewise were angry with Queen Elizabeth about religious reform. Over time, the religious argument and accusations of Lutheranism were dropped in favor of only the stories of the legions of men that Anne slept with and accusations of incest and lifelong promiscuity. *The Tudors* is left referencing some of the most salacious of these accusations without the context for why Anne was so slandered both during and after her lifetime.

Although the details of Anne's story are singular, the way that she has been talked about is anything but original. Denny's pro-Anne and anti-Mary work is also not, in the end, a fresh take on female leadership. Sexual labels and sexual gossip serve to keep women in their place; violence against women is too often justified if those women are thought to be so sexually out of control that they are causing others to misstep too.

Mary Magdalene

There is another biblical woman who has significant parallels to Anne Boleyn and to our conversations about her.

For the Christian imagination, she looms large as a mysterious, controversial, and also hopeful figure. She has had a significant afterlife in the pop culture storytelling of Jesus and his associates, featuring heavily in more recent offerings like *Jesus Christ Superstar*, *Godspell*, *The Last Temptation of Christ*, and *The Da Vinci Code*, as well as in folk tales about Jesus that have cropped up throughout Christian history.

It's Mary Magdalene. Mary was an important leader in Jesus's circle of disciples. All biblical records of Jesus's life agree on the fact that Mary was among the first witnesses of Jesus's resurrection. The accounts differ in who was with Mary on that Sunday at the empty tomb, or whether she encountered the risen Jesus by herself, but all agree that she was the first to see.

She wasn't just important and faithful and courageous enough to have been the one to go to minister to the dead body of a convicted enemy of the state (Jesus), she was also so central to Jesus's life that she was among those who witnessed the horrors of his execution.[7] She was a follower of Jesus throughout his ministry and provided for his work out of her own financial resources.

The Bible tells us that she was healed by Jesus, that she had been possessed by demons and that Jesus successfully exorcised her. This report of demons could mean a lot of things. It could mean certain psychological or physical ailments, including epilepsy. Mary's "demons" might have been a way of talking about how she was perceived as being different, difficult and nonconforming. Jesus's healing of her could have had more to do with accepting her and even empowering her differences. I wouldn't want to dismiss the spiritual realities described in the Bible. Nor would I want to diminish the variety of powerful ways in which healing can happen.

Some of the texts that were written about Jesus's life (and that didn't make the cut for the Bible) describe Mary's relationship with the other male disciples, particularly Peter, as contentious and marred by jealousy. She was questioned for her closeness to Jesus. She was criticized for being too outspoken and presumptuous as a woman.

The reason why Mary Magdalene has been so controversial and so supremely gossiped about in the Christian faith is framed as something other than Mary's strong, faithful, wise, and perhaps "weird" character.

Many Christians have long been under the impression that Mary Magdalene was a prostitute. Prostitutes in every age of history deserve to be treated with dignity and compassion. People of faith should not only be compassionate for the many reasons that people find themselves in a situation where sex work feels like the only option, but should also be committed to the principle, no matter what leads a person into selling sexual services, of treating every person with respect and seeing the image of God in them.

Respect for sex workers aside, there is no Scriptural evidence to suggest that Mary Magdalene took money for sex at any time in her life.

Calling her a prostitute might have been an intentional choice to discredit her. Or calling her a prostitute might have been the language that is just too easily and often adopted to talk about women that don't conform. Anne Boleyn was called the "great whore" throughout the time that she was *not* sleeping with the king. Both women have been slapped with accusations of sexual deviation for their principled, creative, and strong-willed actions.

Mary Magdalene found prominence and power and a voice that was respected and listened to amid a gaggle of men all vying for the attention and favor of Jesus, a man that they suspected might be God's promised savior. She found a way of being a leader, an influencer, a person of significance and impact, in a world where women's roles were strictly managed, where women's subservience to men was assumed, where women's voices, opinions and contributions were rarely welcomed or validated. This isn't the way the story is expected to go; reducing her to a prostitute instead is the all-too-familiar default.

She Refused Sex, and She Was a Whore

I don't subscribe to the view that defending Anne necessitates defending her sexual purity. But it is worth noting that all historical evidence points to the fact that Anne was a virgin until late 1532 when she finally slept with Henry.[8] Had it been found out that Anne had slept with Henry Percy, or any other possible suitor, before the king, she would have been disqualified as a potential wife. In the divorce hearings, Catherine of Aragon's side never raised an argument against the divorce on the grounds of Anne's immorality, even though that certainly would have been pursued if possible. Evidence of adultery, of Anne and Henry's sleeping together while he was seeking an annulment of his marriage to Catherine, would have weakened Henry's claim to be acting on grounds of conscience, but it was never forthcoming.[9]

Most historians agree that Anne went to her death having had just one sexual partner: the king.

Whether we're talking about Mary Magdalene two thousand years ago, female pastors at a community prayer breakfast, or Anne Boleyn and her sister Mary five hundred years ago, we all stand as just a few of the ample examples of how boringly predictable and uncreative society has been in tearing down women who are perceived as threatening. And layered into these accusations is the all-too-popular metaphor of "wanton women" for describing religious viewpoints or religious actions that are deemed corrupt or faithless.

Anne's refusal of the king's bed could have been interpreted as an example of her goodness and piety, had she simply been able to conform to a few more of the expectations placed on her as a woman. When Anne was being excised from the king's life and the royal court, Henry's new love interest, Jane Seymour, would take a page from Anne's book and refuse to sleep with Henry unless he married her. Jane and her family were ambitious too, and this decision was strategic—modeled on Anne's own success in parlaying sexual boundaries into gaining the crown. Jane went on to produce Henry's only legitimate male heir, Edward, and then to die from complications in childbirth. Jane ably fulfilled her womanly duties and died a virtuous death. When Henry told her not to get involved in the politics of the kingdom, she listened and shut up. Jane's conformity to expectations has meant that, in Henry's eyes, Jane's virtue was displayed in her refusal to sleep with him. She didn't have the opportunity then to tarnish that virtue in any way.

In contrast, Anne didn't produce a son, which would have shielded her from the attacks that were always coming at her. Her political and religious influence and ambitions were blatant. Sex, therefore, was interpreted as a weapon that Anne was using to get ahead. "Whore" didn't exactly apply to anything about her sexual choices, but it worked well enough in describing a woman who was judged as both powerful and threatening.

CHAPTER 16

The Mother

The Falcon and the Virgin

At her marriage, Anne adopted the white falcon as her heraldic emblem. It was an animal associated with her family, namely the Butler line, going back to Anne's paternal grandmother. Anne personalized it, with her white falcon alighting on a tree stump bursting with roses, wearing a crown and carrying a scepter.[1]

The imagery was deliberate and layered. This falcon wasn't just connected to her family lineage, it also referenced her anointed position and her embracing the expectation of how she would fulfill God's will, now that she was finally Henry's wife. She was proudly pregnant at her coronation, and Anne was promising that she would make good on this next—most important—order of business.

To do that, the falcon aligned her with Jesus's mother, Mary. The Annunciation is the biblical story of the divine messenger Gabriel telling Mary of Nazareth that she was to give birth to God's son. It is regularly pictured as a white dove descending on Mary, representing for the faithful the belief that Mary's child was conceived by the power of the Holy Spirit and was therefore a child of God. Anne's falcon was depicted in a deliberately similar way and wore a crown. This was reminiscent not just of Anne's queenship, but also of Mary's queenship of heaven.[2] Anne's crest used parallel imagery to tell the people of England that everything in the six-year fight with Rome, the dramatic religious revolution, and now Anne's marriage and coronation, was divinely ordained. Anne's white falcon descending on the tree stump, symbolizing Henry, proclaimed that the child the royal couple expected was heaven-sent.

Mary of Nazareth, commonly referred to as the Virgin Mary, is a tricky one with whom to align, even when being crowned queen of England and carrying the heir to the English throne. This long-ago Mary inadvertently set an impossible standard for women: She is a mother *and* a virgin. She is forever known for her sexual purity while also accomplishing the most romanticized role a woman can take. The Mary of the Bible was a strong, hardheaded, visionary, revolutionary, opinionated woman. But those are rarely the things associated with her. She is a model of holiness. She is a beacon of hope to those who wish to be mothers, those who struggle to be mothers, and those who suffer as mothers.

Mary was given a title that inspired considerable debate in the early church: *Theotokos*, God-bearer. This was thought to be a radical step in recognizing Mary's participation in the salvation of the world. I don't think the name goes far enough in recognizing the fullness of Mary's role, not just as a mother, but as a person whose entire being was involved in forming the person who would be called the Christ. She wasn't merely a God-bearer, a vessel of purity and passivity shuttling Jesus from heaven to earth. Her DNA was Jesus's DNA. And from what little we know about Mary, we can see that Jesus's most prophetic, radical, and world-changing ideas were learned from his mother. Mary wasn't just a God-bearer. She was a God-shaper, a God-teacher, a God-influencer.

This undoubtedly was not on Anne's mind in aligning her symbols with Mary's. Anne wanted her power and influence legitimized. But here on this coronation day, what she also wanted was the blessing of one heavenly mother to one who might have been a queen on earth but was newly and exceptionally vulnerable.

Anne had talked a good talk. She had utterly convinced Henry and herself that together they would make the kingdom right with God. Now she needed to prove that what they had fought for was true. Now her job description was abruptly changed from keeping Henry's nerve directed toward remaking the church, from politicking and religious reform, to becoming a mother.

If she wanted to make the kingdom right with God, she needed to start having children. Especially sons.

Mothers are Communal Property

It is not uncommon for women to be on the receiving end of thoughts from family members, friends, and even relative (or complete) strangers about when they should have babies and what pregnancy should look like. It is still fair game for random people to touch a woman's body if she looks like she has a baby growing inside.

It was almost four years between my wedding and the arrival of our first baby. For much of that time, my body was subject to constant commentary. If I made an unusual clothing choice and my stomach ended up looking a little more round than normal, or if I put on a few holiday pounds in the summer months or Christmas season, I had people asking if I was pregnant. If I was very obviously not pregnant, then well-meaning colleagues, and occasionally parishioners, would offer their unsolicited advice about how I shouldn't wait too long before trying to get pregnant. When I was pregnant, the commentary went up an astonishing number of notches. I was asked how much weight I had gained; I was told that I looked like I was carrying twins; I was affirmed for carrying "the right amount" of weight; I was told horror stories of other women's deliveries; I was patted on the belly by friends and strangers; I was told that I should eat whatever I want and enjoy it; I was warned that I should be careful about carbs and fruit and potential extra pounds; I was told my baby bump was beautiful; I was reminded to hold my stomach in.

Congregations can assume a family identity and therefore an intimacy that also emboldens people to say out loud the parts that are not supposed to be said out loud. Although the volume of advice, guessing, critique, and affirmation about what was going on with my body might be higher than normal because I am a parish priest, the content of these conversations is quite typical of a general and widespread attitude that women's wombs represent communal property.

I knew that I wanted to be a mother before I knew anything else about myself. I wanted children more than I wanted any career or vocation, more than marriage, more than money or success or publishing deals. I have tried to listen to a sense of calling in my work and service: What am I being asked to do? But motherhood was the thing *I* most definitely wanted. I wanted children so much it hurt. A day doesn't go by that I don't feel profound gratitude that I was able to have children and that I get to parent the two miraculous people that I was part of bringing into this world.

Perhaps the world treats women as communal property when babies are on the horizon because if someone is a mother, then we can pin them down and figure them out. We assume we know what is going to drive them, what will be most important, what shapes their day and gets them up out of bed. We know what kind of person they are . . . or at least what kind of person they should be. Their legacy is assured. If the world feels safe when women are kept in check, pinned down, contained, figured out, then motherhood is the surefire way of doing that.

It took me a few years into parenting before I started to realize that being a mom hadn't given me a personality transplant. I still had a sense of calling to serve the church and the wider community. I still got drawn into too many passion projects of writing and leadership. I still wanted to learn new things and take on interesting challenges. My two children are at the center of my whole life. And also, I am a person with things to offer and ideas to share and thoughts that I get lost in and new horizons that call my name to come and see, to learn and grow.

Good Mother

In the heady days of her courtship with Henry, Anne and the king wrote love notes to one another during morning Mass in the royal chapel. They were inked into another illuminated copy of a Book of Hours. This back-and-forth comes up in most histories of Anne's life, and some interpret it as irreverent. However, it is clear from studying other inscriptions in other prayer books—in Anne's personal volumes and in the books that Henry and his last wife Kateryn Parr had together—that writing notes in books was part of the joy of being someone who loved books.

Below the picture of Jesus as the "Man of Sorrows," Henry wrote:

> If you remember my love in your prayers as strongly as I adore you, I shall hardly be forgotten, for I am yours.
>
> Henry R. forever.

Anne replied under a miniature of the Annunciation:

By daily proof you shall me find
To be to you both loving and kind.[3]

It was one more example of Henry's obsession with Anne. It was also revealing of both the intrinsic and explicit promise Anne represented, and she wasn't above reminding Henry of this promise through the long debacle of their premarriage relationship. Here, she was promising the same thing she would at her coronation: She was aligned with the Virgin Mary; she, like Mary, would have children, sent from God.

Anne did embrace the role of mother with enthusiasm and optimism and accepted that bearing children, particularly boys, was the job for which she was ultimately applying. She was initially less active in public affairs after her marriage in 1533. She settled into the maternal role. She exercised her influence in private and enjoyed a brief truce with her enemies. Her marriage and Elizabeth's birth had somewhat settled the issues in which she had been a combatant.[4]

Anne, without complaint, subjected herself to the suffocating circumstances expected of a pregnant woman at the end of her term. She was to begin her "lying in" a month before her expected due date, which involved shutting herself into her chambers with all curtains drawn and any cracks or crevices of fresh air blocked up to guard superstitiously against evil spirits getting into the room. Fires were kept burning in the hearth, even though it was late summer when Anne began her confinement with Elizabeth. The queen was attended only by women for the duration of her pregnancy. Anne might have been unconventional in many ways, but she wouldn't risk going against any of the protocols assigned to pregnant women. It was the dawn of a new era, with intellectual freedom in the air and circulating in print, and also, prescientific ideas of pregnancy and childbirth were still in full swing.

Elizabeth was either a little premature, or Anne miscalculated the due date (possibly deliberately), because she didn't have a month's confinement; she gave birth just twelve days later, on September 7, 1533.[5]

Elizabeth was a disappointment. Anne surely must have been disappointed too, given the very public pronouncements she had made about the son she expected to deliver. Elizabeth was born on the eve of the Feast of Mary's Nativity, and Anne was quick to point this out after Elizabeth's birth. "A virgin is now born," she stated, "on the vigil of that auspicious day when the church commemorates the nativity of our blessed lady the Virgin Mary."[6]

If that disappointment was there, it wasn't obvious. Anne showed herself to be a devoted mother who defied conventions around royal child-rearing and insisted on having her daughter close to her on a velvet cushion in court, even campaigning (unsuccessfully) to breastfeed.[7] After just a few months, Elizabeth was sent to her own palace with her own staff and court. This was an indication of the princess's status, but separation from her baby also served the practicality of hurrying Anne's body to be primed and ready for the next pregnancy.

Anne's reputation has been largely defined by the other tropes that we often use to understand women, but for one person in the world, Anne's identity would be as a mother.

Wicked Stepmother

To many others, Anne fulfilled a different female trope: wicked stepmother.

This narrative isn't without substance. Anne was not known to have shown any compassion to the women that she was throwing out of court and, in fact, was openly antagonistic to them. She was competitive about securing the succession of any of the children she was sure to have with Henry, and that involved Mary being declared illegitimate and Catherine being sent to live in the countryside as if she had never been queen. When Elizabeth was born, it was Henry who insisted that Mary, no longer to be called princess of the realm, be enlisted to serve the new royal baby—a grave indignity. He was trying to force her to conform to the new regime and would struggle with her obstinacy for the rest of his life. Henry never allowed Mary to see her mother again after Catherine's banishment, even when Catherine was dying. Anne, however, got the blame.[8]

Anne, for her part, reportedly uttered threats against both Catherine and Mary. This was at the beginning of 1531, when the dog days of waiting for an annulment that didn't seem to be coming were clearly starting to rattle Anne. She was quoted as saying that she "wished all Spaniards were at the bottom of the sea . . . that she cared not for the queen or any of her family, and that she would rather see her hanged than have to confess that she was her queen and mistress."[9] When Catherine died of cancer, suspicion fell on Anne that she had finally succeeded in having Catherine murdered.

Anne and her stepdaughter, Mary, were often at loggerheads. Mary refused to acknowledge Anne as queen and her mother's marriage as illegitimate, which was a direct threat to the legitimacy of Elizabeth and any other heirs that might come along. Anne was known to have made at least three overtures for a better relationship with Mary, if Mary would only accept her as queen.[10] Her relationship with Mary reveals a rare insecurity that Anne allowed to be visible. She desperately wanted Mary's acceptance and affirmation.

Anne has been unfavorably compared to her successors Jane Seymour and Kateryn Parr, each of whom were conciliatory stepmothers and unifying forces in the king's household. Mary and Jane were very fond of each other, and Kateryn was held in high esteem by all three of Henry's children. Their positions, however, were remarkably different from Anne's. Jane had a son and then died, so she never had to fight for her child's right to rule; he was granted it by his gender, and she was excused from having to defend her position by dying. Kateryn didn't have any children by Henry and outlived him, so she, too, was afforded the luxury of not having to fight that battle.

Henry was reported to have said to his illegitimate son, Henry Fitzroy, on the night of Anne's arrest that "He and his sister [Mary] owed God a great debt for having escaped the hands of that cursed and poisoning whore who had planned to poison them."[11] At her trial, Anne had to answer the question as to whether she had "poisoned Catherine and had planned to poison Mary." To these questions, she answered a resolute "Nay."[12] Henry of Fitzroy was among the spectators at her execution.

Henry Fitzroy died a few months after Anne. But Mary had time to discover the truth: that her father was the real tyrant. The king was far more determined to get his own way and have people kowtow to his demands than Anne ever was. Henry didn't just put Anne and his fifth wife, Katherine Howard, to death. He threatened execution to his daughter Mary and arrest of his sixth wife Kateryn as well.

Mary was scarred for life by her father's treatment of her.[13]

Failed Mother

Anne was a successful mother, although her success was tempered by having a girl rather than a boy.

Then Anne was a failed mother.

Today, pregnancy for many women can be a plan and a choice. Prospective parents will even decide in which month they want their child to be born and will act accordingly. This freedom of choice can create its own kind of anxiety. Having babies in North America is expensive, and in the United States in particular, paid maternity leave, universal childcare, and universal healthcare are absent. Women who wish to be parents can struggle to find the opportune time between establishing their careers and gaining enough of an economic foothold to make raising children feel realistic. This has seen falling birth rates and much pearl clutching about the evils of women in the workforce choosing careers over procreation, as well as worries about procreational windows closing while women wait to be "ready" to have their families.

It has always been less expensive to romanticize motherhood and to attach religious valor to birthing babies than it is to support women and children with policies and structures that allow parents to choose to have children and to be able to raise those children with as much health and opportunity as possible.

Even with the significant challenges associated with bringing children into the world, many women desperately want babies, and for some getting pregnant is a long and painful struggle. As someone who so desperately wanted children myself, I can imagine something of the psychological hell, the pain and anxiety, that descends on a woman every time a month goes by and the news with which they are met is that no baby is on the way. Even in the twenty-first century, the shame and heartbreak for women who wish to be pregnant and aren't can be immense.

The shame and heartbreak of not producing a male heir in the sixteenth century was both personal and political, and it put Anne's life in danger. She was in good company in being a failed mother. Of Henry's known partners—six wives and two mistresses—only four of them conceived, the last time being the beginning of 1537. Catherine of Aragon had five out of six known pregnancies miscarry. Anne had two of three known pregnancies miscarry.[14] Concerns about the king's sexual incapacity were circulating and were a factor in Anne's death. Of the many embarrassing details constructed to bring Anne down at the expense of Henry's reputation, the one that was most glaring and probably also not fabricated, was Anne's complaint about Henry's impotency. When Henry divorced his fourth wife, Anna of Cleves, the end of the marriage was secured on the grounds of the king's sexual incapacity. Henry blamed Anna for being too ugly.[15]

The common denominator in each procreational woe was Henry. Whether the king suffered from a congenital impairment, or just problems with impotency, can only be speculated.[16] A lot of armchair diagnostics goes on in the twenty-first century not only about Henry's problems with conceiving children, but also what his behavior might suggest about potential personality disorders.

That didn't prevent the women in Henry's life from bearing the blame for the lack of princes.

We don't know what Anne, or any of the other five queens, felt personally about wanting, dreaming, or hoping to become mothers. Catherine and Anne were both known to love and dote on their daughters, but having children was not optional. Motherhood wasn't a choice. It was expected.

Not meeting expectations wasn't just disappointing, it was deadly.

CHAPTER 17

The Witch

TikTok's Brightest Stars

I was intrigued when my daughter, Cecilia, told me that Joan of Arc and Anne Boleyn are two of the historical figures most beloved by her generation.

Joan lived about a hundred years before Anne (ca. 1412–1431). Like Anne, she met a violent death, and her afterlife has seen mixed reviews. Joan was led by heavenly visions, wore men's clothing, and was a fierce and sometimes remarkably effective military leader. She rose from the humblest of beginnings to be taken seriously for both her visions and her military prowess. The name by which she was styled wasn't "Joan of Arc," but rather, "Joan the Virgin." Virginity has a proven track record of making women spiritually more credible. Joan was at the side of Charles VII when he was crowned king of France; she was given leadership in establishing strategy and leading armies into battle against the English.

I went into writing this chapter believing that the thing I knew about Joan was that she died as an accused witch. Discovering otherwise was an interesting lesson in just how thoroughly pop culture can convince us of false stories.

Joan was captured in battle and put on trial for her wayward, unusual, and presumptuous ways. Her visions were condemned as coming from somewhere other than God. She was considered blasphemous for aligning herself so closely with the saints and the Archangel Michael. She was supposed to listen to the church, not imagine she had direct access to the divine. And they didn't like her wearing men's clothing either.[1]

She was burned at the stake as a heretic at the age of nineteen.[2]

When I asked Cecilia to describe her connection to Joan with me, she started with music. More specifically, it started with her complaining about a song: "Bigmouth Strikes Again" by The Smiths. In it, the lead singer Morrissey claims to "know how Joan of Arc felt."

"Not only does he not understand Joan of Arc," Cecilia articulated to me with the most withering of looks and a tone of voice dripping with condescension, "But really? Men have to take Joan of Arc too?"

Cecilia and I looked at the lyrics together. They open with images of violent misogyny: smashing the teeth out of someone's head and bludgeoning them in their bed. It's hard not to read these words onto the countless women who have suffered violence at the hands of men, particularly since Joan of Arc is the organizing metaphor. But we're not meant to be upset by that: He says in the song that he's only joking. Women and marginalized people have been expected to tolerate a lot because of variations on this escape clause. *I didn't mean it, I was only joking, you took it the wrong way. You deserved it, you asked for it, you wanted it*—these have worked wonders too.

Cecilia was appropriately disgusted by those lyrical overtones, but her ire was stoked by those other two main issues. How dare this privileged male rock star think that he understands the persecution and violence done to Joan of Arc because he has been criticized for his opinions? And more importantly, why would this successful man think that he gets to lay claim to one of the rare examples of a prominent story of female nonconformity, bravery, and heroism?

Anxiety and Violence

In 1486, just a handful of years after Joan's death and before Anne's birth, a German clergyman, Heinrich Kramer, wrote the *Malleus Maleficarum* (*The Hammer of Witches*):

> All witchcraft comes from carnal lust, which is in women insatiable. . . . There are three things that are never satisfied, yea, a fourth thing which says not, It is enough; that is, the mouth of the womb. Wherefore for the sake of fulfilling their lusts they consort even with devils. . . . Now there are, as it is said in the Papal Bull, seven methods by which they infect with witchcraft the venereal act and the conception of the womb: first, by inclining the minds of men to inordinate passion; second, by obstructing their generative force; third, by removing the members accommodated to that act; fourth, by changing men into beasts by their magic art; fifth, by destroying the generative force in women; sixth, by procuring abortion; seventh, by offering children to devils.[3]

This was a dog's breakfast of accusations: mixing under the banner of witchcraft a catchall of things that have typically been most disturbing about female power, plus a few extra fabricated worries for good measure. Witchcraft was connected to women's sexual desire, which was considered insatiable and easily led both men and women into the hands of the devil.

Witchcraft also got bound up in generalized anxiety around procreation. If pregnancies didn't happen when they should, if men and women weren't as fruitful in multiplying as was desired, if children died in infancy, then these all-too-common fifteenth-century realities could be blamed on bad women. Even concern about abortion was tied up in witchcraft long before it became the central issue in modern gender politics. The possibility that witches were circulating around castrating men and "turning them into beasts" added fuel to the already paranoid fire concerning evil and unbridled sexuality on the loose in untamed and demonic women.

It was male authorities who alone were entrusted with the ability to distinguish whether a woman was being guided by God or by Satan, which made women particularly vulnerable.[4] Reports vary widely on how many people were killed and of what gender they were. One source claims that 40,000 to 65,000 people were killed as witches in early-modern Europe,[5] with women being the main target (75 percent) in England and other parts of Europe.[6] Another source produces much higher numbers: Up to 4 million people were tortured and killed on suspicion of witchcraft, 85 percent of them women.[7] These are dramatically different statistics, but they add up to bad news for women either way.

Weak-mindedness was the primary characteristic associated with witchery. Those whose mental guardrails were flimsier were more vulnerable to demonic influence, and the cultural assumption was that weak mental guardrails were a female specialty.[8] Many theories have been put forward about who was targeted and why. Understandably, twentieth- and twenty-first-century feminists have been interested in considering what female characteristics were named as especially problematic. No real evidence has supported the theory that this was a way of eradicating earlier women-led pagan religions or that this was explicitly about keeping women from getting too powerful when they otherwise started to gain more opportunities.[9] It also wasn't, as is commonly assumed, a war waged by the church. Witchcraft was a criminal offense, tried in courts of law, not churches.

The concerns mostly boiled down to predictable and mundane problems. The typical accused was "a married middle-aged woman of the lower peasant class" with "a sharp tongue and a filthy temper." Women who quarreled, cursed, and expressed anger in their dealings with neighbors were more likely to be imagined as witches.[10] And anxiety about procreation, about mothers and babies' health, was always lurking around the shadows too. “The witch is the dark other of the early modern woman.” She was an antihousewife and an antimother.[11]

Men were also vulnerable to accusation if they were judged as contravening patriarchal expectations about their social roles as good neighbors.[12] Finally, there was a lot of “cross-fertilization” across the various labels and stereotypes that got applied to problematic people. This included overlap with witchcraft, heresy, and Jewishness.[13] It’s not surprising, given these blurred lines, that what Joan of Arc came to be remembered for was witchcraft, not the less cinematic accusation of heresy.

Anne the Witch

Witches might be popular in fairy tales, but they have also featured heavily in the real world, and not as far in the distant past as we might like to believe. Witch hunting, witch trials, and witch executions happened right up until the late nineteenth century. I have a parishioner who can trace just several generations back in her family tree the execution in New England of two relatives accused of witchcraft.

Anne didn’t play nice or conform to expectations of how women were to behave. She has, as a result, been easily framed as the embodiment of evil, a source of dark magic. She banished the beloved Queen Catherine of Aragon and Princess Mary from their palaces. She held the entire court and ruled from the throne of England with dark power. She seduced the king and led England down a miserable and chaotic path. She miscarried at least two babies. She had a “sharp tongue and filthy temper.”

Nicholas Sander’s posthumous takedown of Anne has become the stickiest of descriptions for Anne’s physical appearance, and although he didn’t stoop to calling her a witch,[14] his portrayal of her became tinder for the witchcraft fire. Sander described Anne as charming, talented, and good-looking (“handsome to look at, with a pretty mouth”), but he also wanted to be clear that she had evil lurking inside. To do this, he described her as

> tall, with black hair, and an oval face of a sallow complexion, as if troubled with jaundice. She had a projecting tooth under the upper lip, and on her right hand six fingers. There was a large wen under her chin, and therefore to hide its ugliness she wore a high dress covering her throat.[15]

Sander was using artistic license in portraying Anne, allowing readers to see the unattractive person beneath her charming exterior. These supposed deformities, however, came to line the popular imagination about Anne. Clearly, she looked like a witch; clearly, her outward appearance was a divine warning against her evil dealings; clearly, a woman like this could not have attracted a king without the use of the supernatural. Sander refers to her 1536 miscarriage as bringing forth "a shapeless mass of flesh,"[16] which implied birth defects that were signs of spiritual evil.

Our friend Eustace Chapuys also crops up again in the witchcraft slander against Anne. He quoted in one of his prolific reports to the emperor an offhand comment he heard second- or thirdhand that Henry made after Anne's miscarriage. The king was reported as claiming that Anne had seduced him with "philters, charms, or otherwise" and that she had "enchanted and bewitched" him.[17] These two details from this antagonistic man have continued to live rent-free in the popular Boleyn consciousness, blaming Anne for her own tremendous personal loss by accusing her of sorcery.

Chapuys doesn't mention this again in his commentary on Anne Boleyn, and nowhere else do the historical records indicate that Henry drew such a conclusion about his second wife, either after her miscarriage or when she was brought to trial. But this proved to be a delicious tidbit in constructing Anne's afterlife. Books, movies, and television shows about Anne love to make hay of the storyline that Henry believed his wild obsession was induced by Anne's supernatural dealings and that her delivery of a deformed child was the turning point in his realizing it.

Many of the accusations written in the *Malleus Maleficarum* were reflected in the most dramatic and disturbing aspects of Anne's life. She inspired uncontrollable lust in the king of England. She was responsible for the lust that broke apart the political and religious landscape of England. And if she and Henry had trouble securing that much-desired male heir, that must have been her nefarious and evil doing too.

Witchcraft offered that anxious catchall squarely on Anne's slender shoulders.

Joan and Anne

Joan of Arc's reputation went in two opposing directions following her death. Reports from the English were condemning. Joan had helped the French beat the English in battle, so their interpretation of her was uncharitable. We can see in the years after her death in some of these British sources how charges of witchcraft and sorcery got layered into the original charge of heresy.[18]

In contrast, the French people for whom Joan fought were invested in vindicating and rehabilitating the young warrior, even if she was a woman. Pope Pius II was writing sympathetically of her by the mid-fifteenth century.[19] A French scholar, Edmond Richer, claimed by 1639 that her visions were divinely sent, and French plays started casting Joan as a romantic heroine.[20] Mere decades after her death, a church rehabilitation trial overturned the original church trial as unjust and fraudulent.[21] Joan of Arc was beatified in 1909 and made a saint in 1920,[22] allowing her official status as one of the patron saints of France.

Anne's reputation as a leader in the Reformation was recognized in her lifetime and in the years following her death. The religious controversy, of which she was such a driving force, was one of the reasons she was so disparaged and had such vitriolic enemies. But in contrast to Joan, that leadership came to be more and more overshadowed by the labels applied to her, the accusations against her, and the dramatic contours of her romantic relationship with the king.

Witchcraft was not one of those accusations lobbed at Anne during her lifetime. She was not one of the thousands of nonconforming and worrisome women who were eliminated by witch-hunting. Joan wasn't either. And yet because both women exerted unusual influence on powerful men, rose above their imagined station, and claimed leadership that they weren't supposed to have, both have come to be associated with charges of witchcraft in the generations after their deaths.

Joan has inspired, like Anne, vastly different representations and an unending stream of romanticization, speculation, fabrication, vitriol, and hero worship. Overall, Joan's reputation became purer, brighter, and saintlier with time, leaving far behind the stain of accusation that her leadership had come from demonic means. Both women led highly unusual and dramatic lives; in the end, the label of "witch" could have been predicted for both. When it comes to problematic women, our repertoire of accusations has been limited.

There Aren't Enough Stories

I was curious about Cecilia's sense that young women of her generation have a gravitational pull toward both Joan of Arc and Anne Boleyn. I wondered if she could explain to me what that might be about.

I felt a shiver of recognition run up my spine as she named out loud the same kinds of feelings that simmered in my soul when I was her age. "I think," she mused to me, "that there are women who grow up defined by a certain stereotype because they are into books and art and philosophy, and that isn't judged as popular or cool. They are in touch with themselves and who they are; they want to give expression to their big feelings and imaginations. They notice and pay attention to the world.

"We want women we can look up to and relate to, but we don't have a lot of examples. Here are these stories of these women who were unexpected for their time. And we feel like . . . here is someone for me."

I thought of the stories that consumed all available corners of my imagination growing up and how I was drawn in equal measure to women who spoke of transformation or nonconformity, for unexpected things below the outward exterior, for beauty that grows and deepens. I thought of how Anne Boleyn came to speak to all of that and more, how connected I felt to her, how much she represented the things I cared about, the person I wanted to be but didn't know how.

Cecilia had more to say. "With both Joan of Arc and Anne Boleyn," she said, "there is this interest in historical female figures who died tragically or unfairly. We have to remember these stories, especially since we don't have a lot of them. They're obviously there, but they've been buried."

She thought a little bit more, considering her words carefully. "It's like when there's a female figure big enough to have made it into the history books, then we have to look for the patterns: patterns of what happened back then and what is still happening today. It's a reminder to be aware, be fearful. What we have right now might not be permanent. White men aren't looking back and thinking, 'Oh yeah, there was a time when I didn't have rights, I couldn't be taken seriously, I could just be married off to the highest bidder.' But women know that what we have can also be taken away again. We know we have to remember that.

"We have to stand strong," she concluded.

"And," she added, "Morrissey damn well doesn't know how Joan of Arc felt."

Postscript

Only a few months after talking to Cecilia about Morrissey, Joan, and Anne, the "Bigmouth Strikes Again" song struck again. I was having a conversation with two of my gay friends, and I was stunned to hear them articulate an entirely different take on this rock star and his music.

The violent imagery of the song didn't speak to them of Morrissey co-opting women's experience as his own, but rather as naming the experience of growing up as "other," being slammed into lockers of high school hallways, fearful of being punched by the jocks and masculinity police for being out of step with what was expected of men, of living in the closet and yet knowing that their sexuality was constantly under suspicion, that the masks they learned to wear were perpetually in danger of slipping off, and if that happened, they would be called out and beaten down.

Men were burned as witches too, and when the history books tell us that it was men who were "judged as contravening patriarchal expectations," that sounds like a gay-coded accusation to me. Seeing a parallel between their experience and Joan of Arc's is understandable. I felt silly for not knowing that this was part of Morrissey's songwriting impact, but then again, that's precisely the issue.

The problem is that we don't know the stories because there aren't enough of them and they haven't been prominent. The problem is that women and LGBTQ+ and other marginalized groups have too few narratives. History has tried to incinerate the experiences, the otherness, the contributions of far too many of us.

At first glance, Morrissey, to my mind and Cecilia's, might seem unqualified to claim to understand Joan of Arc and the legions of women who have been violently silenced. But if the song has a legacy of bringing to light the suppressed experience of some people that we have wanted to shut up and disappear, then I will cosign that.

CHAPTER 18

The Most Happy

At her coronation, Anne took the motto "The Moost Happi," which was a replacement or addition to the earlier *Ainsi sera, groigne qui groigne* ("Let them grumble, that is how it's going to be"), which she had used when opposition to her and the sought-after marriage to Henry was most fierce.

The festivities surrounding Anne Boleyn's coronation had been unspooled over several days, starting with Anne's procession into London by barge just after Parliament declared her marriage to Henry valid. The procession took Anne to the Tower of London, with the royal chambers lavishly refurbished just for the new queen. No foreshadowing of another entrance to that Tower several years later was noted. Anne's gowns and jewels for the occasion were extravagant, as expected of one who was being recognized as royalty. Guns were set off in celebration and about fifty barges full of musicians and flags—including Anne's new heraldic symbol, a white falcon crowned with red and white Tudor roses—were part of the procession.[1]

On June 1, Pentecost, Anne was crowned queen. Her coronation was followed by an elaborate banquet for eight hundred people. There were twenty-eight different dishes for the first part of the banquet and then another twenty-three followed in a gratuitous second act.[2]

This wasn't merely about Henry putting his so-called love for Anne on display. Every detail of the ceremony and pageant was designed to communicate to the people of the realm that Anne was accepted by not only the king, but also the nobility of the land, and especially that she was appointed and anointed by God. "The Bible, chivalry, art and—most original in 1533—the language of humanism, all were mobilized to present Anne as a divine ruler."[3]

The fanfare, the clothing, the spectacle, and the symbolism conferred on Anne the divinely ordained authority of royalty—a feature even of modern coronations, but especially important in 1533 to justify the dramatic circumstances that brought Anne to the throne. Firmly in Henry's mind was the belief that Anne was going to make religion right in England, that Anne was the spiritual and maternal hope that the country needed. He spared no expense in using every tool at royalty's disposal to convince his people of that truth too.

"Happy" was a word that, in Anne's time, would better be equated with "fortunate." It represented Anne's gratitude, a nod of humility in recognition of Henry's (and God's) hand in bringing her to this position. However, the message that Anne deserved to be in this elevated position, or that she was anything other than an arrogant social climber, was generally received as unconvincing. The people of England were not in favor of Catherine's removal or the religious revolution that was underway. Catherine of Aragon was popular, and more particularly, Anne was seen as an inexplicable upstart. Kings weren't supposed to marry for love or lust. They were expected to marry to secure heirs and political alliances. Catherine had done one of these things, even if she had failed in producing a son. If she were to be replaced, the people expected someone more helpful to the English cause than the insignificant daughter of a courtier.

This made the coronation even more important. It was a public relations tool. It was spectacle with purpose. England needed to know that Anne was exactly where she was meant to be, and Anne was resolute in staying on message, no matter how strange and precarious her circumstances might have felt. Anne was insisting that fortune and divine and kingly favor had brought her to the place she wanted—"most happy"—even as she was being cast as gratingly arrogant, her sharp tongue and confident demeanor stoking the hatred against her.

Anne could not allow herself the luxury of wallowing in the negativity that surrounded her. She had to keep her chin up. She had to insist that her way was right and good. She had to believe that all that she was fighting for was ultimately worth it.

The Tightrope

In 2014, I started as the lead priest at St. George's at the age of thirty-five. I was constantly reminded that I was the first woman to hold this position. And not only that, but the wider church also, the diocese of Niagara (in the Anglican church we refer to a geographical region of the church as a diocese) was proudly claiming me as the first woman to lead a cardinal (aka large) parish. I spent those first few years trying to prove myself against attacks and critiques that came at me from many different angles, all variations on the same themes of my age and my gender. I had to quell a bit of fear every time I opened my email, scared for the emotional shrapnel that might be unleashed on me from whatever bitter and angry message could be sitting in my inbox at any given hour of the day. For at least twenty-four months, the primary image that came to mind was walking on a tightrope without a safety net underneath. I felt like I was constantly in danger of one little slip of the foot resulting in a decisive tumble.

I lived by the mantra "A leader leads." Acting like I knew where I was going and therefore where *we* were going seemed the essential thing. Just as I started to feel a little more grounded, a little less riddled with imposter syndrome, I was invited out to lunch by a longtime member of the congregation. We went to a beautiful Italian place down the street from the church, and I ordered a delicious-sounding pasta, looking forward to our time together.

I ended up taking the whole meal home in a takeout container, untouched. As soon as our food arrived, she proceeded to bombard me with stories of how my leadership was being perceived in the congregation. She suggested that, although she supported me, "people" were saying things. Among a variety of critiques about changes to the worship service and focus on the wrong things, the most stinging comments were about "people's" perception that I was too ambitious, that I was using St. George's as a stepping stone to bigger and better things, and that I shouldn't be so career-focused when I had young children at home.

I had the wherewithal for very little in response, but I did manage to tell her that I would prove to her that I was, more than anything, a priest who genuinely cares about the church and its people. I did go on to prove that to her, and we had many years to mend the hurt feelings of that bombshell lunch.

I have continued to struggle, however, in various professional settings to claim the kind of confidence in my own abilities and accomplishments that is often necessary for taking on new leadership positions. It's not just a message that I internalized that day over my uneaten pasta. I remember the way Madonna was endlessly discussed and criticized as the biggest pop superstar in the world when I was growing up. She was judged for being calculating, for making deliberate career decisions about everything from her promiscuous attire to her sensationalistic choreography and lyrics. Although we have little sympathy for women who enter the spotlight and then flame out, we are even more rattled by those who plot their climb to the top and then act as if they enjoy being there. I think of the vicious voices attacking the duchess of Sussex during her brief time on the royal stage, complaining that she is too domineering, hardworking, ambitious, and assertive. A 2020 *Tatler* article, titled "Catherine the Great," took Kate Middleton to task for being cunning, careful, calculated, and intelligent. It described a woman who plans every move and polishes every aspect of her image to perfection. Kensington Palace broke their typical rule of "don't complain, don't explain," to challenge the article's portrayal. The prince and princess read as catastrophic criticism the suggestion that Kate's massive and widely untarnished success as one of the world's biggest celebrities requires intentionality and ambition.

Those are just a few of the celebrity examples that have permeated my consciousness, but of course, they are representative of the more casual comments that get whispered, or not even whispered, about women whose focus, planning, and clarity of purpose are considered alarming. I can't help but feel like I have tripped on a snake in Snakes and Ladders, unable to make any progress through the board game, every time that I finally think that I have proven myself worthy to have me and my ideas welcomed at any particular leadership table, only to be told that what I need is to dial back, soften up, be more vulnerable, and stop making other people feel so insecure.

There are underlying assumptions that have changed little since Tudor England: Female arrogance is perceived as threatening, female ambition is considered unseemly, and female happiness is deemed unnatural.

There is a poignant epilogue in *Three Women* by Lisa Taddeo. The book is a narration of the true stories of three featured women—their relationship with men, with sex, with their families, and with themselves—but in the epilogue, Taddeo locates herself as a character in the book too. She describes her interactions with her dying mother, looking to her mother for some final words of wisdom.

Taddeo is frustrated by the conversation. Her mother refuses to offer the kind of closing remarks she is seeking. After a few false starts and nursing interruptions, this is the wisdom that mother chooses as most important to pass on to daughter: "Don't let them see you happy."

Taddeo responds with surprise. "I thought it was the other way around. . . . Don't let the bastards get you down." Her mother's last words of advice are clear, however. "That's wrong. They can see you down. They should see you down. If they see you are happy, they will try to destroy you."[4]

The Hunt

It is hurtful, demeaning, and disempowering for me, and countless other women, to be so relentlessly and insidiously socialized into dissociating ourselves from our own ambition and achievement. I try to get better about speaking up and saying, "This is me. I have a lot to offer." It is a particularly nasty dimension of misogyny that problematizes intentional accomplishment if it is women doing the accomplishing.

However, there is something about Anne's situation that clarifies for me the more sinister reality that underlies the palpable unease, and even fear, expressed about women's agency and power.

Henry's famous love letters to Anne in 1527–28 articulate an obsessiveness, a determination, a man who is on the hunt. Henry begs and cajoles Anne for answers about whether she returns his affections. He sends her gifts designed to claim her as his own, including a bracelet with his picture in it and a dead buck that he had killed.[5] He laments her distance from him; Anne had retreated to her home of Hever Castle to get space from his pursuit. At times, he offers thinly veiled threats:

> I have been advised that the opinion in which I left you has been wholly changed, and that you will not come to court, either with Madam your mother or in any other way, which report, if true, I cannot enough marvel at.

And:

> Ponder well, my mistress, that absence from you is very grievous to me, hoping that it is not by your will that it is so; but if I understood that in truth you yourself wished it, I could do no other than complain of my ill fortune while abating little by little my great folly.[6]

Henry's feelings for Anne were a problem. His letters reveal a vulnerability and neediness that are representative of the ridicule Henry faced for being so irrationally infatuated with Anne. One ambassador said in a letter to Charles V that the king was "so blindly in love with that lady that he cannot see his way clearly," and Chapuys wrote that "this King's obstinacy and his passion for the Lady are such that there is no chance of recalling him by mildness or fair words to a sense of his duty."[7]

As embarrassing as Henry and his behavior were, though, that was judged as Anne's fault. She was a seductress; she was manipulating him. She was the cause of his irrational behavior. That Henry showed predatory and abusive qualities gets overlooked, and instead the focus is on what Anne was doing to provoke him.

This deflection from Henry's behavior to Anne's is arguably the real agenda in villainizing female agency, female power, female ambition. Women who know what they are doing and what they want are a problem. Women setting goals and going after them are a problem. But ultimately this is all a red herring. If women get attacked for the choices they do make, then maybe we won't notice all the choices that have been taken away.

Maybe we won't notice that Anne was hunted by the king until she relented and joined him in his madcap plan to have her at any cost. Maybe we won't notice how Jane, Kateryn, Katherine, Catherine, and Anna also didn't have a choice in marrying this spoiled and violent monarch. Maybe if we criticize Madonna for taking off her clothes, seemingly because she likes doing it and sex sells, then we won't notice how viciously we sexualize women in the spotlight and how little we have cared about the costs they pay for any modicum of celebrity status. Maybe if we get mad at Meghan Markle for being too aggressive, then we don't have to talk about the startling racism that was unleashed when a black woman joined the royal family. And maybe if Kate Middleton can just keep feeding us the fantasy that glamour and poise don't take massive amounts of planning and effort, then we can overlook how deadly the royal family can be to women who get talked into taking on the job of princess.

Anne's "most happy" insistence tugs at my heartstrings. There is something so poignant in imagining this small woman with her big ideas and her spine of steel insisting that this strange and dangerous position was exactly where she wanted to be.

And I am left feeling frustrated that her bravado has been, for five hundred years, so often identified as the problem. There was so much that she couldn't have, that she didn't have, that was taken from her, that wasn't hers to choose. And still the story ends up being one of resentment and condemnation for the targets she set, for the determination she showed, for the goals she pursued.

A World of Pain Contained in 38 mm

There is a small medal from the time of Queen Anne Boleyn that escaped the deliberate erasure of her existence that followed her execution. It dates from 1534, the midpoint in her brief three-year reign and marriage. This artifact (only 38 mm in diameter) provides the only contemporary likeness of Anne that we have with certainty.[8] Her strong nose and jawline verify the reports that said Anne wasn't a beauty but had a strong and interesting face. On it appears her motto, "The Moost Happi."

That little medal with Anne's determined motto was a prototype that was planned to go into wide production and distribution later in 1534, with the birth of the much-anticipated prince that Anne had explicitly promised to Henry and the people of England. Instead, Anne had a stillbirth, likely in the summer of that year when Anne would have been about seven or eight months along. That half centimeter of lead is held in the British Museum, carefully guarded as an artifact from a reign that was cut short and a prototype that never became anything more than disappointment. That medal hints at the personal pain, fear, loss, and panic that Anne would have undoubtedly felt, compounded on top of the basic grief of losing a child so close to term.

Anne's enemies would have taken that miscarriage as an encouraging comeuppance to someone who thought too highly of herself. Which is exactly why Anne needed to stay so fierce and so proud and so determined in the first place.

If that baby had come along, if Anne had just a little more leverage on her side, if she hadn't needed to step on quite so many toes to get to where she got, if she wasn't so principled, if she could just be quieter and more docile and apologize occasionally, if she were interested in sewing rather than religion and politics, if the world were a bit better primed for the offering of a strong and intelligent and passionate woman. . . So many ifs that didn't fall in Anne's favor.

But that she tried to insist anyway that she was exactly where she wanted to be—*that's* the problem.

CHAPTER 19

. . . Happily Ever After

Historians have recently made the discovery that Catherine of Aragon, Anne Boleyn, and Thomas Cromwell were all gifted the same 1527 Book of Hours, printed from the same French printer. Who bestowed this gift on these three fractured—and sometimes warring—people of power at the same time and for what purpose is a delicious, and unanswered, question.[1]

It was in that printed book that Anne wrote her fanciful rhyming couplet:

> Remember me when you do pray,
> That hope doth lead from day to day.
>
> —Anne Boleyn[2]

I can picture her holding that book, praying with it, delighting in its smell and feel and substance. This particular book connected her to the religious traditions of the past, and it represented the power words now had to travel because of printing. As she wrote those words in the margin in her elegant, well-educated hand, I can imagine her heart nearly bursting with excitement at the prospect of suddenly being a power broker in the affairs of church and state, envisioning for herself a trajectory of impact and influence.

Remember me.

Uncontainable

In 2025, my daughter Cecilia and I joined my parents at a seventieth anniversary of the Orillia chapter of the Canadian Federation of University Women. This is an organization devoted to supporting women's education and advocating for women's voices and women's equality. Their guest speaker at this gala evening was Margaret Atwood.

Cecilia and I were both starstruck. "There is no possible way Margaret Atwood could understand just how important she has been to me," Cecilia whispered to me during our salad course. Atwood was seated two tables away from us, and I tried not to stare at her as she ate. "For a whole year, I was reading *The Handmaid's Tale* and watching *The Handmaid's Tale* and completely absorbed in her world," Cecilia continued. When Atwood walked by us in the hallway after supper, we could do little other than smile foolishly at her and stammer out a word of gratitude.

I had a similar experience with *The Handmaid's Tale* in my last year of high school. I recall the essay I wrote for my final English exam on a stormy January day, about what Atwood's book reveals regarding freedom and choice. Even when freedom is restricted as completely as possible, the human spirit still finds its mode of resistance. I hungrily consumed Atwood's other works of fiction when I went off to university, each book absorbing me with its finely drawn characters and sharp dialogue. The social commentary never felt heavy-handed but emerged out of stories that made me care about the characters and invited me to wrestle with someone else's point of view.

Margaret Atwood has written everything from poetry to treatises on why house cats need to be kept indoors because they are killing the songbirds, but she is best known for her anti–fairy tale dystopia. Like in the world of fairy tales, she uses imagined landscapes to talk about real human dynamics, but there is no magical gloss, just the unraveling of what our current choices could bring to our future horizons.

She wrote *The Handmaid's Tale* forty years prior to this gala evening, but a shiver of electricity crackled across the room as the interviewer detailed aspects of the story that felt all too familiar in 2025: a democracy that had been upended into an autocracy, puritanical Christianity giving legitimacy to an agenda of oppression, women's rights curtailed, women participating in the subjugation of other women because doing so buys some measure of power and privilege, and an inordinate focus on women's wombs and controlling the project of procreation. Atwood warned the four-hundred-plus group of people that the most dangerous thing people could believe about themselves is "that could never happen here."

She spoke about resistance. There is always resistance. If you push and squeeze and curtail too much, there will always be a counterreaction. There will always be those rising up. There will always be creativity and imagination and passion and possibility that can't be contained.

"Is there a role for writers in that resistance?" the interviewer wondered to Atwood.

"I am a firm believer in never telling writers what they should be writing," she said decisively. "Otherwise it just becomes propaganda. Let art happen," she advised.

I thought of Anne, how minutely her actions have been observed and interpreted, and how much has still been missed. She used her words and her books to share in spreading ideas and to participate around the tables of power. She understood that access to these new imaginative landscapes was negotiated; she tried to meet expectations. I thought of the notes she wrote in the margins of her books and of how self-conscious those inkings were and how representative, too, of this one seemingly unimportant voice finding a way to be heard.

I thought of my Grandma Jean. She was a quiet and reserved woman, a teetotalist Christian and the consummate housewife, filling her tidy and well-organized home with delicious baking, innovative cooking, order, and calm. She was an artist and craftswoman, and her spare time was devoted to quilts and handmade teddy bears, each of which was a work of art.

She was also a reader. The books that she consumed were full of challenging ideas, irreverent humor, and sometimes sex and graphic language. She passed the books along to me and in doing so would quietly wonder to me about faith, the existence of God, and what sort of world we live in anyway. She would point out the occasional thorny passage and ask what I thought of it too. Books were my grandma's way of painting outside the lines, of articulating beauty and mystery that her very conventional life didn't even hint at, and to encourage me, her granddaughter, to broaden my own horizons.

I thought of how my grandmother would have been a different person if she had been able to go to school instead of being sent to work to make ends meet in the throes of the Depression. Reading and sharing books was the counterpoint to the choices that were taken from her. I thought of the escape, permission, adventure, and possibility that books have opened for me, of the household my parents created, where books were honored as friends and as part of the fabric of our family's life and lore. I thought of my daughter and my son and the worlds I have gotten to share with them, and hope to continue sharing with them, because we can access and love the written word. I think of the rebellion and resistance and fight for goodness that is in them, and I want that to be nurtured throughout their lives. I want them to feel connected to minds like Margaret Atwood's and so many others that remind them that we must always stand up to be counted for the cause of freedom. If we want a better world, we have to be willing to imagine it and shape it.

There was something sad and magnificent about that gala. There were original charter members of the Orillia chapter there that night. They had been fighting for seventy years for women's rights and the advancement of women's education, and I wondered how tired they must sometimes feel in seeing the world roll back their hard-won progress, at suddenly having to prove again that this matters. But also, it was a room of people still committed to fighting, people who had benefited from being able to access stories and go to school and raise their voices and fight like hell. It was a room full of people who had very obviously used that benefit intentionally to help and equip others. It was a room full of women, but men were there too, applauding and supporting and celebrating. They were there as proof positive, first in line, to say how much better their own lives are, and the institutions and businesses they have served, because women have been at the table.

The happily ever after of fairy tales isn't really about the man and the woman riding off into the sunset together after finding their one true love. Anne's story should stand in resolute contradiction to any notion that when kings choose you and the nuptials are completed there won't be dark dealings to follow.

I see in Anne's story a different sort of fairy tale—a deeper, richer, and more disruptive one. She is the surprising person revealed as beautiful and powerful. She explodes the business as usual of our lives. She tells us to see something new and claim hope that wasn't there before.

Anne's happily ever after is about the little markings in the margins of the written word that tell us that ideas are hard to contain and that the people you least expect are leaving their imprint too.

PART 5

Only a Story

Only a story. Only the things we tell to keep out the darkness. Only the myths and fables that save us from despair, to establish power and destroy it, to teach each other how to be good, to describe the limits of desire, to keep us breathing and fighting and yearning and striving when it'd be so much easier to give in. Only the constituent ingredients of every human society since the Stone Age.

Only a story. Only the most important thing in the whole world.

—Laurie Penny, journalist[1]

CHAPTER 20

Anne and Me; Anne and Us

The Patriarchal Equilibrium

I will sheepishly admit to an obsession with *The Bachelor*, which has been the premiere reality dating show on network television for the past twenty years. Yes, I enjoy watching beautiful people dating in exotic locales around the world. And a show that makes finding a romantic partner into a kind of sport does seem custom-made to appeal to my lifelong love of both competition and fairy-tale romance. But truly my greatest enjoyment in watching the franchise comes from listening to the recap podcast feminists Emma and Claire offer the day after each episode airs. They share an unapologetic love of love. But they also pick apart what each cast member's behavior says about broader cultural norms around love, sex, dating, and gender.

The Bachelor franchise, not surprisingly, represents some pretty standard expectations about how men and women are to interact: that the man will ask for the father's blessing before proposing and that a woman will take a man's last name after being wed, for example. These practices are based on the long-ago premise that women were properties to be negotiated between one man and another, but for us today, they are mostly received as normal, or even romantic, traditions associated with marriage. The show, however, despite its rather titillating premise that one lead will date twenty-five people simultaneously, also regularly represents an even more robustly conservative version of North American gender values. There are women who have explicitly stated their belief that a man's role is to be a provider. There are men who evaluate their prospective partners based on whether they think the woman will be a good mother. On hometown dates, families have been known to articulate their expectation that the man will be head of the household, with the women and children falling under his umbrella-like authority. Fathers have threatened potential suitors with harm should they hurt their daughter and then withheld permission for their daughter to marry that suitor, reinforcing in far less subtle ways the belief that daughters belong to their father . . . until they then belong to their husband.

These cultural narratives, present in so many places other than *The Bachelor*, are not neutral in their effect. They shape how we think about what it means to move through this world. Women can certainly be feminists and also embrace traditional expectations. Women can choose not to work outside the home and enjoy homemaking. I took my husband's name when we got married. Freedom doesn't look like just one thing.

It is the narrative around which gender should do what in a partnership, who should have power and who should not, that has broader, more troubling, consequences. Churches that extoll this complementarian theology—that men are the head of the household, the providers, and women's place is as their subservients—seem to attract young people at rates that are astonishing, while our churches of a more progressive bent are filled primarily with seniors. The rise of tradwife influencers—women who are shrewdly making a living on social media as they extoll the virtues of prioritizing family and homemaking over their career—seem baffling to the generations of women who have fought for equality, for choice, for access, for opportunity, who have proven the worth of their voices and leadership and contributions. We work so hard to gain ground, and then it seems to slip away.

The more generous feminist read on this willing rollback is that women have continued to feel failed even by a world that tells them that they can have it all. After all, it is still women who statistically take on the lion's share of physical and emotional labor in raising a family and caring for a household, but now they are expected to have a career too. It is understandably comforting and appealing to imagine a simpler scenario: Designate the securing of a paycheck to the man; women tend to the domestic domain. Maybe the idea that women can "have it all" has ultimately been just as toxic and disempowering as the message that everyone should stay in their gender-assigned lanes. Rights get thrown away because the so-called advances of feminism are still experienced as an unattainable and burdensome fairy tale to be hauling around.

Feminist scholar Judith Bennett names this "The Patriarchal Equilibrium." We can point to times across history, including the time of Anne Boleyn, where it seems as if a new day is dawning for women. We can see this in the early Christian movement, in the writings of Christine de Pizan, in the leadership of Joan of Arc, in Anne's role model Marguerite d'Angoulême, in Anne's daughter, not to mention at various times of war, change, or unrest where women's voices are heard in a new way and women's offerings are finally received. We have seen advances in North America in the past century around women's suffrage, women's access to education, women's excellence in academic spaces and scholarship and arts, women taking leadership roles in traditionally masculine spaces, and women's securing access to birth control and to safe and legal abortions. But the patriarchy is remarkably effective at reasserting itself, and the ground can close in over these ideas and offerings, as if they never happened.

Feminism Fixed

I played Barbies in an uncomplicated, guilt-free way as a child. I loved the clothes and hair, the miniature household items, the make-believe world. I didn't have a Dreamhouse, but I did have a Dream Kitchen, complete with tiny plastic egg cartons and milk bottles, ice-cube trays and peanut butter. I treasured each detail of every item. My Barbies didn't tend to have any of the high-powered jobs to which I aspired. They did the things that I couldn't: They were models and gymnasts and actors. I never could figure out how to do a cartwheel or handstand, but Barbie could front flip, back flip, and balance on beams. I was happy to wear the same comfortable jogging suits day in and day out, but Barbie dressed in stilettos and shimmering form-fitting gowns. I lived in the world of books; Barbie didn't own books.

I went to the *Barbie* movie with my teenage daughter and son when it came out. Cecilia wanted to see the #Barbenheimer doubleheader, so we watched *Oppenheimer* first. We had fun wearing pink and thought it was hilarious when we ordered the *Oppenheimer* tickets and the person at the wicket saw how we were dressed and rang up tickets for *Barbie* instead.

Cecilia loved *Barbie*. My son, Gordon, and I left feeling that it didn't quite meet our sky-high expectations. I thought the movie could have benefited from a more ruthless editor and that the character development was shallow. Cecilia loved that Barbie was so blatantly co-opted to prey on people's nostalgia and attraction to the pink, blonde, and frothy, stealthily delivering a feminist message to her unsuspecting audience. The emotional monologue by actor America Ferrera toward the end of the movie—previewed in so many trailers I had seen and detailing the contradictions and impossibilities of living as a woman—felt trite. "I've heard all of that before," I said on the way home.

"Yeah," Cecilia snapped in response. "And it's all still a problem, so obviously it needs to be said some more." Point.

I recognized the Barbieland of the movie from my childhood—not just because it brought to life the plastic toys that had so enchanted me, but more particularly because of the worldview it presented. I, like the Barbies, thought that the patriarchy had been fixed. I would be quick to chime in when I identified an obvious unfairness in how I was treated in comparison to my brother, or if I thought that another girl was being left out because of her gender. But I believed my parents and a world that told me I could be anything that I wanted to be. I absorbed the ample evidence around me that assured me of the leadership, intelligence, ambition, insight, and creativity of women. I thought that meant the feminist agenda was won and done.

The observations I make about anyone seeming to be blissfully unaware of the hard-won rights they are throwing away are not made from any moral high ground. I grew up believing that identifying as a feminist was passé. I have participated in the patriarchal equilibrium as well. The *Barbie* movie revealed the same feminism to which I admittedly subscribed: feminism shrouded in a glass ceiling. It is a feminism that doesn't see what it doesn't see.

I didn't see how our history books, music and art programs, science, math, and philosophy teachings all featured—almost exclusively—the work of men. I didn't notice that things like composing music or conducting an orchestra didn't appear on my radar as things I might be able to do. I wore my jogging suits and embraced my geekiness; I didn't realize how much the images of beauty—Barbie being one of them—were impacting my sense of what my body should look like. I didn't know that keeping women hungry and feeling badly about our hips has been one of the most successful and insidious ways of continuing to control us, even when we are becoming more powerful in other arenas. I failed to wonder about the pay gap, or the burden so many working women bear in trying to be successful in their careers while still shouldering most of the unpaid labor of caring for the household. It didn't cross my mind that there might be more than the two genders I saw centered, and I didn't appreciate the violence and trauma nonbinary people have so long known in wildly disproportionate numbers. I worried about racism and the barriers minorities face; I didn't know that feminism has failed if we think it's just about women.

I did grow up with tremendous advantages compared to women in much of the rest of the world and across time. I had strong women in my life. I was encouraged to be strong and smart and ambitious myself. I was encouraged by both the women and the men in my life. It's not just my mother who wanted to see me flourish and reach goals. My father has, at key and challenging moments in my life, been the one to speak up and to tell me that I should not retreat into the background and that he supports me in making decisions that are right for me, even if they might be challenging for others.

There is no doubt that I stand on the shoulders of giants. I run because other women painfully and slowly and step by step insisted on walking. So many women went before me and paid enormous prices to be able to claim possibilities and space and legitimacy for the offerings of women. My life as a woman, and as a woman in leadership, has been made relatively easy and straightforward because of my forebears.

Maybe that should be good enough. Maybe my younger self was on to something in calling this done and dusted, and in believing we can just move on.

Feminism: Not Just About Women

To be a feminist is to stand up against a deep, pervasive, toxic, destructive violence. This violence affects people of all genders, even if it has claimed more female lives than male.

People still suffer violent sexual crimes—women, women of color, and trans people in higher numbers. People can still be executed in our world for sexual nonconformity. To an astonishing degree, skin color, ethnicity, and economics still determine who can access education, healthcare, reproductive care, and legal protection from violence in North America and beyond. Here in Canada, thousands of Indigenous women have gone missing or been murdered. Their case files go cold on police desks, and the public has been scandalously slow to ring any alarm bells or elicit a comprehensive response. In numbers staggeringly out of proportion to non-Indigenous Canada, Indigenous women's lives have been lost, and these losses have been treated with shrugs of shoulders, with the attitude that their lifestyles have been the cause of the violence that they have suffered, and that there isn't much that can be done.

To talk about feminism is to do much more than fight for a world where women have rights and opportunities and equal pay, as important as those things are. To be committed to feminism is to be committed to the valuing of bodies, especially different bodies, and to fight for a world where enough voices are represented and sharing with us a whole host of different perspectives, that we get better at seeing one another as human. We learn how to embrace difference rather than exterminate it.

This impacts every part of the world that we all live in. Feminism claims dignity and worth for all of us.

What Does This Have to Do with Anne?

Telling Anne's story in a more complete way won't solve racial inequality and end sexual violence. Hers is just one story, and in many ways, it's a story of privilege. It's the story of a white, educated, rich woman who came to power and lost everything. There isn't even a tenuous connection between her life and the missing and murdered Indigenous people of Canada today—except that the agenda of colonization was right around the corner for England and would be led by the family Anne married into.

Yet seeing her story more clearly and honoring her voice more fully does matter. It matters in the way that a drop in the bucket matters. I encourage the people of my church not to be afraid of being a drop in the bucket. Don't do nothing because you can't do everything. You need those drops in the bucket if you want a pail of water.

The Bones of Anne Boleyn

In the late nineteenth century, bodies were excavated from the general grave at the Tower of London during renovations to the Chapel Royal of St. Peter ad Vincula. Archeologists took the opportunity to examine the bodies for clues about the realities of their lives. Katherine Howard, the fifth wife of Henry and second to be killed by him, and the dukes of Somerset, Northumberland, and Monmouth were all known to have been buried in the chapel. It was also the final resting place of Anne Boleyn.

Doyne C. Bell documented the findings he and his team of six people made in the excavation, writing *Notices of the Historic Persons Buried in the Chapel of St. Peter Ad Vincula in the Tower of London.*[1]

Records indicated that Anne had been buried in front of the altar by the side of her brother, George. On November 9, 1876, Bell described how the pavement above the spot marked on the plan as Anne's grave was lifted and the earth removed to a depth of two feet. He recorded what they found:

> At this depth the bones of a female were found, not lying in the original order, but which had evidently for some reason or other been heaped together into a smaller space: all these bones were examined by Dr Mouat, who at once pronounced those to be of a female of between twenty-five and thirty years of age, of a delicate frame of body, and who had been of slender and perfect proportions; the forehead and lower jaw were small and especially well formed.
>
> The vertebrae were particularly small, especially the joint next to the skull and so bore witness to the Queen's "lyttel neck." Dr Mouat (Local Government Inspector) asserted that the bones all belonged to the one

female and had been buried for upwards of three hundred years. No other female bones were found in this area.[2]

Everyone on the team concluded that these were the bones of Queen Anne Boleyn.

She was only a slight figure, her slender neck one of her most notable features, along with descriptions of her "intellectual forehead," her oval face and rather square chin. Her skull indicated that she had large eyes. The finger bones revealed small and slender hands. Nothing of a sixth finger was noted.[3] The bones had already been disjointed from one another, so the skeleton's severed head wasn't a noted feature. It is interesting that the skeletal records do support the idea that Anne was younger than historians have generally assumed, but then the technology for dating bones was less developed in 1876 than it is now.

In a technical sense, Anne's remains were reburied and haven't been disturbed since. In other ways though, those bones have never been laid to rest.

This unearthing took place almost a hundred and fifty years ago, but I can almost feel myself there. I can feel the weight of my lifelong fascination with Anne, the stories I know of her, the many things I still want to know, the labels and the gossip and the endless representations—some villainous, some sympathetic—all being brought to bear on this small, fragile collection of bones.

It seems almost too much to consider the flesh and meat and imagining and color, vivid, vivid color, that has been built up and added on to this body that so long ago returned to dust, leaving only this small and disjointed skeleton. I have my own picture, my own construction, the leader and role model and fearsome personality that has so inspired and haunted me.

There lingers at the edges of my life as a priest of the church the need to prove myself legitimately called to serve. The voices that claim that my ordination is a travesty and that my voice should be silenced are always hovering around the edges of my Christian purview.

They're hovering around my non-Christian purview too, and I have listened to too many of them too much: the ones that told me I would be beautiful and valued only if I could lose twenty pounds, the ones that taught me how to play nice and put up with touch and comments I didn't want, the ones that trained me to keep my voice controlled and my opinions palatable and my appearance acceptable enough that people don't notice the parts of my personality that might otherwise be unwelcome.

I place inordinate hope in this one woman, whose story made it into the history books, and if we just look closely enough, we can see past the labels and chatter about her to celebrate how she raised her voice and fought like hell and didn't back down. Despite all attempts to silence and erase her, she stands in witness to a fundamental and critical truth: The church I serve wasn't just man-made; the world I live in was shaped by women too.

It's not only that Anne forces a drastic revision of this fictional church history of a faith formed solely by men. In a more fundamental way, Anne makes room for women to be themselves and for being a woman to be a complex and varied reality. We can be nurturing and hot-tempered, principled and selfish, smart and funny and insightful, ambitious and driven and power-hungry, faithful and shortsighted, motherly and mean, powerful and passionate and flawed and fragile. We can defy the nice, neat categories into which we are usually slotted because it's there that we're better able to be controlled and understood. We can hear women's voices and receive their contributions without feeling we need to dismiss, diminish, or apologize for the ways that their jagged edges tear at the boxes into which we have put them.

I bring to bear on her the things that I want for my children and for the world they are beginning to shape. I want my daughter to have these kinds of role models, to know that there's precedence for those of us who feel too much, whose brains feel ready to explode with our curiosity and imaginings and ambitions and big emotions, and that we have spaces and stories and have left our mark also. I want my son to have these kinds of role models too. I want him to think outside the gender norms we so want to fit people into. I want him to have examples of courage and passion and to see the value in choosing a path other than just being nice. I want him to continue to be empowered to lead and love and support and fight for a world where so many more voices get heard, to be the complex fully formed person he is born to be too.

Anne matters to me. But Anne also matters to us.

Those bones bear a legacy. The reformed Church in England, which would become the global Anglican Communion, was initiated under Anne's ascendancy to power and has her fingerprints all over it. That church bears the imprint of her vision in ways that have allowed people across the world and for the past five hundred years to walk meaningfully in faith. That church also bears the imprint of the violence and misogyny that brought her down. That church is a work in progress and needs to be clarified and re-formed even today.

Anne offers a complex, nuanced, and compelling model of female power, of a woman who was extraordinary and who lived through and contributed to extraordinary times. Her story allows people of any gender to feel that their own mixed bag of good and bad could all be part of how we live as fully realized human beings, that maybe there aren't parts of us that we have to edit out but can instead own and address and grow into. That kind of story is especially important for women because we simply don't have enough of those stories. We have been so well taught how to squeeze the vast, colorful landscape of our lives into packages that will be considered acceptable.

There is also a warning, written literally and physically into the very vertebrae of that skeletal neck. Anne stands as warning for how far we still must go in creating a world where people can speak and serve and lead and learn, regardless of their gender. Her story is one that continues to be told, and far too often. It's a story of how we take female power and diminish and sexualize and label and condemn it. It's a story of female vulnerability, that we can be the objects of desire and violence in equal measure and from the same person.

Anne stands for the estimated one in three women worldwide who have been subjected to physical and/or sexual intimate partner violence or nonpartner violence in their lifetime.[4]

She stands for the 13.5 percent of homicides in the world today committed at the hand of an intimate partner.[5]

In the dust of Anne's remains is one step on the impossibly big project of reclaiming some fraction of the countless stories of women and minorities that have gone unheard, and systemic violence has been done to them because we have failed to account for their humanity.

Anne's is a story of how far we have to go, what pitfalls to watch for, how important it is to keep fighting and insisting and laying claim to a world where there is room for all of us to be who we are and to offer what we have to give, and where that being and offering can be seen and valued in all of their richness and complexity. Hers is a story for our children and their children, and for those who will shape the world to come.

Anne's notoriety has grown and evolved over the past five hundred years since her death. Our fascination with her says something about us, about the stories we always tell and the stories we would like to tell and the stories we're learning to tell.

Our fascination also says something about her—the real, surprising, extraordinary, all-too-human person who lived in a specific time and place, who wasn't obviously destined for greatness or to pop off the pages of history to trouble and intrigue. She should have become Henry's mistress, had some babies, and retreated into the background, and instead she had a personality and voice that wouldn't be contained or tamed. She changed history and revolutionized the church, and we continue to excavate what remains of her story because there are always new things to discover, and because the things we still don't know continue to preoccupy and provoke us.

It is a lot to put on her shapely oval face and little neck. Buried in front of the altar in the Tower of London chapel is the physical reminder of a woman who wasn't a fairy tale or a long-ago archetype, who was so much more than her reputation. She lived and breathed and left her mark and died.

All that is left is a small, dusty set of all-too-human bones.

CHAPTER 21

A Legacy of Misogyny

You need to speak the truth, even if your voice shakes.

—Merrill Bittner, one of the first eleven women to be ordained in The Episcopal Church in the United States[1]

An event of tremendous global significance took place down the street from where I live. On November 30, 1976, at Grace Anglican Church in St. Catharines, two women were ordained as Anglican priests in the Anglican Church of Canada (ACC)—the Reverend Mary Lucas and the Reverend Beverly Shanley. They were among six women ordained that day across Canada, the first ordinations of women in our country and denomination. Police were there to manage protesters and any potential outbreak of violence as a result. The mainstream news media had their cameras and mics to document the unfolding of history. My friends Brian and Beth were part of the service, robed and assisting with the liturgy. They speak with pride and amazement at having witnessed such an important turning point in our church's history.

That summer, the ACC's sister church, the Episcopal Church in the United States, had voted at the General Convention in favor of allowing the ordination of women. It was noted at that convention that "if this is voted in favor, this will be the biggest change in the Episcopal Church since Henry VIII in the sixteenth century."[2] In fact, women had been ordained by some brave renegade (retired) bishops several years earlier. These women would be known as the "Philadelphia Eleven" and the "Washington Four." As much as the institutional church loves its rules and regulations, it has sometimes been the case that rules need to be broken in order to help people to see, and then embrace, what is possible. It was in ordaining women and paying attention to what sorts of offerings their ministry then allowed that paved the way for the institution to catch up.

For the bulk of Anglican history—in North America and around the world—women couldn't participate in leadership either in worship or on church councils, much less be ordained. Women have always found ways of exerting influence, but officially their roles were limited to fundraising and teaching Sunday School. Other parts of the global Anglican Communion watched the ordination of women with alarm.[3] The Church of England would eventually follow suit almost two decades later. Some Anglican provinces still exclusively ordain men.[4]

The arguments against women's ordination are and were vicious and vehement. This move, they said, would lead the church down a faithless dead-end path. Female priests would be the ruin of the church.

I was born two years after this took place, which means that I grew up in a church that has ordained women longer than I have been alive. I went into ministry with a certain naïveté as a result. I have had rude awakenings along the way: men walking out of services when I entered the pulpit to preach, people refusing to take Communion from me, households quitting churches when I arrived as the first female leader of that particular congregation, endless comments about my wardrobe choices and the length of my skirts, sexual harassment from colleagues, outdated or nonexistent maternity-leave policies.

The church I have served has been a mixed bag. Any female leaders in the church today are here because of the bravery of those who went before us, who had to break down so many barriers to make our path easier. It took brave, defiant, visionary people of all genders to get our church to the place where Mary Lucas and Beverley Shanley or the Philadelphia Eleven and the Washington Four could be admitted to priestly orders. Mary, Beverley, and Bishop John Bothwell, the bishop of Niagara who ordained those first women here in my St. Catharines neighborhood, went into that November ordination knowing that threats had been made against them for the path they were pursuing. I have been fortunate enough that for every roadblock I have slammed against because of opposition to women in leadership I have also had a vocal cadre of others—often men—ready to stand up as allies in defending my right to be here.

I have been fortunate, but I am also wise not to forget that I am always working against several millennia of practice that told us that women's roles were restricted and women's voices needed to be silenced. I am the heir of the bravery of many women, including Anne Boleyn. But I am also the heir of the misogyny that labeled, demeaned, and dismissed Anne Boleyn, the same misogyny that allowed Henry VIII to put her to death and to move on with his life and with his next marriage with performative celebration and no backward glance. I am the heir of the misogyny that has framed Anne's execution as just desserts for a woman who was seen as too assertive and ambitious for her own good. I am the heir of the misogyny that has too often dismissed and demeaned and labeled and put to death impactful, faithful women.

That violence exemplified in Henry's signing the death warrant of the wife he had professed to love with all his heart, and then throwing a party—that violence is in the church too.

The church has a long history of sheltering sexual abusers and of disbelieving the voices of survivors or of invalidating the experiences of abuse because those experiences challenge entrenched power structures about who has authority and whose authority can't be challenged. The church has participated in stamping racist policies and abusive systems with some bankrupt notion of God's will. The church has given ammunition to agendas of hate, validity to teachings about the subjugation of women, the evils of nonheterosexual relationships, and even the support of owning and trading other human bodies in the transcontinental slave industry.

The patterns of demeaning and disempowering women, the violence of the patriarchy, didn't start with Anne, and they certainly didn't end with her either. They run as corrosive threads through the witness of faith and the history of the church.

Feminist DNA

The Bible is teeming with complex, inspiring, multilayered, nonconforming female leaders. The church has such an entrenched history of managing the roles that women are allowed to have that a lot of these stories have been overlooked or misrepresented.

Queen Esther of the Bible was selected by both Anne Boleyn and Queen Claude of France as a biblical mentor. I knew of Esther's story growing up in the church, but she wasn't part of our main slate of Sunday school teachings. The lead characters were people like Abraham, Isaac, Jacob, and Joseph, not to mention Noah, Adam and Eve, Moses, and then the various characters surrounding Jesus and his ministry. I had a vague idea of Esther as a beautiful and faithful woman who was to be admired and emulated for those qualities.

It has been surprising as an adult to become more familiar with Esther's story and the stories of other women in the Bible who find themselves in precarious positions, and whose beauty and appeal to powerful men become an important part of their story and their framing as faithful. It has been surprising to preach on these texts and to come across words and commentaries on these stories that were not part of my Sunday school story times.

Women are infrequently the main characters in our biblical narratives, and when they are, it was easy as a child in the church to read them through the same fairy-tale lens that I had learned from so many other stories.

There are two descriptions of Sarah, the wife of Abraham, becoming the object of a foreign king's desire when traveling as a nomad with her husband, prior to settling with him in the Promised Land. In both stories, she was taken by these powerful rulers, and in the first case, raped by the Pharaoh.[5] Abraham did nothing to stop the violations against his wife for fear of his own life and well-being, and in fact, encouraged Sarah to be taken so that he himself would be protected rather than targeted. I was told these stories in a way that made it seem like Sarah's beauty was the point of the story, rather than God's intentional intervention in protecting her and overriding the assumed power structure with a care for this powerless nomadic woman.

There is the story of Ruth, also a foreigner, also powerless, also finding herself extremely vulnerable as a widowed woman in a strange land. Her beauty and desirability were framed as the good, admirable, and central things about her. She had to seduce a powerful landowner, Boaz, to provide safety, security, and a home for her and her mother-in-law Naomi. I guess her story would have turned out differently if she hadn't been beautiful. I guess she wouldn't have had to leverage her body into a safe living situation, but then she and Naomi would likely have died.

Ruth was a non-Israelite who became the savior of her vulnerable mother-in-law and then the great-grandmother of King David. Her story contradicts the concern for racial purity that rears its head through the Hebrew Scriptures, framing the great David as one with a mixed bloodline and telling a story of salvation that is intentionally concerned with the lives of women who would otherwise be counted as nothing. These are powerful things to take from the story, but a word of sorrow should also be offered for how Ruth had to allow herself to be used and objectified to keep herself and her loved one alive. The exploitation of women runs as a constant narrative, as does the scriptural insistence that God cares about these women, about their dignity and well-being, in a way that defies cultural conventions of the time.

Ruth's great grandson David would have his own unhinged desire on full display when he was at the height of his powers. His most famous liaison was with the married woman Bathsheba. As with Anne Boleyn, denying a king who has decided what (or who) he wants is rarely an available choice. David wanted Bathsheba, and he took her. He had her husband strategically killed in battle and made her his wife. Bathsheba has too often been framed as a temptress responsible for leading David astray, even though there is nothing to suggest that David's "having" her involved consent on her part. She was taken to his bed, and she gave birth to the king's offspring—the heroic and wise King Solomon.

Once again, there is a narrative surprise on the pages of the Bible. A prophet of God boldly called David to account for his murderous and exploitative behavior, risking his life to tell the king he did wrong. He wasn't just speaking back to David; he was also speaking up for Bathsheba and the many women like her who find themselves the target of powerful and anointed bullies.

Both Bathsheba and Ruth appear in the genealogy of Jesus (a highly unusual feature on a patriarchal bloodline), along with two other women, Tamar and Rahab, in the long list of men. Tamar was known for tricking her father-in-law Judah into having sex with her after her husband died so that she could become pregnant and continue the family bloodline—also assuring her own protection within the family. Rahab was a prostitute, not Jewish, who helped some Israelite spies and later married into the Jewish people. Of course, Mary is also listed in Jesus's bloodline. Jesus's mother was the object of scandal and potential danger due to her pregnancy outside of marriage. The church has forever labeled her as "Virgin," but her story starts with her tarnished reputation and her being at the mercy of her fiancé, Joseph, to save her and her unborn baby from certain destitution and possible death. We take Mary's virginal status as the ultimate compliment, a title of honor, failing to acknowledge how strange it is to suggest that Mary's sexual purity prior to Jesus's birth is the defining thing about her.

Woven through the Judeo-Christian faith is the DNA for claiming the impact, the influence, the dignity and worth of women in contradiction to the sexual labels otherwise used to frame and contain their stories. It's not that the Christian church didn't become the coziest of bedfellows with the patriarchy anyway, but knowing that women's stories were there too, and that they mattered, that they shaped this faith that I serve, that's not nothing.

Advances and Clawbacks

With the death of Henry VIII's son Edward VI in 1553, what had been a more theoretical debate about the ability of women to be leaders became a live conversation. Mary, the first child of Henry VIII, became the anointed monarch of England. Hot out of the gates was John Knox with his tract *The First Blast of the Trumpet Against the Monstrous Regiment of Women* deriding female leadership as being against God, natural law, and moral justice.

Knox's folly had an upside. He hadn't taken issue with Mary and her Catholicism. He attacked Mary's gender. When Elizabeth came to the throne, many evangelicals were strongly motivated to take Knox to task for his words, as they now had a Protestant hope and defender in England. Merely claiming Elizabeth as an able ruler was no response to Knox's arguments, and so a variety of Protestant men with relatively influential platforms were suddenly defending the right and ability of women to rule.[6]

John Aylmer was one of the first to jump into the fray. Aylmer had been raised to leadership under Anne Boleyn, had gone on to tutor the ill-fated Jane Grey,[7] and had kept his powder dry enough to survive the persecution of Mary. His words from *An Harbor for Faithful and True Subjects Against the Late Blown Blast Concerning the Government of Women* sound somewhat foolish to our modern ears:

> If nature have given it them by birth, how dare we pull it from them by violence? . . . If He able women, shall we unable them? If He meant not that they should minister, He could have provided other. Therefore, the safest way is to let Him do His will. . . . It is a plain argument that for some secret purpose He mindeth the female should reign and govern.[8]

The takeaway from his rather fence-sitting argument is: "If there isn't anyone better, then why get upset?" It was hardly a ringing endorsement for female leadership, although interestingly, he referred to Anne Boleyn as an example for why a female ruler should be accepted, crediting her with "banishing the beast of Rome" from England. He asked, "Was there ever in England a greater feat wrought by any man than this was by woman?"[9]

If things were looking up for women in leadership, first under Mary I and then more convincingly under Elizabeth I, those gains were quickly clawed back. Feminists have a mixed judgment to pronounce on Elizabeth I. While she was a strong, effective, inspiring leader, in considering her succession plan, she was nonetheless steeped in patriarchal assumptions, even as she spent forty-five years reigning in contradiction to them. "I know I have but the body of a weak and feeble woman," she is quoted as saying, "but I have the heart and stomach of a king, and of a king of England too." When Elizabeth died, it was her more distant male heir whom she named as successor, not the girls who were closer to her in bloodline.[10] She was able to embody a new possibility, but she was not able to support or enable that new possibility beyond her own individual life.

We shouldn't judge her too harshly. It is difficult for women in leadership, when they are assailed by attacks on their authority because of their gender and spend so much of their time and energy justifying their right to be there, to be then also able to exit the patriarchal waters in which they are swimming and to chart a new path for women who are still to come. When you're constantly justifying your own position, it's hard to be visionary about the future.

In the groundwork of feminist influence that formed Anne in the early sixteenth century in France, Christine de Pizan was a figure that loomed large in the imaginations of strong women. At the turn of the fifteenth century, Christine de Pizan could imagine a great city of ladies that housed not just small numbers of elite women but women of all classes. This was a city built by women for women, a place where, in the company of other women, every citizen of the city would find herself supported and appreciated.[11]

In actuality, in the Middle Ages there had existed many "cities of ladies"—it was through monasticism and the abbeys housing communities of nuns that women were able to access education, pursue an alternative to marriage and motherhood, and in many ways self-govern. Despite the enthusiasm from female circles for the possibilities opened by the Reformation of the sixteenth century, it also came with a significant downside for women's leadership. As power and literacy and learning were taken out of the monastic world, including the abbeys, the alternative path for female leadership, autonomy, and specialized learning was vastly reduced. That patriarchal equilibrium, and the ways in which it ended up swinging back even when we seemed to have taken such huge steps forward, is all too visible in Anne's and her contemporaries' story.

A Counterpoint

My friend Alex is queer and divorced and grew up in the Roman Catholic Church. She considered a call to ordained ministry, but women can't be ordained in her church. The church would have been well served by Alex in a leadership role. Alex's ability to digest, synthesize, and respond to vast quantities of political and philosophical information is unparalleled, and to those gargantuan intellectual gifts, Alex brings a deep well of compassion, a wicked sense of humor, and a fierce commitment to social justice. She doesn't just care about people in a theoretical sort of way, she has a remarkable ability to see what kinds of actions, policies, and personal commitment can materially make people's lives better. The church may have missed out, but the world is well served by Alex's work with those living with poverty and addiction.

Alex asked me to consider this question, the imprint of misogyny on the Church of England. It didn't begin with Anne, certainly, but a through line of assumptions about the role and voice of women, a denigrating of women's stories, a silencing of women's voices, runs from the start of the church in sixteenth-century England to today in ways that have been hard to shake, even when the church has radically and quite rapidly changed its stance on women in leadership just in my lifetime.

"I wonder about Elizabeth though," she mused. "Elizabeth's leadership was accepted. Elizabeth is well regarded. Elizabeth was able to be this sort of unicorn in the history of politics and the church where she just really didn't get diminished or dismissed in the expected ways. She rose above the gender politics of her day, and her reign is generally held in high esteem."

I agreed. "So what are you saying?" I asked.

"Well, Elizabeth didn't come from nowhere," she reasoned. "She was the daughter of Anne. She took Anne's DNA and some of her distinct characteristics and imprinted that on the church too, in this way that was basically accepted."

"So you think there was a correction to the misogyny too?" I asked.

Alex nodded. Alex had been a server in her church when she was younger and had gone to her local Roman Catholic Church a few years prior to our conversation asking to be a server again. Because Alex is divorced and married to a woman, she was not welcome to be involved in leading worship. Alex has suffered personal harm because of the church's misogyny.

There are a lot of stories of personal harm in the Anglican Church too. Countless. "But maybe there have been some counteractive forces too," Alex said. "Like maybe the misogyny has been tempered, because of influences like Anne—whether it's been named or not."

A Circle of Women and a Spirit of Reform

I have continued to reflect on Alex's words. My experience in the church has had its challenges but has been predominantly positive. My mother grew up in a church where women couldn't read or serve in church services, let alone lead and preach, and just one generation later, I grew up in a church where women can, and do, hold the highest offices of power. In October 2025, the Anglican Church appointed the first female archbishop of Canterbury, meaning that a woman is now the global figurehead of the Anglican Communion. I have served in a church where, more often than not, my voice is valued and my leadership recognized. The Anglican Church has pursued other paths of change as well, like the celebration of equal marriage, the creation of rites of name changes for transgender people who have transitioned, and reconciliation with Indigenous peoples who were so harmed by the agenda of colonization in which the Christian church participated.

While not diminishing the pain that my forebears experienced or that women in leadership in our church still face today, I also recognize a remarkable openness to change that has allowed new possibilities about who can speak and serve and offer and how they can do that.

I suspect that there are general things about the spirit of Anne's age that did get baked into the church that she started, as well as specific things about Anne and the influential circle of women who formed her that planted the seeds five hundred years ago for new directions in the church today.

Anne's exposure to reformist ideals was through the female leaders she met as a teenager growing up in the royal courts of Europe. If we consider what was of greatest interest to the early female reformers of Europe, including Queen Claude and Marguerite d'Angoulême, it was specifically having access to the Scriptures and it was generally the permission to be intellectually curious and to imagine that the world, and the systems of power, could change.

Specifically, the Protestant principle of translating the Bible into the language of the people and then providing access to the Bible through printed materials and education is a direct contradiction to one of the most basic and long-standing ways that women have been disenfranchised from religious leadership.[12] If access to religious knowledge is limited to the elite language of Latin, and if mostly only elite men have access to learning Latin, then religious participation is largely controlled by educated men in power.

These women were able to leave an indelible mark and steer the course of world-altering events because they lived in a time and place where suddenly that not only felt possible, but it was also happening before their eyes.

They didn't all make it out unscathed, and Anne suffered in body and reputation significant violence as she threw herself into the possibilities this new world was teasing, and paid the price for the ways in which that new world was still so much a product of the past, for how fiercely those in power will fight to keep power.

But maybe there were some inoculating seeds planted by those brave women of that different time. At the heart, those seeds were about the basic principle of reform: a commitment to the knowledge that we're not a finished product and that we must be ready to consider a new possibility, try something that hasn't been done yet, or even return to a path that we had lost, and that doing so is an act of profound faithfulness.

Malcolm Gladwell would say that there is a tipping point where there are enough representatives of a particular category of people in a particular space where they cease to be tokens or outliers and instead become able to offer their skills in much the same way the majority group would do.

I imagine this tipping-point principle had a lot to do with why Anne thought she could be a power broker in the kingdom in the first place. It wasn't merely because she was uniquely ambitious or driven or visionary. It's also because she grew up surrounded by women offering leadership and expressing opinions and shaping the world around them. She saw herself as part of a team of women exerting influence in ways that Anne was brought up to see as relatively normal. Her daughter, Elizabeth, benefited from something of that tipping point too. She was able to see her stepmother, Kateryn, write and publish and provide materials for the church and the kingdom; when Henry was off in Europe, Kateryn acted as regent. Elizabeth connected with the writings of Marguerite d'Angoulême and possibly received, or knew of, her mother's books and reading materials, normalizing a world of education and learning and leadership which Elizabeth would inhabit and shape.

Over the years of serving in church leadership, I have witnessed numerous little girls want to put on my liturgical vestments and "play priest." They see a woman at the front, and they imagine that could be them too. Little boys in my congregations have told their mothers that their image of God is of a blonde lady, much the same as how so many of us grew up thinking that God was a man because that's who we saw at the front of our churches addressing the divine.

The church has gotten a whole lot wrong . . . and some things right. This circle of female leadership got sewn into the fabric of the church too. People like me—like Mary Lucas and Beverley Shanley, like Bishop John Bothwell, like the Philadelphia Eleven and the Washington Four and the bishops who ordained those trailblazing women, like the first female Archbishop of Canterbury Sarah Mullally, like my daughter and my son who both care so deeply about being part of a church that fights misogyny—have been blessed by the multicolored fabric of our church's story.

CHAPTER 22

The Riverbed

"That's why the counternarrative is so important," I said to my husband as we were talking through my work about Anne Boleyn on the patio one afternoon. I was on my soapbox about the male-dominated slant on how history has been told and who we have assumed the main characters to be. "We need the story of women's influence, of how female vision has shaped the world, and especially the church, that we now have."

"Is it really a counternarrative though?" Dan asked in response. "Or is there another way of looking at it?"

He wondered with me about the image of a riverbed. The riverbed is a container that doesn't just hold the water, its contours shape the water, direct it, and dictate how that water behaves. The water is what is visible, but it is the riverbed that is providing the form. The riverbed is responsive; as it is shaping the flow of the water it is also being changed by the water—rough edges of stones worn smooth, disruptions to the climate and the surrounding land impacting the shape of the bed beneath. Women's influence isn't a separate river or a different story; it is shot through everything that we think we know about why the water goes in the direction that it does.

He offered, too, the observation about forces. There is positive space, the big visible institutions and power structures, the large-scale bricks and mortar that fill up the stories that we tell. But then there is the negative space, the oxygenated air that is carried into those places between, the fluid that infiltrates and shapes what unfolds before our eyes. It is those shape-shifting forces that seep into everything and that wield power and influence that is remarkable, even when we fail to see it—especially, perhaps, when we fail to see it.

Anne and her story have taken up a lot of space. We have told her story in countless ways with much ink spilled and a bottomless well of fascination generated by examining the minutest details of her life.

And yet, because of our assumptions about who really has their hands on the levers of control, because of our well-entrenched habits of trying to fit women's stories into specific shapes within the grander narrative, the true nature of Anne's influence has not been recognized beyond scholarly circles. We noticed that she burned bright, that destruction and change followed in her wake. Because of our inability to see the more hidden, riverbed-like forms of female storytelling, collaboration, and the handing down of vision, influence, and belief, we have missed seeing not only Anne's impact, but how her impact is part of a foundation of female imagination that shaped her and then changed everything. We didn't notice the purpose and vision in Anne's fire, nor where the oxygen came from to get it going and to keep it burning beyond her early grave.

Sharon Jansen, who offers scholarship on women in leadership in Tudor England, discusses how her research led her to unexpected conclusions. In considering the lives of a few specific women who were put to death during the reign of Henry VIII for treason, she expected to find that they had been misunderstood victims of broader political forces. Instead, what she discovered is that women of all classes, backgrounds, educational levels, and circumstances were very involved in religious and political talk of the time:[1]

> Women were not silent in these congregations and were not only, nor even, following their husbands. Indeed, the authorities grew alarmed by the ardour with which London wives supported causes. . . . This female religious enthusiasm is usually to be glimpsed rather than counted. . . . We cannot know how many women converted others to an evangelical vocation and spurred them to action; how often the courage and zeal of women strengthened their husbands' faltering resolve. But we can guess.[2]

Her conclusions are very similar to those of Micheline White, whose research into the writings of Kateryn Parr has been so revelatory, not just in understanding Parr's impact but also in understanding how women were engaging with new ideas, reading the written word, interacting with books and with one another, and shaping a culture in which women were participating in politics and religion, literally from the margins. It has been specifically in studying the "marginalia"—written notes in the books that Kateryn owned and read—that Kateryn's voice and influence, particularly in the ways she intentionally presented herself and interacted with Henry, become more visible and audible.

In early-sixteenth-century England women did not exercise formal political power. They did not sit in Parliament, hold office, act as justices, or head armies. Yet the sixteenth century was a period when women participated in political comment and protest throughout western Europe.[3] Women did exercise widespread informal political power. That informal power is distinguishable from "authority"—power which is formally recognized and legitimated. Nonetheless, that informal power is not to be ignored or downplayed.[4]

Before the duchess of Sussex, Meghan Markle, evacuated the House of Windsor, she made a very quotable statement. She said that it upsets her when people say that we need to give women a voice. Instead, she said, "Women *have* a voice. They need to be empowered to use it. And people need to be encouraged to listen."

Jansen says something similar about the agency of women in the time of Anne Boleyn:

> The voices of other women have not been silenced. Women were present everywhere—in small towns, in the capital, in the midst of rebellion, and as part of conspiracies. And they were speaking out loud—to one another, to anyone who would listen, to the men who recorded their testimony. . . . [A]t stake were not only problems of succession and religious reformation but also much more fundamental problems of order and obedience.[5]

I have focused on Anne Boleyn and the most visible, powerful, and documented lives of the women in her orbit. However, Jansen's work, and the other seldom-seen stories of female power that I have woven through this book, are testimony to the vast scope of women's influence shaping that riverbed of human history and oxygenating the fires of change.

Historian Diarmaid MacCulloch claims that "the shape of the English Reformation was unique in Europe because it owed so much to two women . . . Queen Anne Boleyn and her daughter Queen Elizabeth. Mischievously, one might say it owed a good deal to a third, Queen Mary I, as well."[6]

He is right. But I would go further.

When I started this book, the image that kept coming to me was of a circle of women, wrapping their linked arms around the story of the English Reformation. My conversation with Dan shifted that image. Instead of hovering over, I now see these women's linked bodies and stories providing a foundation, giving the story a definite, and yet so easily unseen, shape.

If I were to try to represent the story that I was seeing, I would enlist my daughter Cecilia's artist's eye and vast talent to collaborate with me in bringing it to life. I want to visualize the church that I serve with a coven of women holding it with strong caretaking arms, shaping it with creativity and instinct and passion, correcting it with a strong push in a different direction. I would want to picture those women with their arms entwined with one another. And their arms are connected not because they liked and agreed with one another and lived as friends on this side of eternity; instead their arms are linked because in the greater picture of what this church is and what it could be, there is an abiding love that connects us all, even when we so passionately (and sometimes even violently) disagree.

In this picture, I would start with the quartet of women who taught Anne in her formative years what it looks like for women to lead, to set off on adventures, to provoke debate, to be curious, to enact change, to have principles, and to put those principles into concrete action: Margaret of Austria, Louise de Savoy, Queen Claude of France, and Marguerite d'Angoulême. The connective tissue that they provided for Anne and the way that she sought to lead and the ideas that she successfully championed—that needs to be painted in such vivid bright color that it cannot possibly be ignored.

I would put Catherine of Aragon in that picture. And she would be holding Anne's hand. They hated each other. Anne was cruel to Catherine. Catherine was far happier to hate Anne than their asshole husband. But Catherine was the mirror to Anne's determined, opinionated, steadfast ways. They both looked danger in the eye and pressed their foot to the pedal rather than backing down or picking the nicer, easier route. If Catherine hadn't been so fierce, Henry could have easily married Anne. There would have been no break from Rome. The Reformation in England, had it happened at all, would have looked very different. Obstacles in the river shape the river too.

Anne would be next. I would want her to look fearsome and strong and not at all pretty or nice. I would want Anne linked into the riverbed, but I would also want her holding that contradictory image of a white-hot flame. She has always lit up the pages of our history books, refusing to be erased or ignored, but our vision of her has been distorted.

I would link her arms to Kateryn Parr, a woman whom she likely never met, who was the more successful version of her brand of religious passion. Kateryn could hold that flame with Anne above the riverbed. Kateryn was more experienced when she married Henry. Her temperament was calmer. Kateryn claimed remarkable latitude in exerting influence and practicing scholarship in ways highly unusual for a woman at that time. The Reformation in England continued to burn because of her careful, considered, deeply intellectual, hardworking, and strong-willed ways.

The three other wives—Jane Seymour, Anna of Cleves, and Katherine Howard—would need to be there. Jane had a wiliness and strong will that is often overlooked because she was so successful at playing nice and doing what was expected of her. Anna turned a humiliating situation into one of noteworthy personal wealth and autonomy. Katherine was young, high-spirited, and passionate. Very little sympathy has been paid her because she has been judged as silly and stupid for having the affair, at least in affection and words, for which she was accused. She also did not deserve to die at the hands of her violent husband.

Mary and Elizabeth would fill out the picture. Whomever they linked arms with, I would want them to link arms with one another. They were seventeen years apart in age. Mary had every reason to hate Elizabeth, even being forced to act as a servant in Elizabeth's household when her half sister was born. Both would spend many years out of the line of succession and estranged from their father's temperamental affections. When Mary became queen, Elizabeth had to tread carefully and was imprisoned in the Tower of London on Mary's orders. She was housed in the same apartments where her mother spent her final days. At any point Elizabeth could have been accused of trying to overthrow her sister, and there were always Protestant factions who were willing to organize to do just that. Mary must have contemplated putting Elizabeth to death. Mary was desperately mistreated by her father, and it was much easier to blame Elizabeth's hated mother, Anne, for that than for Mary to lash out at Henry, the king.

They had every reason to be enemies in life, and the history books recount how they fought for such vastly different versions of what the church should be. The history books also reveal a relationship of loving care for much of their early lives between these two traumatized and disenfranchised sisters.

And MacCulloch is right. They were both influential in creating the church that would eventually take root in England, even if it has been framed as one of them winning and the other losing. I suspect that they both acted with measures of self-interest, ego, duty, trauma, and genuine faith.

Jane Grey would be there with them, the youngest royal woman to be executed for treason. She, like Elizabeth, was mentored and formed by Kateryn Parr. She was a remarkable intellectual, a fiercely pious Protestant, and the world was robbed of her leadership when she was put to death by her cousin Mary for forces well beyond both women's control. I would want them to be linking arms, all of them, because this is exactly the representation that I want and that we need.

None of these women could be considered for any list of saints without significantly downplaying large parts of their lives. They can't be dismissed so easily if they're allowed to be human. We can't overlook how their story is also about us, about who we have always been and about how we could be different.

If we let them all be in the picture, then there would need to be a lot of room left for others. There would be the biblical women, many of whom have had their stories diminished or distorted, but their influence and faithfulness have never been truly extinguished. There would be the mystics and abbesses, the desert mothers, the cross-dressers, female deacons and early church leaders and preachers, the women of self-possession who have fanned the flames of faith and invited people to draw near to God and to another possibility of how we are to live.

Because it's my picture, I would want my grandmothers and mother represented—Jean, Elma, and Susan—showing something of the bravery and strength, the intelligence and loving-kindness, the curiosity and perseverance that they offered, and the ways that they each figured out how to draw outside of the lines of what was expected for them. There are men in my mind's eye too. Men have had ample opportunity to have their stories made visible, but I would want to make room for depicting how impactful it is when they are also willing to be supporting characters. I have been profoundly blessed by having a father and grandfathers and brother and husband and son and many other strong male friends intentionally lend their voices toward supporting me specifically and supporting women's voices and offerings in general.

We could include, if we had enough paint and a big enough canvas, all the stories of faithful women that we know. But for each one of the women who has made it onto the margins of our historical records, there are countless others—real women, with hopes and dreams and ambitions and brave choices and nonconforming ways, with flaws and beauty and some measure of holiness—who have also slipped through the cracks, oxygenated the air we breathe, lit the fires that occasionally burn long and hot enough to transform the world, and formed the riverbed that shapes the whole story.

Acknowledgments

A question that I get asked frequently is "What possessed you to want to write a book about Anne Boleyn?" The answer to that question starts with my brother, Andrew. He's a tough crowd, which made his interest in Anne the genesis of this whole project. My parents, John and Susan, also deserve thanks in this origin story. They raised us in a home where historical figures got to be main characters in our collective imagination. The reason Anne Boleyn has always fascinated me is because of my parents.

Thank you to my readers along the way: Ann Kelly, David Harrison, Faith Whittaker, Liam Squires, Scott Brain, Kevin Powell, Alice Degan, Justin Anthony, Elizabeth Hadaway, Adam MacNeil, and Valear Howsam. Thank you to Russ Pettifer for research assistance and passing along a number of papers to me that were important in forming the ideas in this book. Thank you to Allison Lynn, Anita Djurkovic, and Brian and Beth Kerley for key encouragement at times when I was doubting my ability to see this project through. I offer a special word of thanks to Ben Crosby for a detailed scholarly read of the material (although any errors still in the document are my own responsibility). And I need to give a tremendous shout-out to Carolyn Boll and Susan Kingsley, the two most engaged, thoughtful, insightful, and generous readers a writer could ever imagine. This would be a very different book if it weren't for them.

St. George's Church has continued to be a community that encourages me as a writer, asking about my ideas, listening to early presentations of the material, and not just accepting but enjoying their priest having this other life moonlighting as an author. Tom Vaughan, Linda Telega, Brad Barnham, and Cheryl Bergie would be the flag bearers of this church's above-and-beyond support. In various ways, it was this cohort who championed my taking both a writing leave and a sabbatical in order to complete this book on a notably ambitious timeline. My delight in having several months of focused writing time is complemented by the delight and gratitude that I have for serving in this remarkable congregation.

Thank you to Fiona Hallowell as the editor of this book. This is our first time working together, and I have felt from our first conversation that she shared and understood my vision for why Anne's story would be captivating and important for a wider audience. Thank you to Church Publishing Incorporated for providing me a writerly home for the past eight years and three books.

I need to conclude these acknowledgments with my thanks to my husband, Dan, and my children, Cecilia and Gordon. They take genuine interest in my ponderings and respond with understanding for my early mornings and constantly distracted thoughts. Cecilia and Gordon are two of the most thoughtful and wise-beyond-their-years human beings I have ever known, and they are the inspiration for why I want to be part of populating our world with the best kinds of stories.

APPENDIX I

Key Characters

While not exhaustive, this appendix provides a quick reference for some of the many players in the story of Anne Boleyn and the Tudor Court.

**Some names appear with an asterisk, indicating different spellings in different historical records and accounts. I have chosen one spelling and used that consistently through the book.*

Marguerite d'Angoulême (also known as Marguerite of Navarre) (1492–1549) was "a princess of France, Duchess of Alençon and Berry, and Queen of Navarre by her second marriage to King Henry II of Navarre. Her brother became King of France, as Francis I, and the two siblings were responsible for the celebrated intellectual and cultural court and salons of their day in France. . . . As an author and a patron of humanists and reformers, she was an outstanding figure of the French Renaissance."[1]

***Catherine of Aragon** (1485–1536)—Youngest daughter of Isabella I of Castile and Ferdinand II of Aragon. She was the first wife of King Henry VIII, after being married briefly to his older brother Arthur.

Elizabeth Boleyn, née Howard (1480–1538)—Countess of Wiltshire, an English noblewoman, and the mother of Anne Boleyn. Her brother was Thomas Howard, duke of Norfolk.

George Boleyn, Viscount Rochford (1504–1536)—Brother of Anne Boleyn (likely younger). He was a courtier and politician. He was married to Jane Boleyn, but they didn't have children. He was executed along with Anne and the other men accused of committing adultery with her.

Jane Boleyn, née Parker, Viscountess Rochford (1505–1542)—Wife to George Boleyn and likely one of the informants against her husband and Anne Boleyn in their downfall. She was later executed with Katherine Howard, Henry's fifth wife, as a coconspirator in Katherine's adultery.

Mary Boleyn (Carey) (1499–1543)—She was married to William Carey, with whom she had two children: Catherine and Henry. She was Henry's mistress for an unknown length of time and there was speculation that at least one of the children might have been the king's. In 1534, behind her sister Anne's back (then queen), she married William Stafford.

Thomas Boleyn (1477–1539)—Earl of Wiltshire, first earl of Ormond, first viscount Rochford. Thomas was an English diplomat and politician and the father of Anne Boleyn. Married to Elizabeth Boleyn.

Charles Brandon, First Duke of Suffolk (1484–1545)—A military leader and courtier, and ultimately one of Henry VIII's closest friends. Brandon's third wife was Henry's sister Mary. Their daughter Frances was the mother of Jane Grey. Both Brandon and Mary were opposed to Anne Boleyn.

William Brereton (ca. 1487/1490–1536)—A courtier from a prominent family who was among the men accused of adultery and treason with Anne Boleyn. He was found guilty and executed.

Cardinal Lorenzo Campeggio (1474–1539)—An Italian politician and cardinal of the church.[2] In 1528, he was sent by the pope to England to the hear the case for divorce between Henry VIII and Catherine of Aragon. It is likely during this time that Henry's letters to Anne were stolen from her personal belongings and smuggled to Rome as evidence against the divorce.

Sir Nicholas Carew (1496–1539)—An English courtier and diplomat during the reign of King Henry VIII. He was appointed to the Privy Chamber in 1528, possibly because of the influence of Anne Boleyn, to whom he was related. He was eventually part of a pro-Catholic alliance that worked to remove Anne from power. Carew was executed in 1539 for his alleged part in the Exeter Conspiracy, a plot to depose the king and replace him with Cardinal Reginald Pole.[3]

George Cavendish (1497–1562)—An English writer, best known for writing the biography of Cardinal Wolsey.

Eustace Chapuys (1489–1556)—A diplomat who served Charles V as imperial ambassador to England from 1529 until 1545 and is best known for his extensive and detailed correspondence.[4]

Charles V, Holy Roman Emperor (1500–1558)—Son of Catherine of Aragon's sister Joanna and Philip the Handsome (son of Emperor Maximilian I). Charles V was elected as the Holy Roman Emperor in 1519. He was archduke of Austria from 1519 to 1556, king of Spain from 1516 to 1556, and lord of the Netherlands as titular duke of Burgundy from 1506 to 1555.[5]

Queen Claude of France (1499–1524)—Claude of France was queen of France from January 1, 1515, as the wife of King Francis I, as well as duchess of Brittany in her own right. She died in 1524. She was the eldest daughter of King Louis XII of France.[6] She gave birth to seven children.

Anna of Cleves (1515–1557)—"In March 1539, negotiations for Anna's marriage to Henry began. Henry believed he needed to form a political alliance with her brother, William . . . a leader of the Protestants of Western Germany, to strengthen his position against potential attacks from Catholic France and the Holy Roman Empire. [Anna] arrived in England in December 1539 and married Henry a week later, but the marriage was declared unconsummated after six months and [Anna] was not crowned queen consort. Following the annulment, Henry gave her a generous settlement and [Anna] was thereafter known as *the King's Beloved Sister*. Remaining in England, she lived to see the reigns of Henry's children, Edward VI and Mary I, and attended Mary's coronation in 1553. [Anna] outlived the rest of Henry's wives."[7]

Thomas Cranmer (1489–1556)—Thomas Cranmer was a theologian, leader of the English Reformation and archbishop of Canterbury during the reigns of Henry VIII, Edward VI, and, for a short time, Mary I. He is honored as a martyr in the Church of England, imprisoned and then executed during Mary's reign for his evangelical beliefs. His lasting legacy has been the writing/curation of the Book of Common Prayer, England's first prayer book to include the complete forms of service for daily and Sunday worship in English.[8] The Book of Common Prayer continues to be used in Anglican churches across the world.

Thomas Cromwell (1485–1540)—An English statesman and lawyer who began his time in the court under the jurisdiction of Cardinal Wolsey. He rose to prominence during the fight for Henry's annulment and the severing of England from the Roman Catholic Church. He served as chief minister to King Henry VIII from 1534 to 1540, when he was beheaded on orders of the king.[9]

John Dudley, First Duke of Northumberland (1504–1553)—Dudley became one of Henry VIII's closer advisors toward the end of Henry's life and was appointed to the Regency Council to lead England until Edward VI was of age to rule as king. He helped to solidify the Protestantism of the English church under Edward VI. When Edward Seymour, duke of Somerset, fell out of favor and then was executed, Dudley was essentially acting as sole regent of England. He was seen as the driving force in Edward's naming of Jane Grey (Dudley's daughter-in-law) as his successor. Dudley was put to death when that plan failed, and Princess Mary came to the throne instead.

King Edward VI (1537–1553)—The only surviving son of Henry VIII. Edward was the son of Jane Seymour and king of England from January 1547 (when he was nine years old) until his death. He was the first monarch of England to be raised as a Protestant.[10]

Queen Elizabeth I (1533–1603)—Elizabeth was the daughter of King Henry VIII and the only surviving child of Anne Boleyn. She was the last and longest reigning monarch of the Tudors and continued to lead the English Reformation after the efforts of her half sister, Mary, to return England to Roman Catholicism. Her time on the throne was seen as so consequential culturally, politically, and religiously that it has been named the Elizabethan era.[11]

Esther, originally Hadassah, is the heroine of the Book of Esther in the Hebrew Bible. According to the biblical narrative, which is set in the Achaemenid Empire, the Persian king Xerxes chooses Esther to marry, and she is able to use her position in the court to save the Jewish people.[12] Both Anne Boleyn and Queen Claude of France saw Esther as a biblical role model.

Francis I, King of France (1494–1547)—The son of Charles, count of Angoulême, and Louise of Savoy. He succeeded his father-in-law Louis XII (father of his wife, Queen Claude, and also Francis's cousin), who died without a legitimate son, becoming the king of France in 1515.[13]

St. Frideswide (650–727)—An English princess and abbess. She is credited as the foundress of a monastery later incorporated into Christ Church, Oxford.

Lady Jane Grey (1537–1554)—Jane was the granddaughter of Henry VIII's sister Mary Tudor and was appointed by her cousin Edward VI to serve as monarch upon his death because her Protestant beliefs mirrored his own and he wanted to bypass his two half sisters (particularly his Catholic sister, Mary). Jane took the throne in July 1553. She is known as the "Nine Days Queen" because she and, most importantly, her supporters were quickly overtaken by Princess Mary. Jane was put to death for treason by Mary in 1554.

Lord Guildford Dudley (1535–1554)—Married to the ill-fated Jane Grey. Guildford was the youngest surviving son of John Dudley, who was seen as the engineer of Jane's accession to the throne. Guildford was put to death for treason along with Jane Grey.

Haman is the main antagonist in the Book of Esther, who according to the Hebrew Bible was an official in the court of the Persian empire under

King Ahasuerus, commonly identified as Xerxes I.[14] Anne Boleyn's almoner, John Skip, likened Haman to Thomas Cromwell in a famous sermon on Passion Sunday 1536.

***Katherine Howard** (1524–1542)—Fifth wife of Henry VIII and cousin of Anne Boleyn. She was married and made queen in July 1540 after Henry annulled his marriage to Anna of Cleves. She was executed for adultery in February 1542.

Thomas Howard, Third Duke of Norfolk (1473–1554)—Uncle of both Anne Boleyn and Katherine Howard. A nobleman and politician, regularly involved in the politics and machinations of Henry's court. After falling from favor in 1546, Norfolk was stripped of his dukedom and imprisoned in the Tower of London, avoiding execution when Henry VIII died. He was released on the accession of the Roman Catholic Queen Mary I, whom he aided in securing the throne.[15]

Margaret of Austria (1480–1530) "was Governor of the Habsburg Netherlands from 1507 to 1515 and again from 1519 until her death in 1530. She was the first of many female regents in the Netherlands. She was variously the Princess of Asturias, Duchess of Savoy, and was born an Archduchess of Austria. . . . She was engaged for three marriage alliances, and completed two, but both husbands died within a few years. . . . [She was successful], according to most historians, [in] the highly important role of regent or governor of the Habsburg Netherlands, for firstly her father Maximilian I, Holy Roman Emperor, then her nephew Charles V . . . were both forced to spend most of their time in Germany."[16] Margaret's brother, Philip the Handsome, was married to Catherine of Aragon's sister Joanna. Her first husband, John, was the brother of Catherine of Aragon.

Queen Mary I (1516–1558)—The daughter of King Henry VIII and only surviving child of Catherine of Aragon. She was crowned queen in July 1553 after several chaotic days when her cousin Jane Grey was appointed queen by her brother Edward's succession plan. She was also queen of Spain as the wife of King Philip II from January 1556 until her death in 1558.[17]

She led the Counter-Reformation in England, reversing the work of the Reformation and returning England, briefly, to Roman Catholicism.

Sir Thomas More (1478–1535)—More, venerated in the Catholic Church as Saint Thomas More, was an English lawyer, judge, social philosopher, author, statesman, theologian, and noted Renaissance humanist.[18] He succeeded Cardinal Wolsey as lord chancellor of England and was executed for refusing to sign the Act of Succession and the Oath of Supremacy because he did not believe the government had the spiritual authority to set King Henry as the "Supreme Head" of the church.

Henry Norris (1482–1536)—As Groom of the Stool to the king, he was one of the people closest to Henry. He was a supporter of Anne Boleyn and among those accused of adultery with her. He was found guilty and executed.

Matthew Parker (1504–1575)—Chaplain to Anne Boleyn, Anne asked Parker to watch over Elizabeth should anything happen to her. Parker was Elizabeth's first archbishop of Canterbury and was seen, along with Thomas Cranmer and later Richard Hooker, as one of the primary theologians in shaping Anglican thought.[19]

***Kateryn Parr** (1512–1548)—The sixth and final wife of Henry VIII, married in July 1543. She was twice married and widowed before Henry. She married Thomas Seymour (brother of Jane Seymour) after Henry's death. She died from complications in childbirth when she gave birth to a daughter, Mary, who is not known to have survived beyond childhood. Kateryn was the first woman to publish in print an original work under her own name in the English language.

Henry Percy, Sixth Earl of Northumberland (1502–1537)—He was said to have been in love with Anne Boleyn, and they were betrothed. He was forced by Cardinal Wolsey to marry Mary Talbot instead, which resulted in a reportedly unhappy marriage.

King Philip II of Spain (1527–1598)—Sometimes known in Spain as Philip the Prudent, was king of Spain from 1556, king of Portugal from

1580, and king of Naples and Sicily from 1554 until his death in 1598. He was married to Queen Mary in 1554. He was the son of the Holy Roman Emperor Charles V and therefore a cousin to Mary.[20]

Popes During Anne's Time:

Julius II—Pope from 1503 to 1513. Pope Julius II gave the dispensation for Henry VIII to marry Catherine of Aragon, his brother's widow, in 1509.

Leo X—Pope from 1513 to 1521.

Clement VII—Pope from 1523 to 1534, the critical period during Henry's annulment suit, marriage to Anne, and break from Rome.

***Nicholas Sander (or Sanders)** (1530–1581)—A writer and English Roman Catholic priest. The writings of Sander formed the basis of later Catholic histories of the English Reformation and its martyrology. His major work in this direction was his unfinished *De Origine Ac Progressu Schismatis Anglicani* (*The Rise and Growth of the Anglican Schism*). This had many editions and was used as a basis for other works.[21]

Louise of Savoy (Louise de Savoie) (1476–1531)—A French noblewoman and mother to King Francis I and Marguerite d'Angoulême. She was politically active and served as the regent of France in 1515, in 1525–1526, and in 1529, during the absence of her son.[22]

Jane Seymour (ca. 1508–1537)—The third wife of King Henry VIII and mother of Edward VI. She died from complications in childbirth less than two weeks after Edward's birth. She was the only wife of Henry VIII to receive a queen's funeral. Henry is buried with her.

Edward Seymour, First Duke of Somerset (ca. 1500–1552)—Edward was the brother of Jane Seymour and a politician who was involved in the plan to replace Anne Boleyn as queen. Although he supported the pro-Catholic faction at that time, he was ultimately a strong evangelical. He served as lord protector of England from 1547 to 1549 during the minority of his nephew King Edward VI. He was forced out of power in 1549 after instituting religious measures that were highly unpopular and for general mismanagement of the country. He was accused of high treason at the end of 1551 and executed at the beginning of 1552.[23]

John Skip (1495–1552)—The almoner to Anne Boleyn and the priest who preached the inflammatory sermon in 1536 against Thomas Cromwell. Skip was appointed bishop of Heresford in 1539.

***Mark Smeton (Smeaton)** (ca. 1512–1536)—Smeton was a court musician and the first to be arrested and accused of committing adultery with Anne Boleyn. He was the only one to confess to the charges, but it has been alleged that his confession was gained through torture or perhaps the promise of a commuted sentence. He was found guilty and executed along with the other men.

Arthur Tudor (1486–1502)—Eldest son of King Henry VII, first husband of Catherine of Aragon, first in line to the throne of England, and prince of Wales until his early death.

Margaret Tudor (1489–1541)—Henry VIII's sister and queen of Scotland from 1503 until 1513 by marriage to King James IV. She then served as regent of Scotland during her son's minority and was the grandmother of Mary, Queen of Scots.[24]

Mary Tudor (1496–1533) was an English princess who was briefly queen of France as the third wife of King Louis XII. Louis was more than thirty years her senior. Mary was the fifth child of Henry VII of England and Elizabeth of York, and the youngest to survive infancy. Following Louis's death, Mary married Charles Brandon, first duke of Suffolk. Performed secretly in France, the marriage occurred without the consent of Mary's brother Henry VIII. Henry eventually pardoned the couple after they paid a large fine. Mary had four children with Suffolk. Through her oldest daughter, Frances, she was the maternal grandmother of Lady Jane Grey, the disputed queen of England for nine days in July 1553.[25]

William Tyndale (ca. 1494–1536)—An English biblical scholar and leader of the English Reformation. His translation of the New Testament from the original Greek circulated widely around England, although doing this work sent him into exile. His writing *The Obedience of a Christian Man* was of great importance in giving Henry, Anne, and their team a case for breaking from the pope's authority, but Tyndale spoke publicly against Henry's divorce from Catherine of Aragon. Tyndale was arrested in exile outside of Brussels, imprisoned, and put to death as a heretic. His translations were used in subsequent publications of the English Bible, including "The Great Bible," authorized by Henry VIII himself, despite Henry's animosity toward Tyndale for condemning his split from Catherine.[26]

Francis Weston (1511–1536)—A gentleman of the Privy Chamber and friend of the king who was among the men accused of adultery and treason and put to death with Anne Boleyn.[27]

Cardinal Thomas Wolsey (1473–1530)—Wolsey was a cardinal of the Roman Catholic Church and lord chancellor to King Henry VIII, the king's chief advisor. By 1514 he was controlling most matters of state. He was charged with treason but died on his way to London to answer the charges.[28]

George Wyatt (1554–1624)—He was a writer and the first biographer of Henry VIII's second queen, Anne Boleyn. His grandfather was Sir Thomas Wyatt the Elder.[29]

Thomas Wyatt (1503–1542)—Sir Thomas Wyatt was a sixteenth-century English politician, ambassador, and lyric poet credited with introducing the sonnet to English literature. He was known as a friend and admirer of Anne Boleyn, and several of his poems are assumed to be written about her.[30]

*__King Xerxes__—In the biblical Book of Esther, the Persian king Ahasuerus is traditionally identified as Xerxes I, who ruled the Achaemenid Empire from 486 to 465 BC.[31] This is supported by scholars who believe the narrative of Esther is linked to the historical figure of Xerxes.

APPENDIX II

Timeline

December 16, 1485	Catherine of Aragon's birth
June 28, 1491	Henry VIII's birth, second son of Henry VII
1501 or 1507 (disputed)	Anne's birth
November 14, 1501	Marriage of Catherine and Arthur, Henry's brother
April 2, 1502	Arthur's death
April 21, 1509	Henry VII dies, Henry VIII becomes king
June 11, 1509	Henry VIII and Catherine of Aragon's marriage
1513	Anne in Margaret of Austria's court
February 18, 1516	Mary born to Catherine and Henry
1515–1521	Anne served in Queen Claude of France's court
June 15, 1519	Birth of Henry Fitzroy, the only illegitimate child of Henry VIII acknowledged by the king
March 1522	Anne's debut in the English court
1527	First petition to Rome to annul marriage of Henry VIII and Catherine of Aragon

November 29, 1530	Death of Cardinal Wolsey
1530–1531	Thomas Cromwell begins his rise to power in the service of Henry VIII
November 1532	Anne and Henry consummate their relationship in Calais on the way home from their time in France meeting Francis I
November 14, 1532	Thought to be the date that Henry and Anne made a formal commitment of marriage to one another
January 25, 1533	Official marriage of Henry and Anne
May 23, 1533	Decision that the king's marriage to Catherine had always been illegal
May 28, 1533	Henry's marriage to Anne was decreed legal
June 1, 1533	Anne's coronation
September 7, 1533	Elizabeth's birth
Late July 1534	Anne has a miscarriage or stillbirth
1535	Anne possibly has another pregnancy and miscarriage
June 22, 1535	Bishop Fisher's execution
July 6, 1535	Thomas More's execution
October 1535	Publishing of complete Bible in English by Miles Coverdale; despite being dedicated to Henry VIII, it was technically still banned
January 7, 1536	Death of Catherine of Aragon
January 24, 1536	Jousting accident
January 29 or 30, 1536	Anne has a stillbirth or miscarriage
March 11, 1536	Bill for the dissolution of the monasteries and all religious houses with an income of less than two hundred pounds a year
April 2, 1536	Passion Sunday sermon by John Skip

April 30, 1536	Mark Smeton arrested; confrontation between Henry and Anne
May 1, 1536	Jousting tournament; last time Henry saw Anne
May 2, 1536	Anne's arrest; Henry Norris and George Boleyn also arrested
May 4, 1536	William Brereton arrested
May 5, 1536	Francis Weston arrested
May 12, 1536	Trial of the men, minus George
May 15, 1536	George's trial, Anne's trial
May 17, 1536	Execution of the men
May 19, 1536	Anne's execution
May 30, 1536	Henry's marriage to Jane Seymour
July 22, 1536	Death of Henry's son, Henry Fitzroy
October 12, 1537	Birth of Edward to Henry VIII and Jane Seymour
October 24, 1537	Death of Jane Seymour
January 6, 1540	Marriage of Henry to Anna of Cleves
July 9, 1540	Marriage to Anna declared annulled
July 28, 1540	Marriage to Katherine Howard
February 13, 1542	Katherine Howard's execution
July 12, 1543	Marriage to Kateryn Parr
January 28, 1547	Death of Henry VIII, son Edward becomes King Edward VI
July 6, 1553	Death of Edward VI, Jane Grey is named queen
Approximately July 19, 1553	Mary, daughter of Henry VIII and Catherine of Aragon is named as queen
November 17, 1558	Death of Queen Mary I; Elizabeth I, daughter of Anne Boleyn, becomes queen

Endnotes

INTRODUCTION "I WANT TO READ THAT BOOK"

1. Tom Holland and Dominic Sandbrook, hosts, *The Rest Is History*, podcast, episode 74, "The Six Wives of Henry VIII," Apple Podcasts, July 12, 2021, 55 min., https://podcasts.apple.com/gb/podcast/the-six-wives-of-henry-viii/id1537788786?i=1000528555129.

PART I THE PROBLEM WITH ANNE

1. Eric Ives, *The Life and Death of Anne Boleyn* (Blackwell Publishing, 2004), 49.

CHAPTER 1 A BRIEF BIOGRAPHY

1. Ives, *Life and Death of Anne Boleyn*, 3.
2. Ibid., 17.
3. Ibid., 6.
4. L. Du Garde Peach, *Henry VIII* (Ladybird Books, 1973), 24.
5. "It was conventional for queens to have their jointures, the income from which could be used for patronage, gifts, luxuries and day-to-day expenses, but what made Anne unique, once Henry had finished transferring further vast quantities of property to her, was the sheer scale of her possessions. In 1535 alone, she gained an income of 5,056 pounds from these estates (worth over 5 million pounds today), considerably more than Catherine had received." From John Guy

and Julia Fox, *Hunting the Falcon: Henry VIII, Anne Boleyn, and the Marriage that Shook Europe* (HarperCollins Publishers, 2023), 283.

CHAPTER 2 THE CUTTING ROOM FLOOR

1. Marlow and Moss, hosts, discuss their reasons for depicting Anne Boleyn as they did in *Not Just the Tudors*, podcast, episode 63, "Henry VIII's Wives on Stage: Six—The Musical," Acast, November 22, 2021, 32 min., https://shows.acast.com/not-just-the-tudors/episodes/henryviiiswivesonstage-six-themusical.

PART II AN OLD WORLD FALLING APART, A NEW WORLD JUST BEGINNING

1. Emily Dickinson, "You cannot put a Fire out—," public domain.

CHAPTER 3 CATACLYSMIC CHANGE

1. Tracy Borman, *Anne Boleyn and Elizabeth I: The Mother and Daughter Who Forever Changed British History* (Atlantic Monthly Press, 2023), 210.
2. Ibid., 211.
3. Diarmaid MacCulloch, *All Things Made New: The Reformation and Its Legacy* (Oxford University Press, 2016), 1.
4. Andrew Pettegree, *Brand Luther: How an Unheralded Monk Turned His Small Town into a Center of Publishing, Made Himself the Most Famous Man in Europe—and Started the Protestant Reformation* (Penguin Press, 2015), 41.
5. This was known as "The Disputation Against Scholastic Theology."
6. Pettegree, *Brand Luther*, 52.
7. Ibid., 54. Pettegree notes that "the printing press made Luther's theses a public matter and would rapidly make of their author a controversial and notorious figure. . . . Luther's movement opened up a new era in the history of cheap print. It was a commercial as much as a theological revolution."
8. It is also not uncommon now for a priest in the Roman Catholic Church, or even occasionally in the Anglican Church, to assign a penance after hearing a person's confession. This might be the invitation to read a particular biblical passage and reflect on it. It may be the regular praying of the Lord's Prayer or other well-known Christian prayers. "Penance" has a connotation of punishment, but it is meant to be the offering of prayer and reflection that draws an individual back into relationship with God.
9. Pettegree, *Brand Luther*, 55.

10. Ibid., 56.
11. Ginny Justice, "The Role of Indulgences in the Building of New Saint Peter's Basilica," Rollins Scholarship Online, April 28, 2011, https://scholarship.rollins.edu/mls/7/.
12. Charles Taylor, *A Secular Age* (Harvard University Press, 2007), 69.
13. Pettegree, *Brand Luther*, 61.
14. Ibid., 75.
15. This was called *Defense of the Seven Sacraments*, written in 1521 and dedicated to Pope Leo X. It is thought to have been mostly penned by Thomas More.
16. Diarmaid MacCulloch, *Christianity: The First Three Thousand Years* (Viking, 2009), 569.
17. MacCulloch, *All Things Made New*, 105.
18. Ibid., 114.
19. Suzannah Lipscomb, host, discusses these books with Dr. Owen Emmerson and Kate McCaffrey and the Hever Castle exhibition on *Not Just the Tudors*, podcast, episode 99, "Anne Boleyn's Early Life," Acast, March 28, 2022, 29 min., https://shows.acast.com/not-just-the-tudors/episodes/becoming-anne.
20. Ives, *Life and Death of Anne Boleyn*, 240. The armillary sphere was one of Queen Claude of France's badges. See Guy and Fox, *Hunting the Falcon*, 204. We will see in the next chapter how influential Claude was on Anne.

CHAPTER 4 THE ROLE MODELS—ANNE HAD A VISION

1. Guy and Fox, *Hunting the Falcon*, 38.
2. Joanna Denny, *Anne Boleyn: A New Life of England's Tragic Queen* (Da Capo Press, 2006), 39.
3. Tracy Adams, "Anne Boleyn: Seductress or Scholar?" in *Female Beauty Systems: Beauty as Social Capital in Western Europe and the United States, Middle Ages to the Present*, edited by Christine Adams and Tracy Adams (Cambridge Scholars Publishing, 2015).
4. Wikipedia, "Margaret of Austria, Duchess of Savoy," last modified October 5, 2025, 22:07 (UTC), https://en.wikipedia.org/wiki/Margaret_of_Austria,_Duchess_of_Savoy.
5. Christine de Pizan, *The Book of the City of Ladies*, translated by Rosalind Brown-Grant (Penguin Books, 1999), https://www.loc.gov/item/2021667679/.
6. Guy and Fox, *Hunting the Falcon*, 40.

7. Adams, "Seductress or Scholar?," 50.
8. Guy and Fox, *Hunting the Falcon*, 41.
9. Ibid., 42.
10. Ibid., 45. Guy and Fox argue that Anne was likely talking about Margaret of Austria on page 46.
11. Ibid., 56.
12. Ibid., 58.
13. Ibid., 58.
14. Guy and Fox dispute this timeline, arguing instead that it was Anne's sister Mary who was part of Mary Tudor's entourage to France, that Anne returned home after relations between Margaret of Austria and England had soured, and then went back to France with her father in 1515 to serve Queen Claude. See Guy and Fox, *Hunting the Falcon*, 51–55.
15. Ives, *Life and Death of Anne Boleyn*, 28.
16. Adams, "Seductress or Scholar?," 50.
17. Guy and Fox, *Hunting the Falcon*, 55.
18. Ives, *Life and Death of Anne Boleyn*, 29.
19. Guy and Fox, *Hunting the Falcon*, 55.
20. Ibid., 348.
21. Ives, *Life and Death of Anne Boleyn*, 30.
22. Wikipedia, "Claude of France," last modified November 1, 2025, 10:31 (UTC), https://en.wikipedia.org/wiki/Claude_of_France.
23. Guy and Fox, *Hunting the Falcon*, 56.
24. Ibid.
25. Wikipedia, "*Miroir de l'âme pécheresse*," last modified May 27, 2025, 02:24 (UTC), https://en.wikipedia.org/w/index.php?title=Miroir_de_l'%C3%A2me_p%C3%A9cheresse.
26. Guy and Fox, *Hunting the Falcon*, 69–70.
27. Ibid., 69.
28. Ives, *Life and Death of Anne Boleyn*, 278.
29. Susan Bordo, *The Creation of Anne Boleyn: A New Look at England's Most Notorious Queen* (Houghton Mifflin Harcourt, 2013), 38.
30. Ibid.
31. Ibid.
32. Borman, *Anne Boleyn and Elizabeth I*, 114–115.
33. Alex Mar, "The Rebel Virgins and Desert Mothers Who Have Been Written Out of Christianity's Early History," Atlas Obscura, January 21, 2016, https://

www.atlasobscura.com/articles/the-rebel-virgins-and-desert-mothers-who-have-been-written-out-of-christianitys-early-history?utm_medium=atlas-page&utm_source=facebook. Mar notes: "Women had long been the managers of their households, and since followers of the new movement met in private, in intimate 'house churches,' women often became the natural leaders of the congregation. Christian women and men alike could become full-fledged ministers. This was back when the church was still a social movement, not yet a political powerhouse, and women were drawn to the possibilities it cracked open for them—as preachers, prophets, and patrons."

34. Ibid.
35. Ibid.
36. Ives, *Life and Death of Anne Boleyn*, 25.
37. The song is "O Death Rock Me Asleep," attributed to Anne and thought to have been written by her in the Tower of London prior to her execution.
38. Ives, *Life and Death of Anne Boleyn*, 34.
39. Henry, Cavendish claimed, was interested in Anne, who "for her excellent gesture and behavior did excel all other." See Ives, *Life and Death of Anne Boleyn*, 63.

CHAPTER 5 THE MATTER OF SEX

1. Laura Lys, "St. Frideswide: Patron Saint of Oxford," Museum of Oxford, https://museumofoxford.org/st-frideswide-patron-saint-of-oxford/.
2. Adams, "Seductress or Scholar?," 48.
3. Hannah Dawson, *Not Just the Tudors*, podcast, episode 26, "Sixteenth-Century Feminists," Acast, July 14, 2021, 38 min., 7 sec., https://shows.acast.com/not-just-the-tudors/episodes/earlymodernfeminists.
4. Guy and Fox, *Hunting the Falcon*, 86.
5. Ibid., 93.
6. Ibid., 95. Most sources believe that Anne became one of Queen Catherine's ladies-in-waiting after her debut. See Guy and Fox, *Hunting the Falcon*, 99.
7. Ives, *Life and Death of Anne Boleyn*, 37.
8. Suzannah Lipscomb discussed this with Dr. Lauren MacKay on *Not Just the Tudors*, podcast, episode 10, "Anne Boleyn: New Discoveries," Acast, May 19, 2021, 43 min., 52 sec., https://shows.acast.com/not-just-the-tudors/episodes/anneboleynspecial2-newdiscoveries.
9. There are stories that suggest Henry was thinking of divorce as early as 1522, but certainly by 1525, when he recognized Henry Fitzroy as his illegitimate

child, this possibility was on the horizon. See Ives, *Life and Death of Anne Boleyn*, 83.

10. Ives, *Life and Death of Anne Boleyn*, 83.
11. Scholar Tracy Adams posits that Henry became attracted to Anne because of her religious devotion and biblical knowledge and became convinced that he needed to make her his wife in order to right his relationship, and England's relationship, with God. We look at the timeline and language in more detail in subsequent chapters.
12. In his sonnet "If waker care," Wyatt refers to Anne as the "Brunet" that "did set our country in a roar." See Guy and Fox, *Hunting the Falcon*, 114.
13. Ives, *Life and Death of Anne Boleyn*, 76.
14. Bordo, *Creation of Anne Boleyn*, 41.
15. Ives, *Life and Death of Anne Boleyn*, 82.
16. Denny, *Tragic Queen*, 92–3.
17. Tracy Adams suggests that Henry VIII's contemporaries would have understood such a marriage as an unacceptable act of self-indulgence that sacrificed the common good. See Adams, "Seductress or Scholar?," 52.
18. Wolsey assumed that Henry intended to marry Princess Renée, the sister of Queen Claude of France. See Guy and Fox, *Hunting the Falcon*, 130.

19 Wikipedia, "Frithuswith," last modified October 27, 2025, 12:56 (UTC), https://en.wikipedia.org/wiki/Frithuswith.

CHAPTER 6 THERE'S SOMETHING ABOUT ANNE

1. Ives, *Life and Death of Anne Boleyn*, 24.
2. Ibid., 40.
3. Ibid., 67.
4. Adams, "Seductress or Scholar?," 60.
5. Bordo, *Creation of Anne Boleyn*, 46.
6. Suzannah Lipscomb, host, *Not Just the Tudors*, podcast, episode 368, "The Tudor World at Hampton Court," Acast, October 23, 2024, 40 min., 19 sec., https://shows.acast.com/not-just-the-tudors/episodes/the-tudor-world-at-hampton-court.
7. It has long been noted in Anne Boleyn biographies that it was early in 1526 when Henry is thought to have declared his romantic interest in Anne. The King held a joust and a banquet, and Henry rode into the joust with a banner carrying a status update on his love life. His symbol was a man's heart gripped

inside a press and surrounded by flames with the motto (in French) "Declare I not." See Guy and Fox, *Hunting the Falcon*, 123. That this was a reference to Henry's feelings for Anne has been interpreted through the rearview mirror of knowing where the story went from here and has been sleuthed out based on clues that have been discerned from Henry's seventeen love letters. However, recent scholarship by Professor Tracy Adams calls into question a long-held interpretation of Henry's offer in one of his letters to make Anne his "sole mistress" and assuming that could be interpreted through our modern understanding of "mistress" or a later understanding of the French word, *maitresse*. Adams, however, has offered careful analysis of the word *maitresse* and tells us instead that the word, in that time, was used by a man toward a woman he intended to make his wife. We know that by August 1527, this was indeed Henry's intent, which suggests a different timeline for their relationship and for the writing of Henry's letters. It also means that the 1526 joust can't be assumed to have been about Henry's interest in Anne. This is discussed on Natalie Grueninger, host, *Talking Tudors*, podcast, episode 298, with Dr. Owen Emmerson, "Was It Love? Henry VIII and Anne Boleyn," YouTube, June 16, 2025, 23 min., https://youtu.be/3EXH1NGDSDs, as well as episode 296, with Professor Tracy Adams, "The Myth of the Seductive Anne Boleyn," YouTube, May 28, 2025, 55 min., https://youtu.be/1z6i2b9ePV4.

8. This timeline is discussed in detail between Natalie Grueninger and Professor Owen Emmerson on the podcast noted above, episode 298 of *Talking Tudors*.
9. Guy and Fox, *Hunting the Falcon*, 127.
10. Despite the letters not being dated, historian Eric Ives believes they can be grouped into four eras of their relationship and a basic chronology established. See Ives, *Life and Death of Anne Boleyn*, 84.
11. As discussed on *Talking Tudors*, "The Myth of the Seductive Anne Boleyn."
12. Guy and Fox, *Hunting the Falcon*, 128.
13. Ibid., 127.
14. Ibid., xxxii.
15. Ives, *Life and Death of Anne Boleyn*, 87.
16. Ibid., 195.
17. Ibid., 217.
18. *Talking Tudors*, episodes 296 and 298.
19. Adams, "Seductress or Scholar?," 61.

20. Adams, "Seductress or Scholar?," 52. It might be argued that Charles V was not sincere in this offer, but it was nonetheless a consideration he was willing to put on the table.
21. Ibid., 52.
22. Ibid., 64.
23. Ibid., 63.
24. Guy and Fox, *Hunting the Falcon*, 150.
25. Adams, "Seductress or Scholar?," 64.
26. David Starkey, *Six Wives: The Queens of Henry VIII* (Harper, 2003), 285–286.
27. Tom Holland and Dominic Sandbrook, hosts, *The Rest Is History*, podcast, episode 74, "The Six Wives of Henry VIII," Apple Podcasts, July 12, 2021, 55 min., https://podcasts.apple.com/gb/podcast/the-six-wives-of-henry-viii/id1537788786?i=1000528555129.

CHAPTER 7 HOW ANNE MOVED THE CHESS PIECES OF REFORM

1. Guy and Fox, *Hunting the Falcon*, 155.
2. Bordo, *Creation of Anne Boleyn*, 81.
3. Guy and Fox, *Hunting the Falcon*, 141.
4. It was Pope Julius II who gave the dispensation for Henry VIII to marry Catherine of Aragon, his brother's widow, back in 1509. Clement VII was Pope for the time we are discussing around Henry's annulment and subsequent marriage to Anne.
5. Guy and Fox, *Hunting the Falcon*, 209.
6. Bordo, *Creation of Anne Boleyn*, 82.
7. Guy and Fox, *Hunting the Falcon*, 215.
8. Ives, *Life and Death of Anne Boleyn*, 97.
9. Adams, "Seductress or Scholar?," 63.
10. Ives suggests that Anne's decision finally to sleep with Henry was very likely a calculation that was made by Anne to "stiffen the king's resolve." That this was the "decisive crisis, sure that if she became pregnant, Henry would have to act." See Ives, *Life and Death of Anne Boleyn*, 170.
11. Denny, *Tragic Queen*, 184.
12. Ibid., 186.
13. Guy and Fox, *Hunting the Falcon*, 142.
14. Ives, *Life and Death of Anne Boleyn*, 64.

15. Diarmaid MacCulloch, *Thomas Cranmer* (Yale University Press, 1996), 44.
16. Ibid., 45.
17. Ibid., 47.
18. Ibid., 82.
19. Ibid., 83.
20. "A papal bull is a type of public decree, letters patent, or charter issued by a pope of the Catholic Church. It is named after the leaden seal . . . traditionally appended to authenticate it." Wikipedia, "Papal bull," last modified October 9, 2025, 13:30 (UTC), https://en.wikipedia.org/wiki/Papal_bull.
21. Guy and Fox, *Hunting the Falcon*, 209.
22. Thomas S. Freeman, "Research, Rumour and Propaganda: Anne Boleyn in Foxe's 'Book of Martyrs,'" *The Historical Journal* 38, no. 4 (1995): 802.
23. Ibid., 800.
24. Ibid., 813.
25. Adams, "Seductress or Scholar?," 62.
26. Freeman, "Research, Rumour and Propaganda," 813.
27. MacCulloch, *Thomas Cranmer*, 83.
28. Freeman, "Research, Rumour and Propaganda," 807.
29. "According to Foxe, every week during the year before her coronation, Anne handed out clothing and 100 pounds in alms to the poor. As queen, she gave generously to widows and poor householders, giving 3 and 4 pounds at a time for the purchase of livestock. She sent her sub-almoner to the towns surrounding her properties to compile lists of the poorest householders and then allocate funds. Every day she carried a little purse with her from which she offered alms to the needy." See Guy and Fox, *Hunting the Falcon*, 321.
30. An almoner's job is technically to distribute money to the poor on behalf of the queen, but Skip performed as a sort of personal chaplain for Anne as well.
31. Freeman, "Research, Rumour and Propaganda," 807.
32. Guy and Fox, *Hunting the Falcon*, 205.
33. Ibid., 206.
34. Adams, "Seductress or Scholar?," 62.
35. Ives, *Life and Death of Anne Boleyn*, 272.
36. Ibid., 269.
37. Ibid.
38. The New Testament and parts of the Old Testament were the result of the translation and scholarship of William Tyndale (Tyndale again!), who by that

time had been arrested as a heretic in Brussels. The rest of the translation was a fairly incoherent mess, so Coverdale's translation did not become widely used in England, although it was important in the campaign toward eventually making English Bibles, printed in England, possible.

39. Denny, *Tragic Queen*, 251.
40. Ives, *Life and Death of Anne Boleyn*, 261.

CHAPTER 8 THE ENEMIES—RELIGION, POLITICS, AND PERSONALITY

1. Ives argues: "Throughout their relationship it had been Anne who had stiffened the king's resolve." See Ives, *Life and Death of Anne Boleyn*, 170.
2. Ives, *Life and Death of Anne Boleyn*, 313.
3. Guy and Fox, *Hunting the Falcon*, 215.
4. Ives, *Life and Death of Anne Boleyn*, 104
5. Guy and Fox, *Hunting the Falcon*, 139.
6. Ives, *Life and Death of Anne Boleyn*, 111.
7. Guy and Fox, *Hunting the Falcon*, 152.
8. Ives, *Life and Death of Anne Boleyn*, 114.
9. Guy and Fox, *Hunting the Falcon*, 187.
10. Ibid., 187.
11. Ibid., 188.
12. Ibid., 188
13. Ives, *Life and Death of Anne Boleyn*, 152.
14. Ibid., 47.
15. Guy and Fox, *Hunting the Falcon*, 185.
16. Ives, *Life and Death of Anne Boleyn*, 292.
17. Ibid., 302.
18. Ibid., 301.
19. Ibid., 303.
20. G. J. Meyer, *The Tudors: The Complete Story of England's Most Notorious Dynasty* (Random House Publishing Group, 2010), 318.
21. Ives, *Life and Death of Anne Boleyn*, 151.
22. Meyer, *The Tudors*, 306.
23. Bordo, *Creation of Anne Boleyn*, 140.
24. Ibid., 140.
25. Ibid., 140.
26. Ibid., 125.

27. Ives, *Life and Death of Anne Boleyn*, 195.
28. Ibid., 303.
29. Guy and Fox, *Hunting the Falcon*, 129.

CHAPTER 9 NOT GUILTY BUT NOT INNOCENT

1. The interpretation of the court and of historians since is that Skip would not have made this connection without Anne's direction.
2. In the biblical Book of Esther, the Persian king Ahasuerus is traditionally identified as Xerxes I, who ruled the Achaemenid Empire from 486 to 465 BC.
3. Denny, *Tragic Queen*, 196.
4. Adams, "Seductress or Scholar?," 64.
5. Ives, *Life and Death of Anne Boleyn*, 307.
6. Bordo, *Creation of Anne Boleyn*, 94.
7. Ives, *Life and Death of Anne Boleyn*, 295.
8. "Even where the monasteries and abbeys were not closed down altogether, with their lands taken away they had lost their means of subsistence." See Wikipedia, "Suppression of monasteries," last modified October 6, 2025, 01:36 (UTC), https://en.wikipedia.org/wiki/Suppression_of_monasteries#:~:text=Even%20where%20the%20monasteries%20and,and%20those%20which%20were%20dissolved.
9. Ibid.
10. Guy and Fox, *Hunting the Falcon*, 346.
11. Ibid., 204.
12. Ibid., 294.
13. Ibid., 294.
14. Ibid., 101.
15. Ibid., 316.
16. Ibid., 310.
17. Ibid., 312.
18. Ibid., 301.
19. Ibid., 314.
20. Ibid., 318.

CHAPTER 10 SHE LAUGHED AT THE KING

1. Emma V. Levitt, "'You Look for Dead Men's Shoes': Tiltyard Friendships and Masculine Competition in the Reign of Henry VIII," Academia.edu, accessed December 8, 2025, https://www.academia.edu/33919921/You_look_for

_dead_mens_shoes_Tiltyard_Friendships_and_Masculine_Competition_in _the_Reign_of_Henry_VIII.

2. Ives, *Life and Death of Anne Boleyn*, 319.
3. Levitt, "Dead Men's Shoes," 4.
4. Two dates should be noted. On April 24 an oyer and terminer commission had been established with the king's approval to investigate matters of treason. On April 27, parliament was summoned "to settle the succession and to repeal statues favouring Anne." See Ives, 320. Some commentators suggest that Henry was unaware of these actions and that Cromwell was acting alone. On Natalie Grueninger, host, *Talking Tudors*, podcast, episode 294, with Dr. Owen Emmerson, "The Fall of Anne Boleyn in 20 Key Moments," YouTube, May 12, 2025, 2 hr., 6 min., 41 sec., https://youtu.be/27HXfoI2s_M. Grueninger and Emmerson suggest the possibility that both Henry and Cromwell were working in concert to put the pieces in place to get rid of Anne, but didn't yet know how. When Smeton was reported as making amorous comments about the queen and then when Anne and Henry Norris had their interchange about "dead men's shoes," they had the evidence that they needed.
5. This detail comes from a poem written by Lancelot de Carles and published in Lyon in 1545. De Carles was a witness to these events, and it is the earliest detailed account of Anne's arrest and execution. See Greg Walker, "Rethinking the Fall of Anne Boleyn," *Historical Journal* 45, no. 1 (March 2002): 10, https://doi.org/10.1017/S0018246X01002126.
6. Walker, "Rethinking the Fall of Anne Boleyn," 11.
7. Ives, *Life and Death of Anne Boleyn*, 335.
8. Ibid., 325.
9. Ibid., 325.
10. Walker, "Rethinking the Fall of Anne Boleyn," 3.
11. Levitt, "Dead Men's Shoes," 9.
12. Ives, *Life and Death of Anne Boleyn*, 319.
13. Bordo, *Creation of Anne Boleyn*, 102.
14. Walker, "Rethinking the Fall of Anne Boleyn," 4.
15. Ibid., 17.
16. Ives, *Life and Death of Anne Boleyn*, 331.
17. Walker, "Rethinking the Fall of Anne Boleyn," 14.
18. Two influential scholars, Greg Walker in his paper "Rethinking the Fall of Anne Boleyn" and Eric Ives in his book *The Life and Death of Anne Boleyn*,

differ somewhat on this point. Walker concludes that Cromwell couldn't have envisioned the range of accusations that would eventually bring Anne and the five accused men down and that it was Henry's jealousy and involvement after Smeton's confession that saw the plot devolve into the eventual outcome of Anne and the five men all being tried and executed for adultery. Ives gives more credit to Cromwell, not necessarily for having a master plan in place all along but for building the case against Anne as material emerged. He seized the opportunity to rid the court of competing influences. Not just Anne, but also some of those previously closest to Henry, including George Boleyn and Henry Norris.

19. Walker, "Rethinking the Fall of Anne Boleyn," 16.
20. Ibid., 16.
21. Ibid., 17.
22. "Sex with a consenting queen was not yet made treason in its own right." See Guy and Fox, *Hunting the Falcon*, 380.
23. Levitt, "Dead Men's Shoes," 7.
24. Ibid., 9.
25. Adams, "Seductress or Scholar?," 65.
26. Ives, *Life and Death of Anne Boleyn*, 327.
27. Ibid., 351.
28. Ibid., 312.
29. Ibid., 349.
30. Ibid., 349.
31. Bordo, *Creation of Anne Boleyn*, 84.
32. Ives, *Life and Death of Anne Boleyn*, 346.
33. Ibid., 348.
34. For example, Jane Boleyn, wife of George and thought to have supplied evidence against Anne and her husband, was executed as a coconspirator in the adultery of Henry's fifth wife, Katherine Howard.
35. Walker, "Rethinking the Fall of Anne Boleyn," 13.
36. Ibid., 15.

CHAPTER 11 FROM A TO E: A BLOODY AND TUMULTUOUS ROAD MAP OF REFORMATION

1. As it turns out, Edward Seymour, brother of Jane, became a powerful Evangelical leader in the reign of his nephew Edward VI.

2. Ives, *Life and Death of Anne Boleyn*, 317.
3. Meyer, *The Tudors*, 292. Kateryn was "skillful at adapting herself to her husband's moods and maintaining a pleasant household not only for him but for all three of his children—the first and only time that Henry's offspring were ever together even intermittently in something resembling a normal family home."
4. Meyer, *The Tudors*, 363.
5. "Wife of Henry VIII Wrote BCP Prayer," Anglican Communion News Service, November 12, 2015, https://www.anglicannews.org/news/2015/11/wife-of-henry-viii-wrote-bcp-prayer.aspx.
6. Meyer, *The Tudors*, 292.
7. Ibid., 329.
8. Ibid., 356.
9. Ibid., 341.
10. She should actually be known as the "Thirteen Days" Queen, if we count her time from the death of Edward.
11. Meyer, *The Tudors*, 414–415.
12. Ibid., 404.
13. Ibid., 419.
14. Rough estimates of the number of executions in Henry's thirty-seven years of reigning are in the 57,000–72,000 range, whereas Mary is estimated to have executed fewer than 300 in her five years on the throne.
15. Borman, *Anne Boleyn and Elizabeth I*, 161.
16. Meyer, *The Tudors*, 439.

CHAPTER 12 HER MOTHER'S DAUGHTER

1. Borman, *Anne Boleyn and Elizabeth I*, 1.
2. Ibid., 163.
3. Ibid., 149.
4. MacCulloch, *All Things Made New*, 202.
5. Meyer, *The Tudors*, 442.
6. MacCulloch, *All Things Made New*, 361.
7. Meyer, *The Tudors*, 446.
8. The words of institution from 1559 were returned, although the articles of religion clearly ruled out a physical presence of Christ in the elements received by the worthy and unworthy alike.

9. Specifically the surplice and the cope.
10. MacCulloch, *All Things Made New*, 201.
11. Ibid., 360.
12. Ibid., 211.
13. Borman, *Anne Boleyn and Elizabeth I*, 159.
14. Ibid., 159.
15. MacCulloch, *All Things Made New*, 211.
16. Meyer, *The Tudors*, 448.
17. Borman, *Anne Boleyn and Elizabeth I*, 160.
18. She was born Catherine Dammartin and was a nun who "left her convent, adopted evangelical views, and married Peter Martyr Vermigli," the first Canon of Christ Church Oxford. They experienced some persecution because of Peter's married status and their evangelical beliefs. Wikipedia, "Catherine Dammartin," last modified March 19, 2023, 17:28 (UTC), https://en.wikipedia.org/wiki/Catherine_Dammartin.
19. Laura Lys, "St. Frideswide: Patron Saint of Oxford," Museum of Oxford, accessed November 10, 2025, https://museumofoxford.org/st-frideswide-patron-saint-of-oxford/.

CHAPTER 13 A NEW WORLD, A NEW CHURCH

1. The historic site of execution was actually several yards away, but I didn't know that at the time. Ives, *Life and Death of Anne Boleyn*, xiii.
2. McLuhan notes, "The personal and social consequences of any medium—that is, of any extension of ourselves—result from the new scale that is introduced into our affairs by each extension of ourselves, or by any new technology." See Marshall McLuhan, *Understanding Media: The Extensions of Man* (The MIT Press, Fourth printing, 1996), 7.
3. Taylor, *Secular Age*, 25.
4. McLuhan, *Understanding Media*, 172.
5. I credit the work of scholar Andrew Root, who in turn credits Charles Taylor, with this analysis.
6. Taylor, *Secular Age*, 3.
7. Bordo, *Creation of Anne Boleyn*, 105.
8. Ibid., 107.
9. Bordo, *Creation of Anne Boleyn*, 112–113.
10. Ibid., 108.

11. Dr. Emily Butterworth talks with Professor Suzannah Lipscomb on *Not Just the Tudors*, podcast, episode 186, "Marguerite de Navarre: Mother of Renaissance France," Acast, February 1, 2023, 47 min., 24 sec., https://shows.acast.com/not-just-the-tudors/episodes/marguerite-de-navarre.
12. Ives, *Life and Death of Anne Boleyn*, 283.
13. To be clear, this term "middle way," which would become so associated with Anglicanism, was not language used for describing the church in Anne's time. Nonetheless, the characteristics of a church that included traditional and reformed components could be seen in Anne's religious leadership, as well as in the principles championed by people like Marguerite d'Angoulême and Queen Claude.
14. Andrew Gerns, "VTS Chapel Update, 6-Toed Jesus Saved," *Episcopal Café*, October 27, 2010, https://episcopal.cafe/vts_chapel_update_6_toed_jesus_saved/.
15. Guy and Fox, *Hunting the Falcon*, xxv.
16. Ibid., xxix.
17. Ibid., xxix.
18. Ibid., xxx.
19. Ives, *Life and Death of Anne Boleyn*, 359.

PART 4 BIGGER THAN THE ARCHETYPES

1. "Mae West Going Strong at 75," *Life* magazine, April 18, 1969, 62C.

CHAPTER 14 THE FAIRY TALES

1. Wikipedia, "Cinderella," last modified November 3, 2025, 23:33 (UTC), https://en.wikipedia.org/wiki/Cinderella.
2. J. R. R. Tolkien, "On Fairy-Stories (1939)" in *Tolkien on Fairy-Stories*, ed. Verlyn Flieger and Douglas A. Anderson, expanded edition (HarperCollins, 2008), 57.
3. Ibid., 75.
4. Nicholas Jubber, *The Fairy Tellers: A Journey into the Secret History of Fairy Tales* (John Murray Publishers, 2022), 101–102.
5. Ives, *Life and Death of Anne Boleyn*, 145.
6. Ibid., 143.
7. Ibid., 141.
8. Ibid., 143.
9. Wikipedia, "Palace of Whitehall," last modified November 5, 2025, 06:22 (UTC), https://en.wikipedia.org/wiki/Palace_of_Whitehall.

10. Guy and Fox, *Hunting the Falcon*, 193.
11. Freeman, "Research, Rumour and Propaganda," 801.
12. Ibid., 802.
13. Ibid., 817.
14. Roland Hui, "Anne of the Wicked Ways: Perceptions of Anne Boleyn as a Witch in History and in Popular Culture," published in *Parergon: Journal of the Australian and New Zealand Association for Medieval and Early Modern Studies*, 35, no. 1 (2018): 115.
15. Ives, *Life and Death of Anne Boleyn*, 359.

CHAPTER 15 THE WHORE

1. "Jeremiah 3, Ezekiel 16 and 23, Hosea 4, and others exploit this prostitution-apostate combination and compare disobedient and idolatrous Israel to a prostitute." See David E. Aune, *Revelation 17–22*, Word Biblical Commentary, eds. Bruce Metzger, David A. Hubbard, and Glenn W. Barker, vol. 52C (Thomas Nelson Publishers, 1998), 919.
2. Jonathan Redding notes in his paper, "Babylon Revisited: A Feminist Inspired Reading of the Whore of Babylon," from 2011, that "Hosea, Ezekiel, Jeremiah, Nahum, and Isaiah use the promiscuous woman metaphor to describe nations, cities, and peoples unfaithful to YHWH." See Redding, "Babylon Revisited," 2.
3. "Then the angel said to me, 'The waters you saw, where the prostitute sits, are peoples, multitudes, nations and languages. The beast and the ten horns you saw will hate the prostitute. They will bring her to ruin and leave her naked; they will eat her flesh and burn her with fire.'" See Revelation 17:15–16 (NIV).
4. Wikipedia, "Whore of Babylon," last modified November 9, 2025, 10:11 (UTC), https://en.wikipedia.org/wiki/Whore_of_Babylon.
5. Hui, "Anne of the Wicked Ways," 99.
6. Nicholas Sander, *Rise and Growth of the Anglican Schism* (Alpha Editions, 2020), cxlvi.
7. "Many women were also there, looking on from a distance; they had followed Jesus from Galilee, ministering to him. Among them were Mary Magdalene, and Mary the mother of James and Joseph, and the mother of the sons of Zebedee." See Matthew 27:55–56 (NRSVUE).
8. Ives, *Life and Death of Anne Boleyn*, 171.
9. Ibid., 171.

CHAPTER 16 THE MOTHER

1. Ibid., 221–2.
2. Ibid., 222.
3. Ibid., 6–7.
4. Ibid., 204.
5. Ibid., 40.
6. Borman, *Anne Boleyn and Elizabeth I*, 41–42.
7. Ibid., 50.
8. Ives, *Life and Death of Anne Boleyn*, 197.
9. Ibid., 138.
10. Ibid., 198.
11. Ibid., 327.
12. Ibid., 340.
13. Ibid., 198.
14. Ibid., 190.
15. Ibid., 191.
16. Ibid., 190.

CHAPTER 17 THE WITCH

1. Contemporary critics of Joan note that she "dressed like a man, and carrying a great stick, with which she struck any of her men who did anything wrong," that she took Communion in men's clothing, and "jumped from a high tower without hurting herself at all," Frances Gies, *Joan of Arc: The Legend and the Reality* (Harper & Row, 1981), 242. Others complained that she rode a horse "like a man" and was willing "to do things that other young maidens both abhorred and were ashamed to do." She was a virgin because of "her foul face, that no man would desire it," Gies, *Joan of Arc*, 244.
2. Encyclopedia Britannica Online, s.v. "St. Joan of Arc," accessed November 11, 2025, https://www.britannica.com/biography/Saint-Joan-of-Arc/Capture-trial-and-execution. Her age isn't known precisely since her birth date was not recorded.
3. Mary Pat Fisher, *Women in Religion* (Pearson Longman, 2007), 21.
4. Ibid., 200.
5. Brian P. Levack, ed., *The Oxford Handbook of Witchcraft in Early Modern Europe and Colonial America* (Oxford University Press, 2013), 452.

6. Ibid., 459. The book notes that in places like Iceland, Normandy, Estonia, and Russia, men were more often accused of witchcraft than women. Men and women were prosecuted in roughly even numbers in Finland, Burgundy, and parts of France.
7. Fisher, *Women in Religion*, 208.
8. Levack, *Handbook of Witchcraft*, 456.
9. Ibid., 452–53.
10. Ibid., 461.
11. Ibid., 463.
12. Ibid., 465.
13. Ibid., 504.
14. Hui, "Anne of the Wicked Ways," 105.
15. Sylvia Barbara Soberton, "'Large Wen' or 'Swelling'? Exploring Myths and Misconceptions About Nicholas Sander's Description of Anne Boleyn and Its Link to Witchcraft," *Royal Studies Journal* 10, no. 2 (December 2023): 240–41, https://doi.org/10.21039/rsj.411.
16. Sander, *Anglican Schism*, 132.
17. Hui, "Anne of the Wicked Ways," 100.
18. A letter from 1433 by the duke of Bedford refers to Joan's using enchantments and sorcery to win battles. See Gies, *Joan of Arc*, 242. A municipal history of 1430 calls Joan a "false witch" (Ibid., 243).
19. Gies, *Joan of Arc*, 247.
20. Ibid., 248.
21. Ibid., 238.
22. Ibid., 239.

CHAPTER 18 THE MOST HAPPY

1. Denny, *Tragic Queen*, 194.
2. Ibid., 197.
3. Ives, *Life and Death of Anne Boleyn*, 218.
4. Lisa Taddeo, *Three Women* (Avid Reader Press, 2019), 297.
5. Guy and Fox, *Hunting the Falcon*, 128–29.
6. Ibid., 130–31.
7. Adams, "Seductress or Scholar?," 52–53.
8. Natalie Grueninger, "Anne Boleyn: 'The Moost Happi' Portrait Medal," *On the Tudor Trail*, July 7, 2012.

CHAPTER 19 . . . HAPPILY EVER AFTER

1. Professor Suzannah Lipscomb discusses this on *Not Just the Tudors*, podcast, episode 227, "Cromwell, Boleyn and Aragon: A New Discovery," Acast, June 14, 2023, 34 min., 21 sec., https://shows.acast.com/not-just-the-tudors/episodes/crom-well-boleyn-aragon-a-new-discovery.
2. Ives, *Life and Death of Anne Boleyn*, 240.

PART 5 ONLY A STORY

1. Laurie Penny, *Bitch Doctrine: Essay for Dissenting Adults* (Bloomsbury, 2017), 98–99.

CHAPTER 20 ANNE AND ME; ANNE AND US

1. Doyne Courtenay Bell, *Notices of the Historic Persons Buried in the Chapel of St. Peter Ad Vincula* (J. Murray, 1877).
2. Natalie Grueninger, "Anne Boleyn's Remains and Restoration of the Chapel of St. Peter Ad Vincula," *On the Tudor Trail*, accessed December 8, 2025.
3. R. L. Weston, "Digging Up Anne Boleyn and Others: Burials in the Chapel of St. Peter Ad Vincula," *History Calling*, YouTube, July 16, 2021, 18 min., 55 sec., https://youtu.be/EjCxVN7V6FA.
4. World Health Organization, "Violence Against Women," World Health Organization, March 25, 2024, https://www.who.int/news-room/fact-sheets/detail/violence-against-women#:~:text=Estimates%20published%20by%20WHO%20indicate,violence%20is%20intimate%20partner%20violence.
5. Heidi Stöckl et al., "The Global Prevalence of Intimate Partner Homicide: A Systematic Review," *Lancet* 382, no. 9895 (September 7–13, 2013): 859–865, https://doi.org/10.1016/S0140-6736(13)61030-2.

CHAPTER 21 A LEGACY OF MISOGYNY

1. Margo Guernsey, dir., *The Philadelphia Eleven*, Time Travel Productions, 2023, 1 hr., 31 min., https://www.philadelphiaelevenfilm.com/.
2. Ibid.
3. The Anglican Communion is a global association of churches that trace their origins to the Church of England.
4. An Anglican province is a self-governing, national, or multinational church within the larger Anglican Communion.
5. Genesis 12:10–20, Genesis 20:1–15.

6. Sharon L. Jansen, *Debating Women, Politics, and Power in Early Modern Europe* (Palgrave Macmillan, 2008), 35.
7. Ibid., 36.
8. Ibid., 36.
9. Ibid., 157.
10. Ibid., 158.
11. Ibid., 171.
12. Silvia Geruza Fernandez Rodrigues, "The Church, Woman, Leadership, and the Body," in *Feminism and Religion: How Faiths View Women and Their Rights*, ed. Michele A. Paludi and J. Harold Ellens (Praeger, 2016), 60.

CHAPTER 22 THE RIVERBED

1. Sharon L. Jansen, *Dangerous Talk and Strange Behavior: Women and Popular Resistance to the Reforms of Henry VIII* (St. Martin's Press, 1996), 142.
2. Ibid., 142.
3. Ibid., 144–45.
4. Ibid., 145.
5. Ibid., 145.
6. MacCulloch, *All Things Made New*, 209.

APPENDIX I KEY CHARACTERS

1. Wikipedia, "Marguerite de Navarre," last modified October 30, 2025, 12:55 (UTC), https://en.wikipedia.org/wiki/Marguerite_de_Navarre.
2. Wikipedia, "Lorenzo Campeggio," last modified June 12, 2025, 22:08 (UTC), https://en.wikipedia.org/wiki/Lorenzo_Campeggio.
3. Wikipedia, "Nicholas Carew (courtier)," last modified January 15, 2026, 17:26 (UTC), https://en.wikipedia.org/wiki/Nicholas_Carew_(courtier).
4. Wikipedia, "Eustace Chapuys," last modified January 25, 2026, 07:36 (UTC), https://en.wikipedia.org/wiki/Eustace_Chapuys.
5. Wikipedia, "Charles V, Holy Roman Emperor," last modified January 28, 2026, 01:48 (UTC), https://en.wikipedia.org/wiki/Charles_V,_Holy_Roman_Emperor.
6. Wikipedia, "Claude of France," last modified November 1, 2025, 10:31 (UTC), https://en.wikipedia.org/wiki/Claude_of_France.
7. Wikipedia, "Anne of Cleves," last modified October 27, 2025, 13:10 (UTC), https://en.wikipedia.org/wiki/Anne_of_Cleves.

8. Wikipedia, "Thomas Cranmer," last modified January 25, 2026, 22:10 (UTC), https://en.wikipedia.org/wiki/Thomas_Cranmer.
9. Wikipedia, "Thomas Cromwell," last modified December 29, 2025, 20:00 (UTC), https://en.wikipedia.org/wiki/Thomas_Cromwell.
10. Wikipedia, "Edward VI," last modified January 19, 2026, 01:13 (UTC), https://en.wikipedia.org/wiki/Edward_VI.
11. Wikipedia, "Elizabeth I," last modified January 28, 2026, 06:36 (UTC), https://en.wikipedia.org/wiki/Elizabeth_I.
12. Wikipedia, "Esther," last modified January 9, 2026, 15:54 (UTC), https://en.wikipedia.org/wiki/Esther.
13. Wikipedia, "Francis I of France," last modified January 14, 2026, 20:33 (UTC), https://en.wikipedia.org/wiki/Francis_I_of_France.
14. Wikipedia, "Haman," last modified January 3, 2026, 04:11 (UTC), https://en.wikipedia.org/wiki/Haman.
15. Wikipedia, "Thomas Howard, 3rd Duke of Norfolk," last modified October 11, 2025, 22:53 (UTC), https://en.wikipedia.org/wiki/Thomas_Howard,_3rd_Duke_of_Norfolk.
16. Wikipedia, "Margaret of Austria, Duchess of Savoy," last modified October 5, 2025, 22:07 (UTC), https://en.wikipedia.org/wiki/Margaret_of_Austria,_Duchess_of_Savoy.
17. Wikipedia, "Mary I of England," last modified January 28, 2026, 07:00 (UTC), https://en.wikipedia.org/wiki/Mary_I_of_England.
18. Wikipedia, "Thomas More," last modified January 24, 2026, 03:01 (UTC), https://en.wikipedia.org/wiki/Thomas_More.
19. Wikipedia, "Matthew Parker," last modified January 23, 2026, 02:13 (UTC), https://en.wikipedia.org/wiki/Matthew_Parker.
20. Wikipedia, "Philip II of Spain," last modified January 20, 2026, 03:18 (UTC), https://en.wikipedia.org/wiki/Philip_II_of_Spain.
21. Wikipedia, "Nicholas Sanders," last modified July 20, 2024, 18:30 (UTC), https://en.wikipedia.org/wiki/Nicholas_Sanders.
22. Wikipedia, "Louise de Savoie," last modified October 26, 2025, 13:48 (UTC), https://fr.wikipedia.org/wiki/Louise_de_Savoie.
23. Wikipedia, "Edward Seymour, 1st Duke of Somerset," last modified January 16, 2026, 20:53 (UTC), https://en.wikipedia.org/wiki/Edward_Seymour,_1st_Duke_of_Somerset.

24. Wikipedia, "Margaret Tudor," last modified January 26, 2026, 13:39 (UTC), https://en.wikipedia.org/wiki/Margaret_Tudor.
25. Wikipedia, "Mary Tudor, Queen of France," last modified October 14, 2025, 11:16 (UTC), https://en.wikipedia.org/wiki/Mary_Tudor,_Queen_of_France.
26. Wikipedia, "William Tyndale," last modified January 24, 2026, 08:00 (UTC), https://en.wikipedia.org/wiki/William_Tyndale.
27. Wikipedia, "Francis Weston," last modified January 24, 2026, 13:34 (UTC), https://en.wikipedia.org/wiki/Francis_Weston.
28. Wikipedia, "Thomas Wolsey," last modified January 27, 2026, 09:43 (UTC), https://en.wikipedia.org/wiki/Thomas_Wolsey.
29. Wikipedia, "George Wyatt (writer)," last modified December 14, 2024, 07:30 (UTC), https://en.wikipedia.org/wiki/George_Wyatt_(writer).
30. Wikipedia, "Thomas Wyatt (poet)," last modified January 2, 2026, 07:31 (UTC), https://en.wikipedia.org/wiki/Thomas_Wyatt_(poet).
31. Wikipedia, "Xerxes I," last modified January 27, 2026, 16:42 (UTC), https://en.wikipedia.org/wiki/Xerxes_I.

Bibliography

Abad-Santos, Alex. "The Death of the Girlboss." Vox.com, June 7, 2021. https://www.vox.com/22466574/gaslight-gatekeep-girlboss-meaning.

Adams, Tracy. "Anne Boleyn: Seductress or Scholar?" In *Female Beauty Systems: Beauty as Social Capital in Western Europe and the United States, Middle Ages to the Present*. Edited by Christine Adams and Tracy Adams. Cambridge Scholars Publishing, 2015.

Adams, Tracy. "Powerful Women and Misogynistic Subplots: Some Comments on the Necessity of Checking the Primary Sources." *Medieval Feminist Forum: A Journal of Gender and Sexuality* 51, no. 2 (2016): 69–81. https://dx.doi.org/10.17077/1536-8742.2038.

Anglican Communion News Source. "Wife of Henry VIII Wrote BCP Prayer." November 12, 2015. https://www.anglicannews.org/news/2015/11/wife-of-henry-viii-wrote-bcp-prayer.aspx.

Aune, David E. *Revelation 17–22*. Word Biblical Commentary. Edited by Bruce M. Metzger, David A. Hubbard, and Glenn W. Barker. Vol. 52C. Thomas Nelson Publishers, 1998.

Bainton, Roland H. *Here I Stand: A Life of Martin Luther*. Abingdon-Cokesbury Press, 1950.

Bell, Doyne Courtenay. *Notices of the Historic Persons Buried in the Chapel of St. Peter Ad Vincula*. J. Murray, 1877.

Bordo, Susan. *The Creation of Anne Boleyn: A New Look at England's Most Notorious Queen*. Houghton Mifflin Harcourt, 2013.

Borman, Tracy. *Anne Boleyn and Elizabeth I: The Mother and Daughter Who Forever Changed British History.* Atlantic Monthly Press, 2023.

Brown, Tina. "The Mouse That Roared: How Has Marriage Changed Princess Diana?" *Vanity Fair*, October 1985. https://archive.vanityfair.com/article/1985/10/the-mouse-that-roared.

Brownlee, Jon. "The Surprising History of Katherine Parr's Prayer for Henry VIII." Carleton University, Faculty of Arts & Social Sciences, 2016. Accessed November 8, 2025. https://carleton.ca/fass/2016/surprising-history-katherine-parrs-prayer-henry-viii/.

Cooper, Kate. *Queens of a Fallen World: The Lost Women of Augustine's Confessions.* Basic Books, 2023.

Dawson, Hannah, ed. *The Penguin Book of Feminist Writing*. Penguin Classics, 2021.

Denny, Joanna. *Anne Boleyn: A New Life of England's Tragic Queen*. Da Capo Press, 2006.

De Pizan, Christine. *The Book of the City of Ladies*. Translated by Rosalind Brown-Grant. Penguin Books, 1999. https://www.loc.gov/item/2021667679/.

Duffy, Eamon. *The Stripping of the Altars: Traditional Religion in England, 1400–1580*. Yale University Press, 1992.

Du Garde Peach, L. *Henry VIII*. Ladybird Books, 1973.

Du Garde Peach, L. *The Story of the First Queen Elizabeth*. Wills & Hepworth Ltd., 1958.

Eisenstein, Elizabeth L. *The Printing Press as an Agent of Change: Communications and Cultural Transformations in Early-Modern Europe.* Cambridge University Press, 1979.

Ettia, Merilee. "Six—The History Behind the Hit: Anne Boleyn." *Theatre Haus*, October 4, 2020. https://www.theatrehaus.com/2020/10/six-the-history-behind-the-hit-anne-boleyn/.

Fine, Jerramy. *In Defense of the Princess: How Plastic Tiaras and Fairytale Dreams Can Inspire Strong, Smart Women*. Running Press, 2016.

Fisher, Mary Pat. *Women in Religion*. Pearson Longman, 2007.

Florer-Bixler, Melissa. "Women Posing Problems: In the Gospels and in the World Today, Women Get in the Way and Make the World New." *Christian Century*, September 2024. https://www.christiancentury.org/voices/women-posing-problems.

Foxe, John. *Foxe's Book of Martyrs* [1563]. Digireads.com, 2018.

Foxe, John. *Foxe's Book of Martyrs: Select Narratives.* Edited by John N. King. Oxford University Press, 2009.

Freeman, Thomas S. "Research, Rumour and Propaganda: Anne Boleyn in Foxe's 'Book of Martyrs.'" *Historical Journal* 38, no. 4 (December 1995): 797–819. https://doi.org/10.1017/S0018246X0002046X.

Garst, Karen L., ed. *Women vs. Religion: The Case Against Faith—and for Freedom.* Pitchstone Publishing, 2018.

Gerns, Andrew. "VTS Chapel Update, 6-Toed Jesus Saved." *Episcopal Café*, October 27, 2010. https://episcopal.cafe/vts_chapel_update_6_toed_jesus_saved/.

Gies, Frances. *Joan of Arc: The Legend and the Reality*. Harper & Row, 1981.

Gladwell, Malcolm. *Revenge of the Tipping Point: Overstories, Superspreaders, and the Rise of Social Engineering*. Little, Brown and Company, 2024.

Grueninger, Natalie. "Anne Boleyn's Remains and Restoration of the Chapel of St. Peter Ad Vincula." *On the Tudor Trail.* Accessed December 8, 2025. https://onthetudortrail.com/Blog/anne-boleyn/anne-boleyns-remains-the-restoration-of-the-chapel-of-st-peter-ad-vincula/.

Guernsey, Margo, dir. *The Philadelphia Eleven*. Time Travel Productions, 2023. 1 hr., 31 min. https://www.philadelphiaelevenfilm.com/.

Guy, John, and Julia Fox. *Hunting the Falcon: Henry VIII, Anne Boleyn, and the Marriage that Shook Europe.* HarperCollins Publishers, 2023.

Harline, Craig. *A World Ablaze: The Rise of Martin Luther and the Birth of the Reformation.* Oxford University Press, 2017.

Hui, Roland. "Anne of the Wicked Ways: Perceptions of Anne Boleyn as a Witch in History and in Popular Culture." *Parergon: Journal of the Australian and New Zealand Association of Medieval and Early Modern Studies* 35, no. 1 (2018): 97–118. https://doi.org/10.1353/pgn.2018.0005.

Hutton, Ronald. *The Witch: A History of Fear, from Ancient Times to the Present.* Yale University Press, 2017.

Ives, Eric. *The Life and Death of Anne Boleyn*. Blackwell Publishing, 2004.

Jansen, Sharon L. *Dangerous Talk and Strange Behavior: Women and Popular Resistance to the Reforms of Henry VIII.* St. Martin's Press, 1996.

Jansen, Sharon L. *Debating Women, Politics, and Power in Early Modern Europe.* Palgrave Macmillan, 2008.

Johnson, Ben. "Dissolution of the Monasteries." *Historic UK.* Accessed November 9, 2025. https://www.historic-uk.com/HistoryUK/HistoryofEngland/Dissolution-of-the-Monasteries/.

Jubber, Nicholas. *The Fairy Tellers: A Journey Into the Secret History of Fairy Tales.* John Murray Press, 2022.

Justice, Ginny. "The Role of Indulgences in the Building of New Saint Peter's Basilica." MA thesis, Rollins College, April 28, 2011. https://scholarship.rollins.edu/mls/7/.

Knight, Leah, Micheline White, and Elizabeth Sauer, eds. *Women's Bookscapes in Early Modern Britain: Reading, Ownership, Circulation.* University of Michigan Press, 2018.

LaValle Norman, Dawn. *Early Christian Women.* Cambridge Elements: Women in the History of Philosophy. Cambridge University Press, 2022.

Levack, Brian P., ed. *The Oxford Handbook of Witchcraft in Early Modern Europe and Colonial America.* Oxford University Press, 2013.

Levitt, Emma V. "'You Look for Dead Men's Shoes': Tiltyard Friendships and Masculine Competition in the Reign of Henry VIII." Paper posted on Academia .edu, n.d. Accessed November 9, 2025. https://www.academia.edu/33919921/You_look_for_dead_mens_shoes_Tiltyard_Friendships_and_Masculine_Competition_in_the_Reign_of_Henry_VIII.

Lipscomb, Suzannah. *1536: The Year That Changed Henry VIII.* Lion, 2009.

Loades, David. *The Six Wives of Henry VIII.* Amberley Publishing Plc, 2009.

Lorde, Audre. *The Master's Tools Will Never Dismantle the Master's House.* Penguin Random House UK, 2017.

Lys, Laura. "St. Frideswide: Patron Saint of Oxford." *Museum of Oxford.* Accessed November 10, 2025. https://museumofoxford.org/st-frideswide-patron-saint-of-oxford/.

MacCulloch, Diarmaid. *All Things Made New: The Reformation and Its Legacy.* Oxford University Press, 2016.

MacCulloch, Diarmaid. *Christianity: The First Three Thousand Years.* Viking, 2009.

MacCulloch, Diarmaid. *Silence: A Christian History.* Penguin Random House UK, 2014.

MacCulloch, Diarmaid. *Thomas Cranmer: A Life.* Yale University Press, 1996.

Mar, Alex. "The Rebel Virgins and Desert Mothers Who Have Been Written Out of Christianity's Early History." Atlas Obscura, January 21, 2006. https://www.atlasobscura.com/articles/the-rebel-virgins-and-desert-mothers-who-have-been-written-out-of-christianitys-early-history.

Marty, Martin E. *Martin Luther.* Viking Penguin, 2004.

Mayfield, D. L. "Claims of Sexual Immorality Have Been Used to Diminish or Discredit Female Religious Figures for Ages." *The Washington Post*, April 20, 2019. https://www.washingtonpost.com/gender-identity/claims-of-sexual-immorality-have-been-used-to-diminish-or-discredit-female-religious-figures-for-ages-heres-how-and-why/.

McLuhan, Marshall. *Understanding Media: The Extensions of Man*. McGraw-Hill, 1964; MIT Press, 1996.

Meyer, G. J. *The Tudors: The Complete Story of England's Most Notorious Dynasty*. Delacorte Press, 2010.

Morris, Sarah and Natalie Grueninger. *In the footsteps of Anne Boleyn*. Amberley Publishing, 2013.

Moss, Candida. *God's Ghostwriters: Enslaved Christians and the Making of the Bible*. Little, Brown and Company, 2024.

Paludi, Michele A., and J. Harold Ellens, eds. *Feminism and Religion: How Faiths View Women and Their Rights*. Praeger, 2016.

Pasternak, Anna. "Catherine the Great: Kate Middleton's Star Is Going Stratospheric as the Country Look to the Monarchy for Morale." *Tatler*, May 25, 2020. https://www.tatler.com/article/the-duchess-of-cambridge-is-the-julyaugust-cover.

Penny, Laurie. *Bitch Doctrine: Essay for Dissenting Adults*. Bloomsbury, 2017.

Pettegree, Andrew. *Brand Luther: How an Unheralded Monk Turned His Small Town into a Center of Publishing, Made Himself the Most Famous Man in Europe—and Started the Protestant Reformation*. Penguin, 2015.

Redding, Jonathan. "Babylon Revisited: A Feminist Inspired Reading of the Whore of Babylon in Revelation." Paper posted on Academia.edu, written for "Feminist Interpretations of Scripture" with Dr. Phyllis Trible, April 30, 2011. https://www.academia.edu/858810/Babylon_Revisited_A_Feminist_Inspired_Reading_of_the_Whore_of_Babylon_in_Revelation.

Renee Taylor, Sonya. *The Body Is Not an Apology: The Power of Radical Self-Love*. Berrett-Koehler Publishers, 2018.

Rex, Richard. *Henry VIII and the English Reformation*. 2nd ed. MacMillan, 1993; Palgrave MacMillan, 2006.

Sander, Nicholas. *Rise and Growth of the Anglican Schism* [1573]. Alpha Edition, 2020.

Saxton, Laura. "The Unblemished Concubine: Representations of Anne Boleyn in the English Written Word, 2000–2012." PhD thesis, National School of Arts, Australian Catholic University, Melbourne, January 9, 2015. https://acuresearchbank.acu.edu.au/items/78d5d30d-631f-4ec9-ba7a-56a51d27da39.

Schrader, Elizabeth, and Joan E. Taylor. "The Meaning of 'Magdalene': A Review of Literary Evidence," *Journal of Biblical Literature* 140, no. 4 (December 2021): 751–773. https://doi.org/10.15699/jbl.1404.2021.6.

Shrimplin, Valerie. "Using Objects to Develop the Narrative of Anne Boleyn: Her Age, Possible Guilt and Legacy as Evidenced by a Letter, a Handkerchief and a Tablecloth." *Art, History and Cosmology* (blog), March 2023. https://www.valerieshrimplin.com/pdfs/2023%20_2_58.pdf.

Soberton, Sylvia Barbara. "'Large Wen' or 'Swelling'? Exploring Myths and Misconceptions About Nicholas Sander's Description of Anne Boleyn and Its Link to Witchcraft." *Royal Studies Journal* 10, no. 2 (December 2023): 239–266. https://doi.org/10.21039/rsj.411.

Stanislas Haller, Tobias, ed. *The Episcopal Handbook*. Rev. ed. Church Publishing Incorporated, 2015.

Stein, Leigh. "The End of the Girlboss Is Here." *GEN*, June 22, 2020. https://gen.medium.com/the-end-of-the-girlboss-is-nigh-4591dec34ed8.

Stöckl, Heidi, Karen Devries, Alexandra Rotstein, Naeemah Abrahams, Jacquelyn Campbell, Charlotte Watts, and Claudia Garcia Moreno. "The Global Prevalence of Intimate Partner Homicide: A Systematic Review." *Lancet* 382, no. 9895 (September 7–13, 2013): 859–865. https://doi.org/10.1016/S0140-6736(13)61030-2.

Stuchbery, Ian. *This Is Our Faith: A Guide to Life and Belief for Anglicans*. Anglican Book Centre, 1990.

Taddeo, Lisa. *Three Women*. Avid Reader Press, 2019.

Taylor, Charles. *A Secular Age*. Harvard University Press, 2007.

Tolkien, J. R. R. "On Fairy-Stories (1939)." In *Tolkien on Fairy-Stories*, edited by Verlyn Flieger and Douglas A. Anderson, 27–84. Expanded ed. HarperCollins, 2008.

Truth and Reconciliation Commission of Canada. *Calls to Action*. Truth and Reconciliation Commission of Canada, 2015. https://www2.gov.bc.ca/assets/gov/british-columbians-our-governments/indigenous-people/aboriginal-peoples-documents/calls_to_action_english2.pdf.

Walker, Greg. "Rethinking the Fall of Anne Boleyn." *Historical Journal* 45, no. 1 (March 2002): 1–29. https://doi.org/10.1017/S0018246X01002126.

White, Micheline. "Katherine Parr's Giftbooks, Henry VIII's Marginalia, and the Display of Royal Power and Piety." *Renaissance Quarterly* 76, no. 1 (Spring 2023): 39–83. https://doi.org/10.1017/rqx.2022.445.

Wolf, William J., ed. *The Spirit of Anglicanism: Hooker, Maurice, Temple*. Morehouse-Barlow Co. Inc., 1979.

World Health Organization. "Violence Against Women." World Health Organization, March 25, 2024. https://www.who.int/news-room/fact-sheets/detail/violence-against-women#:~:text=Estimates%20published%20by%20WHO%20indicate,violence%20is%20intimate%20partner%20violence.

Wurtzel, Elizabeth. *Bitch: In Praise of Difficult Women*. Doubleday, 1998.